Third Edition

The Pocket Wadsworth Handbook

Laurie G. Kirszner
University of the Sciences in Philadelphia

Stephen R. Mandell
Drexel University

THOMSON
WADSWORTH

Australia   Canada   Mexico   Singapore   Spain   United Kingdom   United States

THOMSON
WADSWORTH

The Pocket Wadsworth Handbook, Third Edition
Laurie G. Kirszner, Stephen R. Mandell

Publisher: *Michael Rosenberg*
Senior Acquisitions Editor: *Dickson Musslewhite*
Development Editor: *Karen R. Smith*
Editorial Assistant: *Cheryl Forman*
Technology Project Manager: *Cara Douglass-Graff*
Executive Marketing Manager: *Carrie Brandon*
Marketing Assistant: *Dawn Giovanniello*
Advertising Project Manager: *Patrick Rooney*

Senior Project Manager, Editorial Production: *Lianne Ames*
Senior Print Buyer: *Mary Beth Hennebury*
Permissions Editor: *Chelsea Junget*
Production Service: *Susan McIntyre, Nesbitt Graphics*
Text Designer: *Nesbitt Graphics*
Photo Manager: *Sheri Blaney*
Cover Designer: *Brian Salisbury*
Cover Printer: *Coral Graphics*
Compositor: *Nesbitt Graphics*
Printer: *R.R. Donnelley*

For more information about our products, contact us at:
Thomson Learning Academic Resource Center
1-800-423-0563
For permission to use material from this text or product, submit a request online at
http://www.thomsonrights.com.
Any additional questions about permissions can be submitted by email to **thomsonrights@thomson.com.**

Library of Congress Control Number: 2005920220

Student Edition:
    ISBN 1-4130-1168-3
Instructor's Edition:
    ISBN 1-4130-1170-5

Credits appear on page 371, which constitutes a continuation of the copyright page.

Thomson Higher Education
25 Thomson Place
Boston, MA 02210-1202
USA

Asia (including India)
Thomson Learning
5 Shenton Way
#01-01 UIC Building
Singapore 068808

Australia/New Zealand
Thomson Learning Australia
102 Dodds Street
Southbank, Victoria 3006
Australia

Canada
Thomson Nelson
1120 Birchmount Road
Toronto, Ontario M1K 5G4
Canada

UK/Europe/Middle East/Africa
Thomson Learning
High Holborn House
50–51 Bedford Road
London WC1R 4LR
United Kingdom

How to Use This Book

We would like to introduce you to *The Pocket Wadsworth Handbook*, Third Edition, a quick reference guide for college students. This book was designed to be a truly portable handbook that can fit easily in a backpack or pocket but that can still serve as a valuable resource. Despite its compact size, *The Pocket Wadsworth Handbook* covers all the topics you'd expect to find in a much longer book: the writing process (illustrated by a model student paper); sentence grammar and style; punctuation and mechanics; the research process (illustrated by four model student research papers); and MLA, APA, Chicago, and CSE documentation styles. In addition, the book devotes a full section to practical assignments (including Web site and document design, writing for the workplace, and oral presentations) and includes an entire part that addresses the concerns of ESL writers.

The explanations and examples of writing in *The Pocket Wadsworth Handbook* can guide you not just in first-year courses but throughout your college career and beyond. Our goal throughout is to make the book clear, accessible, useful, and—most of all—easy to navigate. To achieve this goal, we incorporated distinctive design features throughout to make information easy to find and easy to use.

Design Features

- *Computer tips* highlight specific ways in which technology can help you throughout the writing, revising, and editing processes. Each computer tip includes the URL for the book's companion Web site <http://kirsznermandell.wadsworth.com>, which contains a wealth of online resources.

- *Grammar checker boxes* illustrating sample errors show the advantages and limitations of using a grammar checker.

- *Numerous checklists* summarize key information that you can quickly access as needed.

- *Close-up boxes* provide an in-depth look at some of the
more perplexing writing-related issues you will
encounter.

- *Part 7, "Documenting Sources,"* includes
the most up-to-date documentation and
format guidelines from the Modern
Language Association, the American Psychological
Association, the University of Chicago Press, and the
Council of Science Editors.

- *Specially designed documentation directories*—
including a specific icon that designates print
sources and another icon that designates electronic
sources—make it easy for you to locate models
for various kinds of sources, including those
found online from library subscription services
such as InfoTrac® College Edition and LexisNexis™. In
addition, annotated diagrams of sample works-cited
entries clearly illustrate the elements of proper
documentation.

See
3d
- *Marginal cross-references* throughout the book allow
you to flip directly to other sections that treat topics in
more detail.

ESL
43a
- *Marginal ESL cross-references* throughout the book direct you to sections of Part 9, "Resources for Bilingual
and ESL Writers," where concepts are presented as they
apply specifically to second-language writers.

- *ESL tips* are woven throughout the text to explain
concepts in relation to the unique experiences
of bilingual students.

Acknowledgments

We would like to take this opportunity to thank Jessie Swigger, University of Texas at Austin, for allowing us to reprint her essays on computer literacy and the accompanying research activities. We would also like to thank Michelle Metzner, Wright State University, for her work on the MLA citations. In addition, we thank the following reviewers for their advice, which helped us develop the third edition:

William M. Abbott, *Fairfield University*
Candace Barrington, *Central Connecticut State University*
Andrew M. Drozd, *University of Alabama*
Kate Dube, *University of New Hampshire*
Roberta Eisel, *Citrus College*
Deanna L. Fassett, *San José State University*
Dan Ferguson, *Amarillo College*
Charlene Kiser, *Milligan College*
Joan Kopperud, *Concordia College*
Leslie Lawrence, *Tufts University*
Frank C. Manista, *Michigan State University*
Jonelle Denton Moore, *Mesa Community College*
Jamil Mustafa, *Lewis University*
Patricia E. Palermo, *Drew University*
Barbara A. Rasnick, *Arizona State University*
Alice Royer, *Penn State Mont Alto*
Ines Shaw, *Nassau Community College*
Rosemarie Shields, *Milligan College*
Susan F. Tellman, *Ball State University*
Ron Waddy, *Hartnell College*
William D. Young, *Maple Woods Community College*

As we have worked to develop a book that would give you the guidance you need to become self-reliant writers and to succeed in college and beyond, we have had the support of an outstanding team of creative professionals at Wadsworth: Publisher Michael Rosenberg; Senior Acquisitions Editor Dickson Musslewhite; Senior Production Project Manager Lianne Ames; Executive

Marketing Manager Carrie Brandon; and, especially, Development Editor Karen Smith.

We have also had the good fortune to work with an equally strong team outside Wadsworth: the staff of Nesbitt Graphics, Inc.; our very talented Project Manager and Copyeditor, Susan McIntyre; and Catherine Bradish, who adapted the design of *The Wadsworth Handbook*, Seventh Edition, to create this book's clear and inviting design. To these people, and to all the others who worked with us on this project, we are very grateful.

Laurie Kirszner
Steve Mandell
February 2005

Writing Essays and Paragraphs

1 Understanding Purpose and Audience 2
1a Determining Your Purpose 2
1b Identifying Your Audience 3

2 Writing Essays 6
2a Planning Your Essay 6
2b Shaping Your Material 7
2c Drafting and Revising 9
2d Editing and Proofreading 11
2e Model Student Paper 13

3 Writing Paragraphs 19
3a Writing Unified Paragraphs 20
3b Writing Coherent Paragraphs 20
3c Writing Well-Developed Paragraphs 22
3d Writing Introductory and Concluding Paragraphs 22

CHAPTER 1

Understanding Purpose and Audience

Everyone who sets out to write confronts a series of choices. In the writing you do in school, on the job, and in your personal life, your understanding of purpose and audience is essential, influencing the choices you make about content, emphasis, organization, style, and tone.

1a Determining Your Purpose

In simple terms, your **purpose** for writing is what you want to accomplish.

- **Writing to Reflect** In diaries and journals, writers explore private ideas and feelings to make sense of their experiences; in autobiographical memoirs and in personal letters, they communicate their emotions and reactions to others.
- **Writing to Inform** In newspaper articles, writers report information, communicating factual details to readers; in reference books, instruction manuals, textbooks, and the like (as well as in catalogs, cookbooks, and government-sponsored Web sites), writers provide definitions and explain concepts or processes, trying to help readers see relationships and understand ideas.
- **Writing to Persuade** In proposals and editorials, as well as in advertising and in some business communication, writers try to convince readers to accept their positions on various issues.
- **Writing to Evaluate** In reviews of books, films, or performances and in reports, critiques, and program evaluations, writers assess the validity, accuracy, and quality of information, ideas, techniques, products, procedures, or services, perhaps assessing the relative merits of two or more things.

Although writers write to reflect, to inform, to persuade, and to evaluate, these purposes are certainly not mutually exclusive, and writers may have other purposes as well. And, of course, in any piece of writing a writer may have a primary aim and one or more secondary purposes; in fact, a writer may even have different purposes in different sections—or different drafts—of a single document.

Checklist: Determining Your Purpose

Is your purpose

- ☐ to express emotions?
- ☐ to inform?
- ☐ to persuade?
- ☐ to explain?
- ☐ to amuse or entertain?
- ☐ to evaluate?
- ☐ to discover?
- ☐ to analyze?
- ☐ to debunk?
- ☐ to draw comparisons?
- ☐ to make an analogy?
- ☐ to define?
- ☐ to criticize?
- ☐ to motivate?

- ☐ to satirize?
- ☐ to speculate?
- ☐ to warn?
- ☐ to reassure?
- ☐ to take a stand?
- ☐ to identify problems?
- ☐ to suggest solutions?
- ☐ to identify causes?
- ☐ to predict effects?
- ☐ to reflect?
- ☐ to interpret?
- ☐ to instruct?
- ☐ to inspire?

1b   Identifying Your Audience

Most of the writing you do is directed at an **audience,** a particular reader or group of readers.

(1) Writing for an Audience

At different times, in different roles, you address a variety of audiences.

- **As a citizen,** consumer, or member of a community, civic, political, or religious group, you may respond to pressing social, economic, or political issues by writing letters to a newspaper, a public official, or a representative of a special interest group.
- **In your personal life,** you may write notes and email messages to friends and family.
- **As an employee,** you may write letters, memos, and reports to your superiors, to staff members you supervise, or to coworkers; you may also be called on to address customers or critics, board members or stockholders, funding agencies or the general public.

- **As a student,** you write essays, reports, and other papers addressed to one or more instructors, and you may also participate in <u>peer review</u>, writing evaluations of classmates' essays and writing responses to their comments about your own work.

See 1b2

As you write, you shape your writing in terms of what you believe your audience needs and expects. Your assessment of your readers' interests, educational level, biases, and expectations determines what information you include, what you emphasize, and how you arrange your material.

Checklist: Identifying Your Audience

- ☐ Who will read your paper?
- ☐ What are your audience's needs? Expectations? Biases? Interests?
- ☐ Does your audience need you to supply definitions? Overviews? Examples? Analogies?
- ☐ What does your audience expect in terms of document design? Format? Documentation style? Method of collecting and reporting data? Use of formulas and symbols or specialized vocabulary?

---

(2) The College Writer's Audience

Most of the writing you do in college is directed either at your instructors or at other students.

Writing for Your Instructor As a student, you usually write for an audience of one: the instructor who assigns the paper. Instructors want to know what you know and whether you can express what you know clearly and accurately. They assign written work to encourage you to think, so the way you organize and express your ideas can be as important as the ideas themselves.

Because they are trained as careful readers and critics, your instructors expect accurate information, standard grammar and correct spelling, logically presented ideas, and a reasonable degree of stylistic fluency. They also expect you to define your terms and to support your generalizations with specific examples. Finally, every instructor also expects you to draw your own conclusions and to provide full and accurate <u>documentation</u> for ideas that are not your own.

See Pt. 7

Writing for Other Students Before you submit a paper to an instructor, you may have an opportunity to participate in **peer review,** sharing your work with your fellow students and responding in writing to their work.

- **Writing Drafts** If you know that other students will read a draft of your paper, you need to consider how they might react to your ideas. For example, are they likely to agree with you? To be shocked or offended by your paper's language or content? To be confused, or even mystified, by any of your references? Even if your readers are your own age, you cannot assume that they share your cultural frame of reference. It is therefore very important that you maintain an appropriate tone and use moderate language in your paper and that you explain any historical, geographical, or cultural references that might be unfamiliar to your audience.

- **Writing Comments** When you respond in writing to another student's paper, you need to take into account how your audience will react to your comments. Here too, your tone is important: you want to be encouraging and polite, offering constructive comments that can help your classmate write a stronger essay.

Checklist: Audience Concerns for Peer-Review Participants

- ☐ **Know your audience.** To be sure you understand what the writer needs and expects from your comments, read the paper several times before you begin writing your response.
- ☐ **Focus on the big picture.** Don't get bogged down on minor problems with punctuation or mechanics or become distracted by a paper's proofreading errors.
- ☐ **Look for a positive feature,** zeroing in on what you think is the paper's greatest strength.
- ☐ **Be positive throughout.** Try to avoid words like *weak, poor,* and *bad*; instead, try using a compliment before delivering the "bad news": "Paragraph 2 is very well developed; can you add this kind of support in paragraph 4?"
- ☐ **Show respect.** It is perfectly acceptable to tell a writer that something is confusing or inaccurate, but don't go on the attack.

(continued)

Audience concerns for peer-review participants (continued)

☐ **Be specific.** Avoid generalizations like "needs more examples" or "could be more interesting"; instead, try to offer helpful, focused suggestions: "You could add an example after the second sentence in paragraph 2"; "Explaining how this process operates would make your discussion more interesting."

☐ **Don't give orders.** Ask questions, and make suggestions.

☐ **Include a few words of encouragement,** emphasizing the paper's strong points.

CHAPTER 2

Writing Essays

Writing is a constant process of decision making—of selecting, deleting, and rearranging material as you plan, shape, draft, revise, edit, and proofread your paper.

2a   Planning Your Essay

See Ch. 1 Once you understand your <u>purpose</u> and <u>audience</u>, you are ready to begin planning your essay: choosing a topic to write about and deciding what to say about it.

(1) Choosing a Topic

Most of the time, your instructor will steer you toward a topic by giving you an assignment. This assignment will usually specify the required length and format and give you a general subject (or a list of subjects from which to choose); sometimes the assignment will pose a question for you to answer.

Assignment: Write a short essay about a problem students face in adjusting to college.

Topic: Overcoming computer illiteracy

Before you begin to write, be sure your topic is narrow enough for your purpose, your audience, and your page limit. If it is not, you will need to narrow it further.

(2) Finding Something to Say

Once you decide on your topic, you can begin to collect ideas for your paper, using one (or several) of the strategies listed below:

- **Reading and Observing** As you read textbooks, magazines, and newspapers and browse the Internet, as you engage in conversation with friends and family, and as you watch films and TV shows, look for ideas you can use.
- **Keeping a Journal** Try recording your thoughts about your topic in a journal, where you can explore ideas, ask questions, and draw tentative conclusions.
- **Freewriting** Try doing timed, unstructured writing. Writing informally for five to ten minutes without stopping may unlock ideas and encourage you to make free associations about your topic.
- **Brainstorming** On an unlined sheet of paper, write down everything you can think of about your topic—comments, questions, lists, single words, and even symbols and diagrams.
- **Asking Questions** If you prefer an orderly, systematic way of finding material to write about, apply the familiar journalistic questions—*who? what? why? where? when?* and *how?*—to your topic.

ESL Tip

Some ESL students spend little time generating ideas for their writing because they are primarily concerned about writing grammatically correct sentences. But remember, the purpose of writing is to convey ideas. If you want to find material to write about, you will need to devote plenty of time to the activities described in this section.

2b Shaping Your Material

Once you have collected material for your essay, your next step is to organize it. The essays you write for your college courses will have a thesis-and-support structure.

A **thesis-and-support essay** includes a **thesis state-ment** (which expresses the **thesis,** or main idea, of the essay) and the specific information that explains and de-velops that thesis.

See 3d   Your essay will consist of several paragraphs: an <u>intro-ductory paragraph</u>, which introduces your thesis; a <u>concluding paragraph</u>, which gives your essay a sense of completion, perhaps restating your thesis; and a number of **body paragraphs,** which provide the support for your essay's thesis.

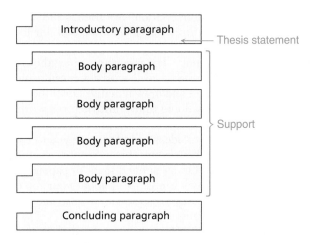

Introductory paragraph ← — Thesis statement

Body paragraph
Body paragraph   } Support
Body paragraph
Body paragraph

Concluding paragraph

Close-up: Writing Effective Thesis Statements

An effective thesis statement has four character-istics:

1. **An effective thesis statement clearly communicates your essay's main idea.** It tells your readers not only what your essay's topic is, but also how you will ap-proach that topic and what you will say about it. Thus, your thesis statement reflects your essay's purpose.

2. **An effective thesis statement is more than a gen-eral subject, a statement of fact, or an announce-ment of your intent.**

   Subject: Computers in college
   Statement of Fact: Computers are used extensively in college.
   Announcement: The essay that follows will show that computer literacy is important in college.
   Thesis Statement: Students who enter college with weak computer skills are at a significant disadvantage.

3. **An effective thesis statement is carefully worded.**
   Your thesis statement—usually expressed in a single, concise sentence—should be direct and straightforward. Avoid vague phrases, such as *centers on*, *deals with*, *involves*, *revolves around*, or *is concerned with*. Do not include phrases like *As I will show*, *I plan to demonstrate*, and *It seems to me*, which weaken your credibility by suggesting that your conclusions are based on opinion rather than on reading, observation, and experience.

4. **Finally, an effective thesis statement suggests your essay's direction, emphasis, and scope.** Your thesis statement should not make promises that your essay will not fulfill. It should suggest the major points you will cover, the order in which you will introduce them, and where you will place your emphasis.

NOTE: As you write and rewrite, you may modify your essay's direction, emphasis, and scope; if you do so, you must reword your thesis statement.

2c Drafting and Revising

(1) Writing a Rough Draft

When you write a rough draft, you get ideas down on paper so you can react to them. You will generally do several drafts of your essay, and you should expect to add or delete words, to reword sentences, to rethink ideas, to reorder paragraphs—even to take an unexpected detour that may lead you to a new perspective on your topic. To make revision easier, leave room on the page so that you can add material or rewrite. When you type, triple-space. Print out every draft, and edit by hand on the hard copy, typing in your changes on subsequent drafts.

(2) Revising Your Drafts

When you revise, you "re-see" what you have written and write additional drafts. Everyone's revision process is different, but the following specific strategies can be helpful at this stage of the process:

- <u>Outline</u> **your draft.** An outline can help you check the logic of your paper's structure. See 28h1

- **Participate in peer review.**   Ask a classmate to give you feedback on your draft.
- **Use instructors' comments.**   Study your instructor's written comments on your draft, and arrange a conference if necessary.
- **Use revision checklists.**   Revise in stages, first looking at the whole essay and then turning your attention to the individual paragraphs, sentences, and words. Use the revision checklists that follow to guide you through the process.

Checklist: Revising the Whole Essay

- ☐ Are thesis and support logically related, with each body paragraph supporting your thesis statement? **(See 2b)**
- ☐ Is your thesis statement clearly and specifically worded? **(See 2b)**
- ☐ Have you discussed everything promised in your thesis statement? **(See 2b)**

Checklist: Revising Paragraphs

- ☐ Does each body paragraph focus on one main idea, expressed in a clearly worded topic sentence? **(See 3a)**
- ☐ Are the relationships of sentences within paragraphs clear? **(See 3b)**
- ☐ Are your body paragraphs fully developed? **(See 3c)**
- ☐ Does your introductory paragraph arouse interest and prepare readers for what is to come? **(See 3d1)**
- ☐ Does your concluding paragraph review your main points? **(See 3d2)**

Checklist: Revising Sentences

- ☐ Have you used correct sentence structure? **(See Chapters 4 and 5)**
- ☐ Are your sentences varied? **(See Chapter 10)**
- ☐ Have you eliminated nonessential words and unnecessary repetition? **(See 11a–b)**
- ☐ Have you avoided overloading your sentences with too many words, phrases, and clauses? **(See 11c)**
- ☐ Have you avoided potentially confusing shifts in tense, voice, mood, person, or number? **(See 12a)**

□ Are your sentences constructed logically? **(See 12b–c)**

□ Have you strengthened sentences by using parallel constructions? **(See 13a)**

□ Have you placed modifiers clearly and logically? **(See Chapter 14)**

Checklist: Revising Words

□ Have you eliminated jargon, pretentious diction, clichés, and biased language from your writing? **(See 15b–c)**

Close-up: Choosing a Title

- A title should convey your essay's focus, perhaps using key words and phrases from your essay or echoing the wording of your assignment.

- A title should arouse interest, perhaps with a provocative question, a quotation, or a controversial position.

Assignment: Write about a problem students face in adjusting to college.

Topic: Overcoming computer illiteracy

Possible Titles:

Computer Illiteracy: A Problem for College Students (echoes wording of assignment and uses key words from essay)

Can College Students Really Use Their Computers? (provocative question)

College Campuses and the "Digital Divide" (quotation)

The Plugged-In and the Unplugged: An Unfair Imbalance on College Campuses (controversial position)

2d Editing and Proofreading

When you **edit,** you concentrate on grammar, spelling, punctuation, and mechanics. When you **proofread,** you reread every word carefully to make sure you did not make any errors as you typed.

Close-up: Proofreading Strategies

To help you proofread more effectively, try using these strategies:

- Read your paper aloud.
- Have a friend read your paper aloud to you.
- Read silently word by word, using your finger or a sheet of paper to help you keep your place.
- Read your paper's sentences in reverse order, beginning with the last sentence.

http://kirsznermandell.wadsworth.com

Computer Tip: Editing and Proofreading

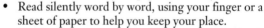

- As you edit, look at only a small portion of text at a time. Reduce the size of your window so that you can see only one or two lines of text at a time.
- Use the Search or Find command to look for words or phrases in usage errors that you commonly make—for instance, confusing *it's* with *its*. You can also uncover <u>sexist language</u> by searching for words such as *he*, *his*, *him*, or *man*.

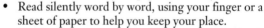

See
15c2

- Remember that a spell checker will not catch a typo that creates a correctly spelled word—for example, *there* for *their* or *form* for *from*. Even after you run a spell check, you still must proofread your papers carefully.

2e   Model Student Paper

Romney 1

Kimberly Romney

Professor Wilson

English 101

10 October 2004

Computer Illiteracy: A Problem for
College Students

Today, most colleges expect entering
students to be familiar with computers.
From registering for courses to contacting
professors, students are required to use
computers on a daily basis. For this
reason, students who enter college with
weak computer skills are at a significant
disadvantage.

Computers are increasingly important
in today's society. As Henry Louis Gates
Jr. writes in his article "One Internet,
Two Nations," many people are concerned
that there is a division between those who
have access to the Internet and those who
do not. He writes, "Today we stand at the
brink of becoming two societies, one
largely white and plugged in and the other
black and unplugged" (500). The gap
between those who are technologically
literate and those who are not extends
beyond race and ethnicity to include the
elderly, the disabled, and those who live
in rural areas. This "digital divide" is
particularly obvious among college students.

Introduction

Thesis statement

Importance of computers in society

Romney 2

Importance of computers in college

Entering college students are expected to be familiar with a variety of software programs. Most professors, for example, require their students to use <u>Microsoft Word</u> to write their papers, and many instructors expect their students to use <u>PowerPoint</u> to present their papers or research projects.

Importance of the Internet

Students are also expected to be familiar with the Internet. For example, registration for classes is often conducted online. Professors and administrators use the Internet to post information about campuswide events, and many professors create their own Web pages where they post their syllabi and class assignments. Finally, professors expect their students to use the Internet when conducting research.

A good understanding of how email works is also necessary for college success. Discussion questions for class are often posted on listservs. If a student wants to communicate with someone in the class, email

Importance of email

is one of the most efficient ways to do so. Email is also vital for communicating with professors. For example, if a student cannot attend office hours, he or she can still ask the professor a question.

Despite the importance of a strong working knowledge of computers and the

Romney 3

Internet, many students arrive at college
with very little experience with either.
In fact, computer illiteracy is a real
problem for entering college students.
Some students have poor computer skills
because they did not have access to a
computer at home. Some families cannot
afford computers, and others simply do not
see a computer as a necessity.

Other students may not have been
taught computer skills in elementary or
high school. A recent study of efforts to
bridge the "digital divide" in elementary
and high schools reported that although
many schools are improving their access to
computers, teachers still might not use
them in the classroom:

> These results paint an alarming
> picture: despite the expenditure
> of literally billions of dollars
> in classroom technology, fully
> 14% of U.S. K-12 teachers make
> no use whatsoever of computers
> for instructional purposes, and
> nearly half (45%) use it with
> their students less than 15
> minutes per week—equivalent to
> just 3 minutes per day! (Norris
> et al. 17-18)

Those students who arrive at college
with weak computer skills face serious

Reason for students' poor skills: lack of access at home

Reason for students' poor skills: lack of access at school

Problems caused by weak computer skills

consequences. For example, registering for classes on the Internet and contacting professors or other students via email become time-consuming (rather than timesaving) tasks. Students may be so embarrassed by their weak computer skills that they do not ask for help. Without help, they have difficulty improving their skills. As a result, they do not benefit from the opportunities offered by the Internet (such as faster and more thorough research) or by sophisticated software programs (such as professional-looking papers and presentations).

Colleges and universities recognize the problems these students face and offer programs to help them. For example, our campus has an outreach program aimed at students with sub-par computer skills.

Possible solution to problems: classes

Once a week, the computer lab offers classes on software programs such as <u>Microsoft Word</u>, <u>PowerPoint</u>, and <u>Dreamweaver</u>. A class about email not only gives students basic information (such as how to send and open attachments), but also tells them how to use programs (such as <u>Outlook Express</u>) to track their daily schedules and appointments. The library also offers several classes, both general and more discipline-specific, about how to use the Internet for research.

However, while this outreach program can provide students with opportunities to improve their skills, many do not know about it. Students are not given information about these classes at orientation, and they are not well advertised in the student newspaper, or even at the computer lab and library. The administration is also not very sensitive to the embarrassment that many students feel about having poor computer skills. Many students might avoid asking a librarian or computer lab proctor for help, and this is a problem that a good advertising campaign would remedy.

As a student from a small town where computer classes were not a part of the high school curriculum, I have personal experience with this problem. I came to college with very limited computer skills. Although I had some knowledge of <u>Microsoft Word</u> and had used the Internet and email, I was not very comfortable using computers. One of my first classes here was a writing class that was held in a computer lab. I was confronted with my problem every Monday, Wednesday, and Friday, and because I was embarrassed about my poor computer skills, I did not want to ask the professor for help. Trying to find help on my own was difficult. It took me two weeks to figure out when and where classes on <u>Microsoft</u>

Limitations of classes

Personal experience: problems in college

<u>Word</u> and the Internet were held. However, after taking these classes, my skills were greatly improved.

Personal experience: changes in high school

Through my own experience, I have come to realize that more efforts need to be made at the high school level to educate students about technology. In my own hometown, such efforts are already underway: the school district instituted a computer literacy class for all high school freshmen the year after I graduated.

According to my high school English teacher, Vicky Wellborn, students really enjoy this class: they go to the new computer lab during breaks or after school, and the lab is frequently full. In addition, the district now requires teachers to take a computer literacy class so that they are better prepared to answer students' questions (Wellborn).

Conclusion

Despite my own frustrating experiences, I am optimistic about the future. As high schools continue to make efforts to incorporate technology into the classroom, students entering college will be better prepared for the technological challenges they will face. And as they become more computer literate, the "digital divide" will close.

Romney 7

Works Cited

Gates, Henry Louis Jr. "One Internet, Two
    Nations." <u>The Blair Reader</u>. 4th ed.
    Ed. Laurie G. Kirszner and Stephen R.
    Mandell. Upper Saddle River, NJ:
    Prentice, 2002. 499-501.

Norris, Cathleen, et al. "No Access, No
    Use, No Impact: Snapshot Surveys of
    Educational Technology in K-12."
    <u>Journal of Research on Technology in
    Education</u> 36.1 (2003): 15-27. <u>Expanded
    Academic ASAP</u>. Gale Group Databases.
    U of Texas Lib. System. 15 Sept. 2004
    〈http://www.galegroup.com〉.

Wellborn, Vicky. "Re: Computer Literacy."
    Email to the author. 23 Sept. 2004.

CHAPTER 3

Writing Paragraphs

A **paragraph** is a group of related sentences. It may be complete in itself or part of a longer piece of writing.

Checklist: When to Begin a New Paragraph

☐ Begin a new paragraph whenever you move
    from one major point to another.
☐ Begin a new paragraph whenever you move your
    readers from one time period or location to another.
☐ Begin a new paragraph whenever you introduce a
    major new step in a process or sequence.

(continued)

When to begin a new paragraph (continued)

☐ Begin a new paragraph when you want to emphasize an important idea.
☐ Begin a new paragraph every time a new person speaks.
☐ Begin a new paragraph to signal the end of your introduction and the beginning of your conclusion.

3a Writing Unified Paragraphs

A paragraph is **unified** when it develops a single idea. Each paragraph should have a **topic sentence** that states the main idea of the paragraph; the other sentences in the paragraph support that idea.

Topic sentence
Support

I was a listening child, careful to hear the very different sounds of Spanish and English. Wide-eyed with hearing, I'd listen to sounds more than words. First, there were English (*gringo*) sounds. So many words were still unknown that when the butcher or the lady at the drugstore said something to me, exotic polysyllabic sounds would bloom in the midst of their sentences. Often the speech of people in public seemed to me very loud, booming with confidence. The man behind the counter would literally ask, "What can I do for you?" But by being so firm and so clear, the sound of his voice said that he was a *gringo;* he belonged in public society. (Richard Rodriguez, *Aria: A Memoir of a Bilingual Childhood*)

NOTE: A topic sentence usually comes at the beginning of a paragraph, but it may appear in the middle or at the end—or even be implied.

3b Writing Coherent Paragraphs

A paragraph is **coherent** when all its sentences are logically related to one another. **Transitional words and phrases** clarify the relationships among sentences by establishing the spatial, chronological, and logical connections within a paragraph.

Topic sentence
Transitional words and phrases establish

Napoleon certainly made a change for the worse by leaving his small kingdom of Elba. After Waterloo, he went back to Paris, and he abdicated for a second time. A hundred days after his return from Elba, he fled to Rochefort in hope of escaping to America. Finally, he gave himself up to the English captain of the ship *Bellerophon*.

chronol- Once again, he suggested that the Prince Regent grant
ogy of him asylum, and once again, he was refused. In the end, all
events he saw of England was the Devon coast and Plymouth
Sound as he passed on to the remote island of St. Helena.
After six years of exile, he died on May 5, 1821, at the age
of fifty-two. (Norman Mackenzie, *The Escape from Elba*)

Using Transitional Words and Phrases

To Signal Sequence or Addition
again, also, besides, furthermore, moreover, in addition,
first . . . second . . . third, one . . . another, too

To Signal Time
after, afterward, as soon as, at first, at the same time, before, earlier, finally, in the meantime, later, meanwhile,
next, now, since, soon, subsequently, then, until

To Signal Comparison
also, by the same token, likewise, in comparison,
similarly

To Signal Contrast
although, but, despite, even though, however, in contrast, instead, meanwhile, nevertheless, nonetheless, on
the contrary, on the one hand . . . on the other hand,
still, whereas, yet

To Introduce Examples
for example, for instance, namely, specifically

To Signal Narrowing of Focus
after all, indeed, in fact, in other words, in particular,
specifically, that is

To Introduce Conclusions or Summaries
as a result, consequently, in summary, therefore, in conclusion, in other words, thus, to conclude

To Signal Concession
admittedly, certainly, granted, naturally, of course

To Introduce Causes or Effects
accordingly, as a result, because, consequently, hence,
since, so, then, therefore

NOTE: Parallel constructions ("He was a patriot. . . . He   See
12a
was a reformer. . . . He was an innovator. . . .") and repeated key words and phrases ("He invented a new type

of printing press. . . . <u>This</u> printing press. . . .") can also
help writers achieve coherence.

3c   Writing Well-Developed Paragraphs

A paragraph is **well developed** when it contains all
the support—examples, statistics, expert opinion, and so
on—that readers need to understand its main idea.

Topic
sentence

> From Thanksgiving until Christmas,
> children are bombarded with ads for violent
> toys and games. Toy manufacturers persist
> in thinking that only toys that appeal to
> children's aggressiveness will sell. One
> television commercial praises the merits of
> a commando team that attacks and captures a
> miniature enemy base. Toy soldiers wear
> realistic uniforms and carry automatic

Specific
examples

> rifles, pistols, knives, grenades, and
> ammunition. Another commercial shows
> laughing children shooting one another with
> plastic rocket fighters and tank-like
> vehicles. Despite claims that they (unlike
> action toys) have educational value, video
> games have increased the level of violence.
> The most popular video games involve
> children in strikingly realistic combat
> situations. One game lets children search

Specific
examples

> out and destroy enemy fighters in outer
> space. Other best-selling games graphically
> simulate hand-to-hand combat on city
> streets. The real question is why parents
> buy these violent toys and games for their
> children. (student writer)

NOTE: Length alone does not determine whether a paragraph is well developed. To determine the amount and
kind of support you need, you need to consider your audience, your purpose, and the scope and complexity of
your paragraph's main idea.

3d   Writing Introductory and Concluding Paragraphs

(1) Introductory Paragraphs

An **introductory paragraph** prepares readers for the essay to follow and makes them want to read further. Typi-

cally, it introduces the subject, narrows it, and then states the essay's thesis.

Thesis statement
> Although it has now faded from view, the telegraph lives on within the communications technologies that have subsequently built upon its foundations: the telephone, the fax machine, and, more recently, the Internet. <u>And, ironically, it is the Internet—despite being regarded as a quintessentially modern means of communication—that has the most in common with its telegraphic ancestor.</u> (Tom Standage, *The Victorian Internet*)

An introductory paragraph may arouse readers' interest with a relevant quotation, a compelling question, an unusual comparison, or a controversial statement.

NOTE: Avoid introductions that simply announce your subject ("In my paper I will talk about Lady Macbeth") or that undercut your credibility ("I don't know much about alternative energy sources, but I would like to present my opinion").

Checklist: Revising Introductions

☐ Does your introduction include your essay's thesis statement?
☐ Does it lead naturally into the body of your essay?
☐ Does it arouse your readers' interest?
☐ Does it avoid statements that simply announce your subject or that undercut your credibility?

---

(2) Concluding Paragraphs

A **concluding paragraph** provides closure to an essay by reminding readers what they have read. Typically, it begins with specifics—for example, a review of the essay's main points—and then moves to more general statements.

> As an Arab-American, I feel I have the best of two worlds. I'm proud to be part of the melting pot, proud to contribute to the tremendous diversity of cultures, customs and traditions that make this country unique. But Arab-bashing— public acceptance of hatred and bigotry—is something no American can be proud of. (Ellen Mansoor Collier, "I Am Not a Terrorist")

A concluding paragraph may also offer a prediction, a warning, a recommendation, or a pertinent quotation.

NOTE: Avoid conclusions that just repeat your introduction in different words or that cast doubt on your concluding points ("I may not be an expert" or "At least this is my opinion"). If possible, end with a statement that readers will remember.

Checklist: Revising Conclusions
☐ Does your conclusion sum up your essay, perhaps by reviewing the essay's main points?
☐ Does it do more than just repeat the introduction?
☐ Does it avoid apologies?
☐ Does it end memorably?

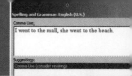

Writing Grammatical Sentences

4 Revising Comma Splices and Fused Sentences 26
4a Recognizing Comma Splices and Fused Sentences 26
4b Correcting Comma Splices and Fused Sentences 27

5 Revising Sentence Fragments 28
5a Recognizing Sentence Fragments 28
5b Correcting Sentence Fragments 29
5c Using Fragments Intentionally 31

6 Understanding Agreement 32
6a Making Subjects and Verbs Agree 32
6b Making Pronouns and Antecedents Agree 36

7 Using Verbs 38
7a Using Irregular Verbs 38
7b Understanding Tense 41
7c Understanding Mood 43
7d Understanding Voice 44

8 Using Pronouns 45
8a Understanding Pronoun Case 45
8b Determining Pronoun Case in Special Situations 47
8c Revising Pronoun Reference Errors 48

9 Using Adjectives and Adverbs 50
9a Using Adjectives as Subject Complements 50
9b Using Adverbs Appropriately 51
9c Using Comparative and Superlative Forms 51

CHAPTER 4

Revising Comma Splices and Fused Sentences

4a Recognizing Comma Splices and Fused Sentences

See A2.3 A **run-on sentence** is created when two independent clauses are joined incorrectly.

A **comma splice** is a run-on that occurs when two independent clauses are joined by just a comma. A **fused sentence** is a run-on that occurs when two independent clauses are joined with no punctuation.

> **Comma Splice:** Charles Dickens created the character of Mr. Micawber, he also created Uriah Heep.

> **Fused Sentence:** Charles Dickens created the character of Mr. Micawber he also created Uriah Heep.

Grammar Checker: Identifying Comma Splices

Your word processor's grammar checker will highlight comma splices and prompt you to revise them. It may also offer suggestions for revision.

> Comma Use:
> I went to the mall, she went to the beach.

Checklist: Revising Comma Splices and Fused Sentences

To revise a comma splice or fused sentence, use one of the following strategies:

- ☐ Add a period between the clauses.
- ☐ Add a semicolon between the clauses.
- ☐ Add an appropriate coordinating conjunction.
- ☐ Subordinate one clause to the other, creating a complex sentence.

4b   Correcting Comma Splices and Fused Sentences

(1) Using a Period

You can add a period between the independent clauses, creating two separate sentences. This is a good strategy to use when the clauses are long or when they are not closely related.

> In 1894 Frenchman Alfred Dreyfus was falsely con-
> victed of treason, *His* his struggle for justice pitted the
> army against the civil libertarians.

(2) Using a Semicolon

You can add a <u>semicolon</u> between two closely related clauses that convey parallel or contrasting information.   See 18a

> Chippendale chairs have straight legs *;* however, Queen
> Anne chairs have curved legs.

NOTE: When you use a <u>transitional word or phrase</u> (such as *however, therefore,* or *for example*) to connect two independent clauses, the transitional element must be preceded by a semicolon and followed by a comma. If you use a comma alone, you create a comma splice. If you omit punctuation entirely, you create a fused sentence.   See 3b

(3) Using a Coordinating Conjunction

You can use a coordinating conjunction (*and, or, but, nor, for, so, yet*) to join two closely related clauses of equal importance into one <u>compound sentence</u>. The coordinating conjunction you choose indicates the relationship between the clauses: addition (*and*), contrast (*but, yet*), causality (*for, so*), or a choice of alternatives (*or, nor*). Be sure to add a comma before the coordinating conjunction.   See 10a1

> Elias Howe invented the sewing machine, *and* Julia Ward
> Howe was a poet and social reformer.

(4) Using a Subordinating Conjunction or Relative Pronoun

When the ideas in two independent clauses are not of equal importance, you can use an appropriate subordinating

See
10a2
conjunction or a relative pronoun to join the clauses into one <u>complex sentence</u>, placing the less important idea in the dependent clause.

Stravinsky's ballet *The Rite of Spring* shocked Parisians in 1913, _{because} its rhythms seemed erotic.

Lady Mary Wortley Montagu _{, who} had suffered from smallpox herself ~~she~~ helped spread the practice of inoculation.

CHAPTER 5

Revising Sentence Fragments

5a   Recognizing Sentence Fragments

A **sentence fragment** is an incomplete sentence—a clause or a phrase—that is punctuated as though it were a sentence. A sentence may be incomplete for any of the following reasons:

- It lacks a subject.

  Many astrophysicists now believe that galaxies are distributed in clusters. <u>And even form supercluster complexes.</u>

- It lacks a verb.

  Every generation has its defining moments. <u>Usually the events with the most news coverage.</u>

- It lacks both a subject and a verb.

  Researchers are engaged in a variety of studies. <u>Suggesting a link between alcoholism and heredity.</u> (*Suggesting* is a **verbal**, which cannot serve as a sentence's main verb.)

See
A1.3

See
A2.3
- It is a <u>dependent clause</u>, a clause that begins with a subordinating conjunction or relative pronoun.

  Bishop Desmond Tutu was awarded the 1984 Nobel Peace Prize. <u>Because he struggled to end apartheid.</u>

The pH meter and the spectrophotometer are two scientific instruments. <u>That changed the chemistry laboratory dramatically.</u>

Grammar Checker: Identifying Fragments

Your grammar checker will identify many (although not all) sentence fragments. However, not every word group identified as a fragment will actually be a fragment. You, not your grammar checker, will have to make the final decision and correct any errors.

> Fragment:
> Present and past, town and country, familiar and foreign.

Checklist: Revising Sentence Fragments

To revise a sentence fragment, use one or more of the following strategies:

☐ Attach the fragment to an adjacent independent clause that contains the missing words.
☐ Delete the subordinating conjunction or relative pronoun.
☐ Supply the missing subject or verb (or both).

5b Correcting Sentence Fragments

(1) Attaching the Fragment to an Independent Clause

In most cases, the simplest way to correct a fragment is by attaching it to an adjacent independent clause that contains the missing words.

President Johnson did not seek reelection, ~~For~~ *for* a number of reasons. (**prepositional phrase** fragment) See A2.3

Students sometimes take a leave of absence, ~~To~~ *to* decide on definite career goals. (**verbal phrase** fragment) See A2.3

The pilot changed course, *, realizing* ~~Realizing~~ that the weather was worsening. (verbal phrase fragment)

See
8b3

Brian was the star forward of the Blue Devils, <del>The</del> ^, the^ team with the most wins. (**appositive** fragment)

Fairy tales are full of damsels in distress, <del>Such</del> ^, such^ as Rapunzel. (appositive fragment)

People with dyslexia have trouble reading, <del>And</del> ^and^ may also find it difficult to write. (part of compound predicate)

They took only a compass and a canteen, <del>And</del> ^and^ some trail mix. (part of compound object)

See
A2.3

Property taxes rose sharply, <del>Although</del> ^although^ city services declined. (**dependent clause** fragment)

The battery is dead, <del>Which</del> ^, which^ means the car won't start. (dependent clause fragment)

Close-up: Lists

See
21a1

When a fragment takes the form of a <u>list</u>, add a colon to connect the list to the independent clause that introduces it.

Tourists often outnumber residents in four European cities, ^:^ Venice, Florence, Canterbury, and Bath.

---

(2) Deleting the Subordinating Conjunction or Relative Pronoun

When a fragment consists of a dependent clause that is punctuated as though it were a complete sentence, you can correct it by attaching it to an adjacent independent clause, as illustrated in **5a1**. Alternatively, you can simply delete the subordinating conjunction or relative pronoun.

Property taxes rose sharply. <del>Although</del> ^City^ city services declined. (subordinating conjunction *although* deleted)

The battery is dead. <del>Which</del> ^This^ means the car won't start. (relative pronoun *which* replaced by *this*, a word that can serve as the sentence's subject)

NOTE: Simply deleting the subordinating conjunction or relative pronoun is usually the least desirable way to revise a sentence fragment. It is likely to create two choppy sentences and obscure the connection between them.

(3) Supplying the Missing Subject or Verb

Another way to correct a fragment is to add the missing words (a subject or a verb or both) that are needed to make the fragment a sentence.

>   *It was divided*
> In 1948, India became independent. ~~Divided~~ into the nations of India and Pakistan. (verbal phrase fragment)

> A familiar trademark can increase a product's sales.
> *It reminds*
> ~~Reminding~~ shoppers that the product has a longstanding reputation. (verbal phrase fragment)

Close-up: Fragments Introduced by Transitions

    Many fragments are word groups that are introduced by <u>transitional words and phrases</u>, such as *also*, *finally*, *in addition*, and *now*, but are missing subjects and verbs. To correct such a fragment, you need to add the missing subject and verb.

See 3b

>   *he found*
> Finally, a new home for the family.

>   *we need*
> In addition, three new keyboards for the computer lab.

5c   Using Fragments Intentionally

Fragments are often used in speech and informal writing as well as in journalism, creative writing, and advertising. In professional and academic writing, however, sentence fragments are generally not acceptable except in certain special situations.

Checklist: Using Fragments Intentionally

☐ In lists
☐ In captions that accompany visuals

(continued)

Using fragments intentionally (continued)

☐ In topic outlines
☐ In quoted dialogue
☐ In *PowerPoint* presentations
☐ In titles and subtitles of papers and reports

CHAPTER 6

Understanding Agreement

Agreement is the correspondence between words in number, gender, or person. Subjects and verbs agree in _{See 12a4} number (singular or plural) and person (first, second, or third); pronouns and their antecedents agree in number, person, and gender.

6a Making Subjects and Verbs Agree

Singular subjects take singular verbs, and plural subjects _{See 7b1} take plural verbs. Present tense verbs, except *be* and *have*, add *-s* or *-es* when the subject is third-person singular. (Third-person singular subjects include nouns; the personal pronouns *he*, *she*, *it*, and *one*; and many indefi- _{See 6a4} nite pronouns.)

The President has the power to veto congressional legislation.

She frequently cites statistics to support her points.

In every group somebody emerges as a natural leader.

Present tense verbs do not add *-s* or *-es* when the subject is a plural noun, a first-person or second-person pronoun (*I*, *we*, *you*), or a third-person plural pronoun (*they*).

Experts recommend that dieters avoid processed meat.

At this stratum, we see rocks dating back ten million years.

They say that some wealthy people default on their student loans.

In some situations, making subjects and verbs agree can cause problems for writers.

(1) Words between Subject and Verb

If a modifying phrase comes between the subject and the verb, the verb should agree with the subject, not with a word in the modifying phrase.

> The <u>sound</u> of the drumbeats <u>builds</u> in intensity in Eugene O'Neill's play *The Emperor Jones*.

> The <u>games</u> won by the intramural team <u>are</u> few and far between.

This rule also applies to phrases introduced by *along with*, *as well as*, *in addition to*, *including*, and *together with*.

> Heavy <u>rain</u>, along with high winds, <u>causes</u> hazardous driving conditions.

(2) Compound Subjects Joined by *And*

Compound subjects joined by *and* usually take plural verbs.

> <u>Air bags and antilock brakes</u> <u>are</u> standard on all new models.

There are, however, two exceptions to this rule. First, when a compound subject joined by *and* stands for a single idea or person, it is treated as a unit and takes a singular verb: <u>Rhythm and blues</u> <u>is</u> a forerunner of rock and roll.

Second, when *each* or *every* precedes a compound subject joined by *and*, the subject takes a singular verb: <u>Every desk and file cabinet</u> <u>was</u> searched before the letter was found.

(3) Compound Subjects Joined by *Or*

Compound subjects joined by *or* may take either singular or plural verbs. If both subjects are singular, use a singular verb; if both are plural, use a plural verb. If a singular and a plural subject are linked by *or* (or by *either . . . or*, *neither . . . nor*, or *not only . . . but also*), the verb agrees with the subject that is nearer to it.

> <u>Either radiation treatments or chemotherapy</u> <u>is</u> combined with surgery for effective results.

> <u>Either chemotherapy or radiation treatments</u> <u>are</u> combined with surgery for effective results.

(4) Indefinite Pronouns

ESL
43c3 Most <u>indefinite pronouns</u>—*another, anyone, everyone, one, each, either, neither, anything, everything, something, nothing, nobody,* and *somebody*—are singular and take singular verbs.

<u>Anyone</u> <u>is</u> welcome to apply for this grant.

Some indefinite pronouns—*both, many, few, several, others*—are always plural and take plural verbs.

<u>Several</u> of the articles <u>are</u> useful.

A few indefinite pronouns—*some, all, any, more, most,* and *none*—can be singular or plural, depending on the noun they refer to.

Of course, <u>some</u> of this trouble <u>is</u> to be expected. (*Some* refers to *trouble*.)

<u>Some</u> of the spectators <u>are</u> getting restless. (*Some* refers to *spectators*.)

Grammar Checker: Subject-Verb Agreement

Your word processor's grammar checker will highlight and offer revision suggestions for many subject-verb agreement errors, including errors in sentences that have indefinite pronoun subjects.

```
Subject-Verb Agreement:
All of these little details makes the contract
hard to understand.


Suggestions:
make
```

---

(5) Collective Nouns

A **collective noun** names a group of persons or things—for instance, *navy, union, association, band*. When a collective noun refers to the group as a unit (as it usually does), it takes a singular verb; when it refers to the individuals or items that make up the group, it takes a plural verb.

To many people, the royal family *symbolizes* Great Britain. (The family, as a unit, is the symbol.)

The family *eat* at different times. (Each member eats separately.)

Phrases that name fixed amounts—*three-quarters, twenty dollars, the majority*—are treated like collective nouns. When the amount denotes a unit, it takes a singular verb; when it denotes part of the whole, it takes a plural verb.

Three-quarters of his usual salary is not enough to live on.

Three-quarters of the patients improve dramatically after treatment.

(6) Singular Subjects with Plural Forms

A singular subject takes a singular verb, even if the form of the subject is plural.

Statistics deals with the collection and analysis of data.

When such a word has a plural meaning, however, use a plural verb.

The statistics prove him wrong.

(7) Inverted Subject-Verb Order

Even when the verb comes before the subject (as it does in questions and in sentences beginning with *there is* or *there are*), the subject and verb must agree.

Is either answer correct?

There are currently thirteen circuit courts of appeals in the federal system.

(8) Linking Verbs

A linking verb should agree with its subject, not with the subject complement. See 9a

The problem was termites.

Termites were the problem.

(9) Relative Pronouns

When you use a relative pronoun (*who, which, that,* and so on) to introduce a dependent clause, the verb in the dependent clause should agree in number with the pronoun's **antecedent,** the word to which the pronoun refers. See A1.2

The farmer is among the <u>ones</u> who <u>suffer</u> during a grain embargo.

The farmer is the only <u>one</u> who <u>suffers</u> during a grain embargo.

6b   Making Pronouns and Antecedents Agree

Singular pronouns—such as *he, him, she, her, it, me, myself,* and *oneself*—should refer to singular antecedents. Plural pronouns—such as *we, us, they, them,* and *their*—should refer to plural antecedents.

(1) Compound Antecedents

In most cases, use a plural pronoun to refer to a **compound antecedent** (two or more antecedents connected by *and*).

<u>Mormonism and Christian Science</u> were similar in <u>their</u> beginnings.

However, there are several exceptions to this general rule:

- Use a singular pronoun when a compound antecedent is preceded by *each* or *every.*

  <u>Every programming language and software package</u> has <u>its</u> limitations.
- Use a singular pronoun to refer to two or more singular antecedents linked by *or* or *nor.*

  <u>Neither Thoreau nor Whitman</u> lived to see <u>his</u> work read widely.
- When one part of a compound antecedent is singular and one part is plural, the pronoun agrees in person and number with the antecedent that is nearer to it.

  <u>Neither the boy nor his parents</u> had <u>their</u> seatbelts fastened.

(2) Collective Noun Antecedents

If the meaning of a collective noun antecedent is singular (as it will be in most cases), use a singular pronoun. If the meaning is plural, use a plural pronoun.

The teachers' <u>union</u> announced <u>its</u> plan to strike. (The members act as a unit.)

The <u>team</u> moved to <u>their</u> positions. (Each member acts individually.)

(3) Indefinite Pronoun Antecedents

Most <u>indefinite pronouns</u>—*each, either, neither, one, anyone,* and the like—are singular and take singular pronouns.

See 6a4

<u>Neither</u> of the men had <u>his</u> proposal ready by the deadline.

<u>Each</u> of these neighborhoods has <u>its</u> own traditions and values.

(A few indefinite pronouns are plural; others can be singular or plural.)

> ### Close-up: Pronoun-Antecedent Agreement
>
> In speech and in informal writing, many people use the plural pronouns *they* or *their* with singular indefinite pronouns that refer to people, such as *someone, everyone,* and *nobody.*
>
> <u>Everyone</u> can present <u>their</u> own viewpoint.
>
> In college writing, however, you should avoid using a plural pronoun with a singular subject. Instead, you can use both the masculine and the feminine pronoun.
>
> <u>Everyone</u> can present <u>his or her</u> own viewpoint.
>
> Or, you can make the sentence's subject plural.
>
> <u>All participants</u> can present <u>their</u> own viewpoints.
>
> The use of *his* to refer to a singular indefinite pronoun (Everyone can present *his* own viewpoint) is considered <u>sexist language</u>.

See 15c2

> ### Grammar Checker: Pronoun-Antecedent Agreement
>
> Your word processor's grammar checker will highlight and offer revision suggestions for many pronoun-antecedent agreement errors.
>
> | Pronoun Use: |
> | --- |
> | Someone should take responsibility for their actions. |
>
> | Suggestions: |
> | --- |
> | his or her |

CHAPTER 7

Using Verbs

7a Using Irregular Verbs

A **regular verb** forms both its past tense and its past participle by adding *-d* or *-ed* to the **base form** of the verb (the present tense form of the verb that is used with *I*).

Principal Parts of Regular Verbs		
Base Form	**Past Tense Form**	**Past Participle**
smile	smiled	smiled
talk	talked	talked

Irregular verbs do not follow this pattern. The chart that follows lists the principal parts of the most frequently used irregular verbs.

Frequently Used Irregular Verbs		
Base Form	**Past Tense Form**	**Past Participle**
arise	arose	arisen
awake	awoke, awaked	awoke, awaked
be	was/were	been

Base Form	Past Tense Form	Past Participle
beat	beat	beaten
begin	began	begun
bend	bent	bent
bet	bet, betted	bet
bite	bit	bitten
blow	blew	blown
break	broke	broken
bring	brought	brought
build	built	built
burst	burst	burst
buy	bought	bought
catch	caught	caught
choose	chose	chosen
cling	clung	clung
come	came	come
cost	cost	cost
deal	dealt	dealt
dig	dug	dug
dive	dived, dove	dived
do	did	done
drag	dragged	dragged
draw	drew	drawn
drink	drank	drunk
drive	drove	driven
eat	ate	eaten
fall	fell	fallen
fight	fought	fought
find	found	found
fly	flew	flown
forget	forgot	forgotten, forgot
freeze	froze	frozen
get	got	gotten
give	gave	given
go	went	gone
grow	grew	grown
hang (suspend)	hung	hung
have	had	had
hear	heard	heard
keep	kept	kept
know	knew	known
lay (place/put)	laid	laid
lead	led	led
lend	lent	lent
let	let	let
lie (recline)	lay	lain
make	made	made
prove	proved	proved, proven

(continued)

Frequently used irregular verbs (continued)

Base Form	Past Tense Form	Past Participle
read	read	read
ride	rode	ridden
ring	rang	rung
rise	rose	risen
run	ran	run
say	said	said
see	saw	seen
set (place)	set	set
shake	shook	shaken
shrink	shrank, shrunk	shrunk, shrunken
sing	sang	sung
sink	sank	sunk
sit	sat	sat
speak	spoke	spoken
speed	sped, speeded	sped, speeded
spin	spun	spun
spring	sprang	sprung
stand	stood	stood
steal	stole	stolen
strike	struck	struck, stricken
swear	swore	sworn
swim	swam	swum
swing	swung	swung
take	took	taken
teach	taught	taught
throw	threw	thrown
wake	woke, waked	waked, woken
wear	wore	worn
wring	wrung	wrung
write	wrote	written

Close-up: Lie/Lay and Sit/Set

Lie means "to recline" and does not take an object ("He likes to *lie* on the floor"); *lay* means "to place" or "to put" and does take an object ("He wants to *lay* a rug on the floor"):

Base Form	Past Tense Form	Past Participle
lie	lay	lain
lay	laid	laid

Sit means "to assume a seated position" and does not take an object ("She wants to *sit* on the table"); *set* means "to place" or "to put" and usually takes an object ("She wants to *set* a vase on the table"):

Base Form	Past Tense Form	Past Participle
sit	sat	sat
set	set	set

7b Understanding Tense

<u>Tense</u> is the form a verb takes to indicate when an action occurred or when a condition existed.

ESL 43a2

English Verb Tenses

Simple Tenses
Present (I *finish*, he or she *finishes*)
Past (I *finished*)
Future (I *will finish*)

Perfect Tenses
Present perfect (I *have finished*, he or she *has finished*)
Past perfect (I *had finished*)
Future perfect (I *will have finished*)

Progressive Tenses
Present progressive (I *am finishing*, he or she *is finishing*)
Past progressive (I *was finishing*)
Future progressive (I *will be finishing*)
Present perfect progressive (I *have been finishing*)
Past perfect progressive (I *had been finishing*)
Future perfect progressive (I *will have been finishing*)

---

(1) Using the Simple Tenses

The **simple tenses** include *present*, *past*, and *future*.

The **present tense** usually indicates an action that is taking place at the time it is expressed or an action that occurs regularly.

I see your point. (an action taking place when it is expressed)

We wear wool in the winter. (an action that occurs regularly)

> ### Close-up: Special Uses of the Present Tense
>
> The present tense has four special uses.
>
> **To Indicate Future Time:** The grades <u>arrive</u> next Thursday.
>
> **To State a Generally Held Belief:** Studying <u>pays</u> off.
>
> **To State a Scientific Truth:** An object at rest <u>tends</u> to stay at rest.
>
> **To Discuss a Literary Work:** *Family Installments* <u>tells</u> the story of a Puerto Rican family.

The **past tense** indicates that an action has already taken place.

John Glenn <u>orbited</u> the Earth three times on February 20, 1962. (an action completed in the past)

As a young man, Mark Twain <u>traveled</u> through the Southwest. (an action that occurred once or many times in the past but did not extend into the present)

The **future tense** indicates that an action will or is likely to take place.

Halley's Comet <u>will reappear</u> in 2061. (a future action that will definitely occur)

The housing boom in Nevada <u>will</u> probably <u>continue</u>. (a future action that is likely to occur)

(2) Using the Perfect Tenses

The **perfect tenses** indicate actions that were or will be completed before other actions or conditions. The perfect tenses are formed with the appropriate tense form of the auxiliary verb *have* plus the past participle.

The **present perfect** tense can indicate either of two kinds of continuing action beginning in the past.

Dr. Kim <u>has finished</u> studying the effects of BHA on rats. (an action that began in the past and is finished at the present time)

My mother <u>has invested</u> her money wisely. (an action that began in the past and extends into the present)

The **past perfect** tense indicates an action occurring before a certain time in the past.

By 1946, engineers <u>had built</u> the first electronic digital computer.

The **future perfect** tense indicates that an action will be finished by a certain future time.

By Tuesday, the transit authority <u>will have run</u> out of money.

(3) Using the Progressive Tenses

The **progressive tenses** indicate continuing action. They are formed with the appropriate tense of the verb *be* plus the present participle.

The **present progressive** tense indicates that something is happening at the time it is expressed in speech or writing.

The volcano <u>is erupting</u>, and lava <u>is flowing</u> toward the town.

The **past progressive** tense can indicate either of two kinds of past action.

Roderick Usher's actions <u>were becoming</u> increasingly bizarre. (a continuing action in the past)

The French revolutionary Marat was stabbed to death while he <u>was bathing</u>. (an action occurring at the same time in the past as another action)

The **future progressive** tense indicates a continuing action in the future.

The treasury secretary <u>will be monitoring</u> the money supply very carefully.

The **present perfect progressive** tense indicates action continuing from the past into the present and possibly into the future.

Rescuers <u>have been working</u> around the clock.

The **past perfect progressive** tense indicates that a past action went on until another one occurred.

Before President Kennedy was assassinated, he <u>had been working</u> on civil rights legislation.

The **future perfect progressive** tense indicates that an action will continue until a certain future time.

By eleven o'clock we <u>will have been driving</u> for seven hours.

7c   Understanding Mood

Mood is the form a verb takes to indicate whether a writer is making a statement, asking a question, giving a command, or expressing a wish or a contrary-to-fact statement. There are three moods in English: the *indicative*, the *imperative*, and the *subjunctive*.

The **indicative** mood states a fact, expresses an opinion, or asks a question: Jackie Robinson <u>had</u> a great impact on professional baseball.

The **imperative** mood is used in commands and direct requests: <u>Use</u> a dictionary.

The **subjunctive** mood is used to express wishes, contrary-to-fact conditions, and requests or recommendations:

- The **present subjunctive** is used in *that* clauses after words such as *ask, suggest, require, recommend,* and *demand*. The present subjunctive uses the base form of the verb, regardless of the subject.

  Captain Ahab insisted that his crew <u>hunt</u> the white whale.

  The report recommended that doctors <u>be</u> more flexible.

- The **past subjunctive** is used in **conditional statements** (statements beginning with *if, as if,* or *as though* that are contrary to fact and statements that express a wish). The past subjunctive has the same form as the past tense of the verb, except for the verb *be*, which uses *were*, even with singular subjects.

  If John <u>went</u> home, he could see Marsha. (John is not home.)

  The father acted as if he <u>were</u> having the baby. (The father couldn't be having the baby.)

  I wish I <u>were</u> more organized. (expresses a wish)

NOTE: Because the subjunctive can seem formal or stiff, many people use the indicative in everyday speech: I wish I *was* better organized. In college writing, however, always use the subjunctive in the situations described above.

7d   Understanding Voice

Voice is the form a verb takes to indicate whether the subject of a sentence acts or is acted upon. When the subject of a verb does something—that is, acts—the verb is in the **active voice.** When the subject of a verb receives the action—that is, is acted upon—the verb is in the **passive voice.**

Active Voice: Hart Crane <u>wrote</u> *The Bridge.*

Passive Voice: *The Bridge* <u>was written</u> by Hart Crane.

Because the active voice emphasizes the person or thing performing an action, it is usually clearer and more emphatic than the passive voice. Whenever possible, use active voice in your college writing.

The students chose investigative

~~Investigative~~ reporter Bob Woodward ~~was chosen by the students~~ as the graduation speaker.

Some situations, however, do call for the use of the passive voice—for example, when the actor is unknown or when the action itself is more important than the actor. This is usually the case in scientific and technical writing.

Grits <u>are eaten</u> throughout the South. (Passive voice emphasizes the fact that grits are eaten; who eats them is not important.)

A study <u>was conducted</u> by the Department of Health and Human Services to determine the seriousness of the problem. (Passive voice emphasizes the study; the government agency that carried out the study is less important.)

DDT <u>was found</u> in soil samples. (Passive voice emphasizes the discovery of DDT; who found it is not important.)

CHAPTER 8

Using Pronouns

8a Understanding Pronoun Case

Pronouns change **case** to indicate their function in a sentence. English has three cases: *subjective, objective,* and *possessive.*

Pronoun Case Forms							
Subjective							
I	he, she	it	we	you	they	who	whoever
Objective							
me	him, her	it	us	you	them	whom	whomever
Possessive							
my	his, her	its	our	your	their	whose	
mine	hers		ours	yours	theirs		

(1) Subjective Case

A pronoun takes the **subjective case** in the following situations.

> **Subject of a Verb:** I bought a new mountain bike.
>
> **Subject Complement:** It was he for whom the men were looking.

(2) Objective Case

A pronoun takes the **objective case** in these situations.

> **Direct Object:** Our sociology teacher asked Adam and me to work on the project.
>
> **Indirect Object:** The plumber's bill gave him quite a shock.
>
> **Object of a Preposition:** Between us we own ten shares of stock.

Close-up: Pronoun Case in Compound Constructions

I is not necessarily more appropriate than *me*. In compound constructions like the following, *me* is correct.

> Just between you and me [not *I*], I think the data are incomplete. (*Me* is the object of the preposition *between*.)

---

(3) Possessive Case

A pronoun takes the **possessive case** when it indicates ownership (*our* car, *your* book). The possessive case is also used before a gerund.

See
A1.3

Napoleon approved of <u>their</u> [not *them*] ruling Naples. (*Ruling* is a gerund.)

8b Determining Pronoun Case in Special Situations

(1) Comparisons with *Than* or *As*

When a comparison ends with a pronoun, the pronoun's function in the sentence determines your choice of pronoun case. If the pronoun functions as a subject, use the subjective case; if it functions as an object, use the objective case. (You can determine the function of the pronoun by completing the comparison.)

Darcy likes John more than <u>I</u>. (*I* is the subject: more than *I* like John.)

Darcy likes John more than <u>me</u>. (*Me* is the object: more than she likes *me*.)

(2) *Who* and *Whom*

The case of the pronouns *who* and *whom* depends on their function *within their own clause*. When a pronoun serves as the subject of its clause, use *who* or *whoever*; when it functions as an object, use *whom* or *whomever.*

The Salvation Army gives food and shelter to <u>whoever</u> is in need. (*Whoever* is the subject of the dependent clause.)

I wonder <u>whom</u> jazz musician Miles Davis influenced. (*Whom* is the object of *influenced* in the dependent clause.)

Close-up: Pronoun Case in Questions

To determine the case of *who* at the beginning of a question, use a personal pronoun to answer the question. The case of *who* should be the same as the case of the personal pronoun.

<u>Who</u> wrote *The Age of Innocence?* (<u>She</u> wrote it—subject)

<u>Whom</u> do you support for mayor? (I support <u>her</u>—object)

---

(3) Appositives

An <u>appositive</u> is a noun or noun phrase that identifies or renames an adjacent noun or pronoun. The case of a   ESL 43c4 pronoun in an appositive depends on the function of the word the appositive identifies.

> We heard two Motown recording artists, Smokey Robinson and <u>him</u>. (*Artists* is the object of the verb *heard*, so the pronoun in the appositive *Smokey Robinson and him* takes the objective case.)

> Two Motown recording artists, <u>he</u> and Smokey Robinson, recorded for Motown Records. (*Artists* is the subject of the sentence, so the pronoun in the appositive *Smokey Robinson and he* takes the subjective case.)

(4) *We* and *Us* before a Noun

When a first-person plural pronoun directly precedes a noun, the case of the pronoun depends on the way the noun functions in the sentence.

> <u>We</u> women must stick together. (*Women* is the subject of the sentence, so the pronoun *we* takes the subjective case.)

> Teachers make learning easy for <u>us</u> students. (*Students* is the object of the preposition *for*, so the pronoun *us* takes the objective case.)

8c   Revising Pronoun Reference Errors

^{ESL}
^{43c1} An <u>antecedent</u> is the word or word group to which a pronoun refers. The connection between a pronoun and its antecedent should always be clear.

(1) Ambiguous Antecedents

Sometimes it is not clear to which antecedent a pronoun—for example, *this*, *that*, *which*, or *it*—refers. In such cases, eliminate the ambiguity by substituting a noun for the pronoun.

> The accountant took out his calculator and completed the tax return. Then, he put ^*the calculator* it into his briefcase. (The pronoun *it* can refer either to *calculator* or to *tax return*.)

Sometimes a pronoun—for example, *this*—does not seem to refer to any specific antecedent. In such cases, supply a noun to clarify the reference.

Some one-celled organisms contain chlorophyll yet are considered animals. This ^paradox^ illustrates the difficulty of classifying single-celled organisms. (Exactly what does *this* refer to?)

(2) Remote Antecedents

The farther a pronoun is from its antecedent, the more difficult it is for readers to make a connection between them. If a pronoun's antecedent is far away from it, replace the pronoun with a noun.

> During the mid-1800s, many Czechs began to immigrate to America. By 1860, about 23,000 Czechs had left their country. By 1900, 13,000 Czech immigrants were coming to ^America's^ ~~its~~ shores each year.

(3) Nonexistent Antecedents

Sometimes a pronoun refers to an antecedent that does not appear in the sentence. In such cases, replace the pronoun with a noun.

> Our township has decided to build a computer lab in the elementary school. ^Teachers^ ~~They~~ feel that fourth-graders should begin using computers. (*They* refers to an antecedent the writer has failed to mention.)

Close-up: *Who, Which,* and *That*

In general, *who* refers to people or to animals that have names. *Which* and *that* refer to objects, events, or unnamed animals. When referring to an antecedent, be sure to choose the appropriate pronoun (*who, which,* or *that*).

> David Henry Hwang, <u>who</u> wrote the Tony Award-winning play *M. Butterfly*, also wrote *Family Devotions* and *FOB*.

> The spotted owl, <u>which</u> lives in old-growth forests, is in danger of extinction.

> Houses <u>that</u> are built today are usually more energy efficient than those built twenty years ago.

NOTE: *Which* introduces <u>nonrestrictive clauses</u>, which
See 17d1 are set off by commas. *That* introduces <u>restrictive</u> <u>clauses</u>, which are not set off by commas. *Who* can introduce either restrictive or nonrestrictive clauses.

CHAPTER 9

Using Adjectives and Adverbs

Adjectives modify nouns and pronouns. **Adverbs** modify verbs, adjectives, or other adverbs—or entire phrases, clauses, or sentences.

The function of a word, not its form, determines whether it is an adjective or an adverb. Although many adverbs (such as *immediately* and *hopelessly*) end in *-ly*, others (such as *almost* and *very*) do not. Moreover, some words that end in *-ly* (such as *lively*) are adjectives.

ESL Tip

For information on correct placement of adjectives and adverbs in a sentence, **see 43d1.** For information on correct order of adjectives in a series, **see 43d2.**

9a Using Adjectives as Subject Complements

See A1.3 Be sure to use an adjective, not an adverb, as a subject complement. A <u>subject complement</u> is a word that follows a linking verb and modifies the sentence's subject, not its verb. A **linking verb** does not show physical or emotional action. *Seem, appear, believe, become, grow, turn, remain, prove, look, sound, smell, taste, feel,* and the forms of the verb *be* are or can be used as linking verbs.

Michelle seemed <u>brave</u>. (*Seemed* shows no action and is therefore a linking verb. Because *brave* is a subject complement that modifies the noun *Michelle*, it takes the adjective form.)

Michelle smiled <u>bravely</u>. (*Smiled* shows action, so it is not a linking verb. *Bravely* modifies *smiled*, so it takes the adverb form.)

NOTE: Sometimes the same verb can function either as a linking verb or as an action verb.

He looked <u>hungry</u>. (*Looked* is a linking verb; *hungry* modifies the subject.)

He looked <u>hungrily</u> at the sandwich. (*Looked* is an action verb; *hungrily* modifies the verb.)

9b   Using Adverbs Appropriately

Be sure to use an adverb, not an adjective, to modify verbs, adjectives, or other adverbs—or entire phrases, clauses, or sentences.

Most students did ~~great~~ _∧*very well* on the midterm.

My parents dress a lot more conservative*ly* than my friends do.

Close-up: Using Adjectives and Adverbs

In informal speech, adjective forms such as *good*, *bad*, *sure*, *real*, *slow*, *quick*, and *loud* are often used to modify verbs, adjectives, and adverbs. Avoid these informal modifiers in college writing.

The program ran ~~real good~~ *really well* the first time we tried it, but the new system performed ~~bad~~ *badly*.

9c   Using Comparative and Superlative Forms

Comparative and Superlative Forms		
Form	**Function**	**Example**
Positive	Describes a quality; indicates no comparisons	big
Comparative	Indicates comparisons between two qualities (greater or lesser)	bigger
Superlative	Indicates comparisons among more than two qualities (greatest or least)	biggest

NOTE: Some adverbs, particularly those indicating time, place, and degree (*almost, very, here, yesterday,* and *immediately*), do not have comparative or superlative forms.

(1) Regular Comparatives and Superlatives

To form the comparative and superlative, all one-syllable adjectives and many two-syllable adjectives (particularly those that end in *-y, -ly, -le, -er,* and *-ow*) add *-er* or *-est:* slow<u>er</u>, funni<u>er</u>; slow<u>est</u>, funni<u>est</u>. (Note that a final *y* becomes *i* before the *-er* or *-est* is added.)

Other two-syllable adjectives and all long adjectives form the comparative with *more* and the superlative with *most:* <u>more</u> famous, <u>more</u> incredible; <u>most</u> famous, <u>most</u> incredible.

Adverbs ending in *-ly* also form the comparative with *more* and the superlative with *most:* <u>more</u> slowly; <u>most</u> slowly. Other adverbs use the *-er* and *-est* endings: soon<u>er</u>; soon<u>est</u>.

All adjectives and adverbs indicate a lesser degree with *less* (<u>less</u> lovely; <u>less</u> slowly) and the least degree with *least* (<u>least</u> lovely; <u>least</u> slowly).

Close-up: Using Comparatives and Superlatives

- Never use both *more* and *-er* to form the comparative, and never use both *most* and *-est* to form the superlative.

  Nothing could have been ~~more~~ easier.

  Jack is the ~~most~~ meanest person in town.

- Never use the superlative when comparing only two things.

  Stacy is the ~~oldest~~ *older* of the two sisters.

- Never use the comparative when comparing more than two things.

  We chose the ~~earlier~~ *earliest* of the four appointments.

---

(2) Irregular Comparative and Superlative Forms

Some adjectives and adverbs have irregular comparative and superlative forms.

Irregular Comparative and Superlative Forms

	Positive	**Comparative**	**Superlative**
Adjectives:	good	better	best
	bad	worse	worst
	a little	less	least
	many, some, much	more	most
Adverbs:	well	better	best
	badly	worse	worst

Close-up: Illogical Comparative and Superlative Forms

Adjectives and adverbs that denote absolute states can logically exist only in the positive degree. For example, words such as *perfect, unique, empty, excellent, impossible, parallel,* and *dead* cannot have comparative or superlative forms.

I read ~~the most~~ excellent story.
     an

The bobblehead in her collection was ~~very~~ unique.

Spelling and Grammar: English (U.S.)

Wordiness:
It is important to learn the true facts before we proceed.

Suggestions:
Facts

Writing Effective Sentences

10 Writing Varied Sentences 56
10a Using Compound and Complex Sentences 56
10b Varying Sentence Length 57
10c Varying Sentence Openings 59

11 Writing Concise Sentences 59
11a Eliminating Nonessential Words 59
11b Eliminating Unnecessary Repetition 61
11c Tightening Rambling Sentences 62

12 Revising Awkward or Confusing Sentences 64
12a Revising Unwarranted Shifts 64
12b Revising Mixed Constructions 65
12c Revising Faulty Predication 66

13 Using Parallelism 66
13a Using Parallelism Effectively 67
13b Revising Faulty Parallelism 67

14 Placing Modifiers Carefully 68
14a Revising Misplaced Modifiers 69
14b Revising Intrusive Modifiers 70
14c Revising Dangling Modifiers 70

15 Choosing Words 71
15a Choosing the Right Word 71
15b Avoiding Inappropriate Language 73
15c Avoiding Biased Language 74

CHAPTER 10

Writing Varied Sentences

10a Using Compound and Complex Sentences

See A2.2 Paragraphs that mix <u>simple sentences</u> with compound and complex sentences are more varied—and therefore more interesting—than those that do not.

(1) Compound Sentences

A **compound sentence** consists of two or more independent clauses joined with *coordinating conjunctions, transitional words and phrases, correlative conjunctions, semicolons,* or *colons.*

Coordinating Conjunctions

The pianist made some mistakes, <u>but</u> the concert was a success.

NOTE: Use a comma before a coordinating conjunction— See A2.3 *and, or, nor, but, for, so,* and *yet*—that joins two <u>independent clauses</u>.

Transitional Words and Phrases

The saxophone does not belong to the brass family; <u>in fact</u>, it is a member of the woodwind family.

NOTE: Use a semicolon—not a comma—before a transitional word or phrase that joins two independent clauses. See 3b Frequently used <u>transitional words and phrases</u> include conjunctive adverbs like *consequently, finally, still,* and *thus* as well as expressions like *for example, in fact,* and *for instance.*

Correlative Conjunctions

<u>Either</u> he left his coat in his locker, <u>or</u> he left it on the bus.

Semicolons

Alaska is the largest state; Rhode Island is the smallest.

Colons

He got his orders: he was to leave for Iraq on Sunday.

(2) Complex Sentences

A **complex sentence** consists of one independent clause and at least one <u>dependent clause</u>. In a complex sentence, a **subordinating conjunction** or **relative pronoun** links the independent and dependent clauses and indicates the relationship between them. See A2.3

        (dependent clause)   (independent clause)
[After the town was evacuated], [the hurricane began].

      (independent clause)   (dependent clause)
[Officials watched the storm], [which threatened to destroy the town].

                    (dependent clause)
Town officials, [who were very concerned], watched the storm.

Frequently Used Subordinating Conjunctions

after	before	until
although	if	when
as	once	whenever
as if	since	where
as though	that	wherever
because	unless	while

Relative Pronouns

that	whatever	who (whose, whom)
what	which	whoever (whomever)

10b Varying Sentence Length

Strings of short simple sentences can be tedious—and sometimes hard to follow, as the following paragraph indicates.

> John Peter Zenger was a newspaper editor. He waged and won an important battle for freedom of the press in America. He criticized the policies of the British governor. He was charged with criminal libel as a result. Zenger's lawyers were disbarred by the governor. Andrew Hamilton defended him. Hamilton convinced the jury that Zenger's criticisms were true. Therefore, the statements were not libelous.

You can revise choppy sentences like these by using *coordination, subordination,* or *embedding* to combine them with adjacent sentences.

Coordination pairs similar elements—words, phrases, or clauses—giving equal weight to each.

Two choppy sentences linked with and, creating compound sentence John Peter Zenger was a newspaper editor. He waged and won an important battle for freedom of the press in America. <u>He criticized the policies of the British governor, and he was charged with criminal libel as a result.</u> Zenger's lawyers were disbarred by the governor. Andrew Hamilton defended him. Hamilton convinced the jury that Zenger's criticisms were true. Therefore, the statements were not libelous.

ESL Tip

Some ESL students rely on simple sentences and coordination in their writing because they are afraid of making sentence structure errors. The result is a monotonous style. To add variety, try using **subordination** and **embedding** (explained below) in your sentences.

Subordination places the more important idea in an independent clause and the less important idea in a dependent clause.

Simple sentences become dependent clauses, creating two complex sentences <u>John Peter Zenger was a newspaper editor who waged and won an important battle for freedom of the press in America.</u> He criticized the policies of the British governor, and he was charged with criminal libel as a result. <u>When Zenger's lawyers were disbarred by the governor, Andrew Hamilton defended him.</u> Hamilton convinced the jury that Zenger's criticisms were true. Therefore, the statements were not libelous.

Embedding is the working of additional words and phrases into sentences.

The sentence Hamilton convinced the jury . . . becomes the phrase convincing the jury John Peter Zenger was a newspaper editor who waged and won an important battle for freedom of the press in America. He criticized the policies of the British governor, and he was charged with criminal libel as a result. <u>When Zenger's lawyers were disbarred by the governor, Andrew Hamilton defended him, convincing the jury that Zenger's criticisms were true.</u> Therefore, the statements were not libelous.

This final revision of the original paragraph's choppy sentences is interesting and readable because it is composed of varied and logically linked sentences. The final short simple sentence has been retained for emphasis.

10c　Varying Sentence Openings

Rather than beginning every sentence with the subject, begin some with modifying words, phrases, or clauses.

Words

<u>Proud</u> and <u>relieved</u>, they watched their daughter receive her diploma. (adjectives)

Phrases

<u>For better or worse</u>, credit cards are now widely available to college students. (prepositional phrase)

<u>Located on the west coast of Great Britain</u>, Wales is part of the United Kingdom. (participial phrase)

<u>His interests widening</u>, Picasso designed ballet sets and illustrated books. (absolute phrase)

Clauses

<u>After Woodrow Wilson was incapacitated by a stroke</u>, his wife unofficially performed many presidential duties. (adverb clause)

CHAPTER 11

Writing Concise Sentences

A sentence is not concise simply because it is short; a concise sentence contains only the words necessary to make its point.

11a　Eliminating Nonessential Words

Whenever possible, delete nonessential words—*deadwood, utility words,* and *circumlocution*—from your writing.

(1) Eliminating Deadwood

The term **deadwood** refers to unnecessary phrases that take up space and add nothing to meaning.

Many
~~There were many~~ factors ~~that~~ influenced his decision
to become a priest.

Shoppers ~~who are~~ looking for bargains often go to
outlets.

an exhausting
They played a racquetball game ~~that was exhausting~~.

This
~~In~~ this article ~~it~~ discusses lead poisoning.

Deadwood also includes unnecessary statements of
opinion, such as *I feel*, *it seems to me*, and *in my opinion*.

The
~~In my opinion, I believe the~~ characters seem undeveloped.

This
~~As far as I'm concerned, this~~ course looks interesting.

(2) Eliminating Utility Words

Utility words function as filler; they contribute nothing
to the meaning of a sentence. Utility words include
nouns with imprecise meanings (*factor, situation, type, as-
pect*, and so on); adjectives so general that they are almost
meaningless (*good, bad, important*); and common adverbs
denoting degree (*basically, actually, quite, very, definitely*).
Often you can just delete a utility word; if you cannot, replace it with a more precise word.

Registration
~~The registration situation~~ was disorganized.

an
The scholarship ~~basically~~ offered Fran ~~a good~~ opportunity to study Spanish.

It was ~~actually~~ a worthwhile book, but I didn't ~~com-
pletely~~ finish it.

(3) Eliminating Circumlocution

Circumlocution is taking a roundabout way to say
something (using ten words when five will do). Instead of
complicated constructions, use concise, specific words
and phrases that come right to the point.

The
~~It is not unlikely that the~~ trend toward lower con-
probably
sumer spending will continue.

while
Joe was in the army ̭ ~~during the same time that~~ I was
in college.

Close-up: Revising Wordy Phrases

If you cannot edit a wordy construction, substitute a more concise, more direct term.

Wordy	Concise
at the present time	now
due to the fact that	because
in the vicinity of	near
have the ability to	be able to

11b Eliminating Unnecessary Repetition

Redundant word groups (repeated words or phrases that
say the same thing) and other kinds of unnecessary repetition can annoy readers and obscure your meaning. Correct unnecessary repetition by using one of the following
strategies.

(1) Deleting Redundancy

People's clothing ~~attire~~ can reveal a good deal about
their personalities.

Grammar Checker: Deleting Redundancy

Your word processor's grammar checker will
often highlight redundant expressions and offer suggestions for revision.

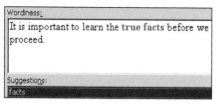

---

(2) Substituting a Pronoun

Fictional detective Miss Marple has solved many
                                                    her
crimes. *The Murder at the Vicarage* was one of ̭ ~~Miss
Marple's~~ most challenging cases.

(3) Creating an Appositive

Red Barber, was a sportscaster, He was known for his colorful expressions.

(4) Creating a Compound

John F. Kennedy was the youngest man ever elected president, *and* He was the first Catholic to hold this office.

(5) Creating a Complex Sentence

Americans value freedom of speech, *which* Freedom of speech is guaranteed by the First Amendment.

11c Tightening Rambling Sentences

The combination of nonessential words, unnecessary repetition, and complicated syntax creates **rambling sentences.** Revising rambling sentences frequently requires extensive editing.

(1) Eliminating Excessive Coordination

When you string a series of clauses together with coordinating conjunctions, you create a rambling, unfocused *See 10a1* compound sentence. To revise such sentences, first identify the main idea or ideas, and then subordinate the supporting details.

Benjamin Franklin, was the son of a candlemaker, but he later apprenticed with his half-brother as a printer, and this *an* experience *that* led to his buying *The Pennsylvania Gazette,* *which* and he managed this periodical with great success.

(2) Eliminating Adjective Clauses

See A2.3 A series of adjective clauses is also likely to produce a rambling sentence. To revise, substitute concise modifying words or phrases for adjective clauses.

Moby-Dick, which is a novel about a white whale, was *revised the first draft at the urging of his* written by Herman Melville, who was friendly with

Nathaniel Hawthorne,~~who urged him to revise the first draft.~~

(3) Eliminating Passive Constructions

Excessive use of the <u>passive voice</u> can create rambling sentences. Correct this problem by changing passive voice to active voice.

See 7d

Concerned Americans are organizing
"Buy American" rallies ~~are being organized by con-~~
hoping
~~cerned Americans who hope~~ that jobs ~~can be saved by~~
can save jobs.
such gatherings,

Grammar Checker: Eliminating Passive Constructions

Your word processor's grammar checker will highlight passive voice constructions in your writing and offer revision suggestions.

> **Passive Voice:**
> High test scores that will improve his grade point average are being achieved by the student.
>
> **Suggestions:**
> The student is achieving high test scores that will improve his grade point average

---

(4) Eliminating Wordy Prepositional Phrases

When you revise, substitute adjectives or adverbs for wordy <u>prepositional phrases</u>.

See A2.3

dangerous *exciting*
The trip was ~~one of danger~~ but also ~~one of excitement.~~

confidently *authoritatively.*
He spoke ~~in a confident manner~~ and ~~with a lot of au-~~
~~thority,~~

(5) Eliminating Wordy Noun Constructions

Substitute strong verbs for wordy <u>noun phrases</u>.

See A2.3

decided
We have ~~made the decision~~ to postpone the meeting
appear
until ~~the appearance of~~ all the board members.

CHAPTER 12

Revising Awkward or Confusing Sentences

The most common causes of awkward or confusing sentences are *unwarranted shifts*, *mixed constructions*, *faulty predication*, and *illogical comparisons*.

12a Revising Unwarranted Shifts

(1) Shifts in Tense

See
7b;
ESL
43a2

Verb <u>tense</u> in a sentence or in a related group of sentences should not shift without good reason—to indicate changes of time, for example. Unwarranted shifts in tense can be confusing.

I registered for the advanced philosophy seminar because I wanted a challenge. However, by the first week
I s̶t̶a̶r̶t̶ *started* having trouble understanding the reading. (unwarranted shift from past to present)

Jack Kerouac's novel *On the Road* follows a group of
friends who d̶r̶o̶v̶e̶ *drive* across the United States in the
1950s. (unwarranted shift from present to past)

NOTE: The present tense is used in discussions of literary works.

(2) Shifts in Voice

See
7d
ESL
43a6

Unwarranted shifts from active to passive <u>voice</u> (or from passive to active) can be confusing. In the following sentence, for instance, the shift from active (*wrote*) to passive (*was written*) makes it unclear who wrote *The Great Gatsby*.

F. Scott Fitzgerald wrote *This Side of Paradise*, and
later *wrote* *The Great Gatsby* w̶a̶s̶ w̶r̶i̶t̶t̶e̶n̶.

NOTE: Sometimes a shift from active to passive voice within a sentence may be necessary to give the sentence proper emphasis: Even though consumers <u>protested</u>, the

64

sales tax was <u>increased</u>. (To say *the legislature increased the sales tax* would draw the sentence's emphasis away from *consumers.*)

(3) Shifts in Mood

Unwarranted shifts in <u>mood</u> can also create awkward sentences. ^{See 7c}

> Next, heat the mixture in a test tube, and ~~you should make~~ ^{be} sure it does not boil. (unwarranted shift from imperative to indicative)

(4) Shifts in Person and Number

<u>Person</u> indicates who is speaking (first person—*I, we*), ^{ESL 43a1} who is spoken to (second person—*you*), and who is spoken about (third person—*he, she, it,* and *they*). Unwarranted shifts between the second and the third person are most often responsible for awkward sentences.

> ^{you}
> When ~~someone~~ looks for a car loan, you compare the interest rates of several banks. (unwarranted shift from third to second person)

<u>Number</u> indicates one (singular—*novel, it*) or more than one (plural—*novels, they, them*). Singular pronouns should refer to singular **antecedents** and plural pronouns to plural antecedents. ^{See 8c; ESL 43c1}

> ^{he or she}
> If a person does not study regularly, ~~they~~ will have a difficult time passing Spanish. (unwarranted shift from singular to plural)

12b Revising Mixed Constructions

A **mixed construction** is created when a dependent clause, prepositional phrase, or independent clause is incorrectly used as the subject of a sentence.

> Because she studies every day, ~~explains why~~ she gets good grades. (dependent clause incorrectly used as subject)

> ^{, you can}
> By calling for information, ~~is the way to~~ learn more about the benefits of ROTC. (prepositional phrase incorrectly used as subject)

Being
~~He was~~ late ~~was what~~ made him miss Act 1. (independent clause incorrectly used as subject)

12c Revising Faulty Predication

Faulty predication occurs when a sentence's predicate does not logically complete its subject. Faulty predication is especially common in sentences that contain a linking verb—a form of the verb *be*, for example—and a subject complement.

caused
Mounting costs and decreasing revenues ~~were~~ the downfall of the hospital.

Faulty predication also occurs in one-sentence definitions that contain a construction like *is where* or *is when*. *Is* must be preceded and followed by a noun or noun phrase.

the construction of
Taxidermy is ~~where you construct~~ a lifelike representation of an animal from its preserved skin.

Finally, faulty predication occurs when the phrase *the reason is* precedes *because*. In this situation, *because* (which means "for the reason that") is redundant and can be deleted.

that
The reason we drive is ~~because~~ we are afraid to fly.

CHAPTER 13

Using Parallelism

Parallelism—the use of matching words, phrases, clauses, or sentence structures to express equivalent ideas—adds unity, balance, and force to your writing. Effective parallelism can help you write clearer sentences, but faulty parallelism can create awkward sentences that obscure your meaning and confuse readers.

13a Using Parallelism Effectively

(1) With Items in a Series

<u>Eat</u>, <u>drink</u>, and <u>be</u> merry.

<u>Baby food consumption</u>, <u>toy production</u>, and <u>mini-van sales</u> are likely to decline as the U.S. population ages.

(2) With Paired Items

Paired words, phrases, or clauses should be presented in parallel terms.

The thank-you note was <u>short</u> but <u>sweet</u>.

<u>Ask not what your country can do for you</u>; <u>ask what you can do for your country</u>. (John F. Kennedy)

Paired items linked by **correlative conjunctions** (such as *not only . . . but also* and *either . . . or*) should always be parallel.

The designer paid attention not only <u>to color</u> but also <u>to texture</u>.

Either <u>repeat physics</u> or <u>take calculus</u>.

Parallelism is also used with paired elements linked by *than* or *as*.

Richard Wright and James Baldwin chose <u>to live in Paris</u> rather than <u>to remain in the United States</u>.

NOTE: Elements in <u>outlines</u> and <u>lists</u> should also be parallel.

See 28h1, 38c

13b Revising Faulty Parallelism

Faulty parallelism occurs when elements that have the same function in a sentence are not presented in parallel terms.

Many developing countries lack sufficient housing, sufficient food, and _^*sufficient* ~~their~~ health-care facilities ~~are also insufficient~~.

To correct faulty parallelism, match nouns with nouns, verbs with verbs, and phrases or clauses with similarly constructed phrases or clauses.

Popular exercises for men and women include spin-
ning, weight ~~lifters~~, and jogging.
^lifting^

I look forward to hearing from you and to ~~have~~ an
opportunity to tell you more about myself.
^having^

Close-up: Repeating Key Words

Although the use of similar grammatical structures may be enough to convey parallelism, sometimes
sentences are even clearer if certain key words (for example, prepositions that introduce items in a series) are also
parallel. In the following sentence, repeating the preposition *by* makes it clear that *not* applies only to the first
phrase.

Computerization has helped industry by not allowing la-
bor costs to skyrocket, ^by^ increasing the speed of production, and ^by^ improving efficiency.

Grammar Checker: Revising Faulty Parallelism

Grammar checkers are not very useful for identifying
faulty parallelism. Although your grammar checker may
highlight some nonparallel constructions, it may not identify others.

CHAPTER 14

Placing Modifiers Carefully

A **modifier** is a word, phrase, or clause that describes,
limits, or qualifies another word or word group in the
sentence. A modifier should be placed close to its **headword,** the word or phrase it modifies. **Faulty modification** is the confusing placement of modifiers or the modification of nonexistent words.

14a   Revising Misplaced Modifiers

A **misplaced modifier** is a word or word group whose placement suggests that it modifies one word or phrase when it is intended to modify another.

> *Wendy watched the storm, fierce*
> ^Fierce and threatening, ~~Wendy watched the storm.~~
> (The storm, not Wendy, was fierce and threatening.)

(1) Placing Modifying Words Precisely

Limiting modifiers such as *almost*, *only*, *even*, and *just* should come immediately before the words they modify. A different placement will change the meaning of a sentence.

> Nick *just* set up camp at the edge of town. (He did it just now.)

> *Just* Nick set up camp at the edge of town. (He did it alone.)

> Nick set up camp *just* at the edge of town. (His camp was precisely at the edge.)

When a limiting modifier is placed so that it is not clear whether it modifies a word before it or one after it, it is called a **squinting modifier.**

> The life that everyone thought would fulfill her <u>totally</u> bored her.

To correct a squinting modifier, place the modifier so that it clearly modifies its headword.

> The life that everyone thought would <u>totally</u> fulfill her bored her. (She was expected to be totally fulfilled.)

> The life that everyone thought would fulfill her bored her <u>totally</u>. (She was totally bored.)

(2) Relocating Misplaced Phrases

When you revise, relocate misplaced verbal phrases directly before or directly after the words or word groups they modify.

> *Roller-skating along the shore,*
> ^Jane watched the boats. ~~roller-skating along the shore.~~

Place prepositional phrase modifiers immediately after the words they modify.

Venus de Milo is a statue ∧ created by a famous artist ∧ ~~with no arms.~~

[with no arms inserted above after "statue"]

(3) Relocating Misplaced Dependent Clauses

A dependent clause that serves as a modifier must clearly relate to its headword. An **adjective clause** usually appears immediately after the word it modifies.

This diet program ∧ will limit the consumption of possible carcinogens ∧ ~~which will benefit everyone.~~

[, which will benefit everyone, inserted after "program"]

An **adverb clause** may appear in various positions, but its relationship to its headword must be clear and logical.

∧ ~~The~~ parents checked to see that the children were sleeping ∧ ~~after they had a glass of wine.~~

[After they had a glass of wine, the inserted at the start]

14b Revising Intrusive Modifiers

An **intrusive modifier** interrupts a sentence, making the sentence difficult to understand.

Revise when a long modifying phrase comes between an auxiliary verb and a main verb.

∧ She had, ~~without~~ giving it a second thought or considering the consequences, ∧ planned to reenlist.

[Without inserted before "She had"; she had inserted before "planned"]

See A1.3 Revise when a modifier awkwardly "splits" an **infinitive**, coming between the word *to* and the verb.

He hoped to ∧ quickly and easily ∧ ~~defeat his opponent.~~

[defeat his opponent inserted after "to"]

14c Revising Dangling Modifiers

A **dangling modifier** is a word or phrase that cannot logically modify any word or word group in the sentence.

Using this drug, many undesirable side effects are experienced. (Who is using this drug?)

One way to correct this dangling modifier is to create a new subject by adding a word or word group that *using this drug* can modify.

Using this drug, <u>patients</u> experience many undesirable side effects.

Another way to correct the dangling modifier is to change it into a dependent clause.

Many undesirable side effects are experienced <u>when this drug is used</u>.

> **Close-up: Dangling Modifiers and the Passive Voice**
>
>
>
> Most sentences that include dangling modifiers do not include a headword because they are in the passive voice. Changing the <u>passive voice</u> to the <u>active voice</u> corrects the dangling modifier by changing the subject of the sentence's main clause (*side effects*) to a word that the dangling modifier can logically modify (*patients*).
>
> See 7d; ESL 43a6

CHAPTER 15

Choosing Words

15a   Choosing the Right Word

(1) Denotation and Connotation

A word's **denotation** is its basic dictionary meaning—what it stands for without any emotional associations. A word's **connotations** are the emotional, social, and political associations it has in addition to its denotative meaning.

Word	Denotation	Connotation
politician	someone who holds a political office	opportunist; wheeler-dealer

If you use terms without considering their connotations, you run the risk of confusing and possibly angering your readers.

> ### ESL Tip
> Dictionary entries sometimes give a word's con-
> notations as well as its denotations. You can increase your
> understanding of a word's connotations by paying atten-
> tion to the context in which the word appears.

(2) Euphemisms

A **euphemism** is a polite term used in place of a blunt
term that describes a subject that many people consider
offensive or unpleasant. College writing is no place for
euphemisms. Say what you mean—*pregnant*, not *expect-
ing*; *died*, not *passed away*; and *strike*, not *work stoppage*.

(3) Specific and General Words

Specific words refer to particular persons, items, or
events; **general** words denote entire classes or groups.
Queen Elizabeth II, for example, is more specific than
monarch; *jeans* is more specific than *clothing*; and *SUV* is
more specific than *vehicle*. You can use general words to
describe entire classes of items, but you must use specific
words to clarify such generalizations.

(4) Abstract and Concrete Words

Abstract words—*beauty, truth, justice*, and so on—refer
to ideas, qualities, or conditions that cannot be perceived
by the senses. **Concrete** words name things that readers
can see, hear, taste, smell, or touch. The more concrete
your words and phrases, the more vivid the image you
evoke in the reader.

> ### Close-up: Using Specific Words
> Avoid general words such as *nice, great*, and *ter-
> rific* that say nothing and could be used in almost any sen-
> tence. These <u>utility words</u> convey only enthusiasm, not
> precise meanings. Replace them with more specific words.

See
11a2

(5) Commonly Confused Words (Homophones)

Some words, such as *accept* and *except*, are pronounced
alike but spelled differently. Because they are often confused, you should be very careful when you use them.

accept	to receive
except	other than
affect	to have an influence on (*verb*)
effect	result (*noun*); to cause (*verb*)
its	possessive of *it*
it's	contraction of *it is*

For a full list of these and other homophones, along with their meanings and sentences illustrating their use, **see Appendix B.**

15b Avoiding Inappropriate Language

When you write, use language that is appropriate for your audience and purpose.

(1) Jargon

Jargon, the specialized or technical vocabulary of a trade, profession, or academic discipline, is useful for communicating in the field for which it was developed, but outside that field it can be confusing.

The patient had ~~an acute myocardial infarction.~~ *a heart attack.*

(2) Pretentious Diction

Good writing is clear writing, and pompous or flowery language is no substitute for clarity. Revise to eliminate **pretentious diction,** inappropriately elevated and wordy language.

As I fell ~~into slumber,~~ *asleep* I ~~cogitated~~ *thought* about my day ~~ambling~~ *hiking* through ~~the splendor of~~ the Appalachian Mountains.

(3) Clichés

Clichés are trite expressions that have lost all meaning because they have been so overused. Familiar sayings like "last but not least," "crystal clear," and "what goes around comes around," for example, do little to enhance your writing. Avoid the temptation to use clichés in your college writing. Take the time to think of fresh language.

15c Avoiding Biased Language

(1) Offensive Labels

When referring to a racial, ethnic, or religious group, use words with neutral connotations or words that the group itself uses in *formal* speech or writing. Also avoid potentially offensive labels related to age, class, occupation, physical ability, or sexual orientation.

(2) Sexist Language

Be careful to avoid **sexist language**, language that promotes gender stereotypes. Sexist language entails much more than the use of derogatory words such as *hunk* and *bimbo*. Assuming that some professions are exclusive to one gender—for instance, that *nurse* denotes only women or that *engineer* denotes only men—is also sexist. So is the use of job titles such as *mailman* for *letter carrier* and *stewardess* for *flight attendant*.

Sexist language also occurs when a writer fails to apply the same terminology to both men and women. For example, you should refer to two scientists with Ph.D.s not as Dr. Sagan and Mrs. Yallow, but as Dr. Sagan and Dr. Yallow.

In your writing, always use *women*—not *girls* or *ladies*—when referring to adult females. Also avoid using the generic *he* or *him* when your subject could be either male or female. Instead, use the third-person plural or the phrase *he or she* (not *he/she*).

Sexist: Before boarding, each <u>passenger</u> should make certain that <u>he</u> has <u>his</u> ticket.

Revised: Before boarding, <u>passengers</u> should make certain that <u>they</u> have <u>their</u> tickets.

Revised: Before boarding, each <u>passenger</u> should make certain that <u>he</u> or <u>she</u> has a ticket.

NOTE: Be careful not to use *they* or *their* to refer to a singular antecedent.

Drivers
﹏Any ~~driver~~ caught speeding should have their driving privileges suspended.

Close-up: Eliminating Sexist Language

For most sexist usages, there are nonsexist alternatives.

Sexist Usage	Possible Revisions
1. Mankind	People, human beings
Man's accomplishments	Human accomplishments
Man-made	Synthetic
2. Female engineer (lawyer, accountant, etc.), male model	Engineer (lawyer, accountant, etc.), model
3. Policeman/woman	Police officer
Salesman/woman/girl	Salesperson/clerk
Businessman/woman	Businessperson, executive
4. Everyone should complete his application by Tuesday.	Everyone should complete his or her application by Tuesday.
	All students should complete their applications by Tuesday.

Understanding Punctuation

16 Using End Punctuation   78
16a Using Periods   78
16b Using Question Marks   79
16c Using Exclamation Points   80

17 Using Commas   80
17a Setting Off Independent Clauses   80
17b Setting Off Items in a Series   81
17c Setting Off Introductory Elements   82
17d Setting Off Nonessential Material   82
17e Using Commas in Other Conventional Contexts   86
17f Using Commas to Prevent Misreading   86
17g Editing Misused Commas   87

18 Using Semicolons   88
18a Separating Independent Clauses   88
18b Separating Items in a Series   88
18c Editing Misused Semicolons   89

19 Using Apostrophes   90
19a Forming the Possessive Case   90
19b Indicating Omissions in Contractions   91
19c Forming Plurals   92

20 Using Quotation Marks   93
20a Setting Off Quoted Speech or Writing   93
20b Setting Off Titles   96
20c Setting Off Words Used in Special Ways   97
20d Using Quotation Marks with Other Punctuation   97
20e Editing Misused Quotation Marks   98

21 Using Other Punctuation Marks   99
21a Using Colons   99
21b Using Dashes   100
21c Using Parentheses   101
21d Using Brackets   102
21e Using Slashes   102
21f Using Ellipses   103

CHAPTER 16

Using End Punctuation

16a Using Periods

Use a period to signal the end of most sentences, including indirect questions.

Something is rotten in Denmark.

They wondered whether the water was safe to drink.

Also use periods in most abbreviations.

Mr. Spock   Aug.   Dr. Livingstone

9 p.m.   etc.   1600 Pennsylvania Ave.

If an abbreviation ends the sentence, do not add another period.

He promised to be there at 6 a.m.

However, add a question mark if the sentence is a question.

Did he arrive at 6 p.m.?

If the abbreviation falls *within* a sentence, use normal punctuation after the period.

He promised to be there at 6 p.m., but he forgot.

Close-up: Abbreviations without Periods

Abbreviations composed of all capital letters do not usually require periods unless they stand for initials of people's names (E. B. White).

MD   RN   BC

Familiar abbreviations of names of corporations or government agencies and scientific and technical terms do not require periods.

CD-ROM   NYU   DNA   CIA   WCAU-FM

Acronyms—new words formed from the initial letters or first few letters of a series of words—do not include periods.

hazmat   AIDS   NAFTA   CAT scan

Clipped forms (commonly accepted shortened forms of words, such as *gym*, *dorm*, *math*, and *fax*) do not use periods.

Postal abbreviations do not include periods.

TX   CA   MS   PA   FL   NY

Use periods to mark divisions in dramatic, poetic, and biblical references.

Hamlet 2.2.1–5 (act, scene, lines)
Paradise Lost 7.163–167 (book, lines)
Judges 4.14 (chapter, verse)

NOTE: In **MLA parenthetical references**, titles of literary and biblical works are often abbreviated: Ham. 2.2.1-5; Judg. 4.14. See 33a1

Close-up: Electronic Addresses

Periods, along with other punctuation marks (such as slashes and colons), are used in electronic addresses (URLs).

g.mckay@smu.edu.
http://www.nwu.org/nwu

NOTE: When you type an electronic address, do not end it with a period, and do not add spaces after periods within the address.

16b   Using Question Marks

Use a question mark to signal the end of a direct question.

Who was that masked man?

Use a question mark in parentheses to indicate that a date or number is uncertain.

Aristophanes, the Greek playwright, was born in 448 (?) BC and died in 380 (?) BC.

> **Close-up: Editing Misused Question Marks**
>
> Use a period, not a question mark, with an indirect question.
>
> The personnel officer asked whether he knew how to type?.
>
> Do not use a question mark to convey sarcasm. Instead, suggest your attitude through your choice of words.
>
>   *not very*
> I refused his ₍generous (?) offer.

16c Using Exclamation Points

An exclamation point is used to signal the end of an emotional or emphatic statement, an emphatic interjection, or a forceful command.

    Remember the Maine!

    "No! Don't leave!" he cried.

> **Close-up: Editing Misused Exclamation Points**
>
> Except for recording dialogue, do not use exclamation points in college writing. Even in informal writing, use exclamation points sparingly.

CHAPTER 17

Using Commas

17a Setting Off Independent Clauses

Use a comma when you form a compound sentence by linking two independent clauses with a <u>coordinating conjunction</u> (*and, but, or, nor, for, yet, so*) or a pair of <u>correlative conjunctions</u>.

See A1.7

    The House approved the bill, <u>but</u> the Senate rejected it.

    <u>Either</u> the hard drive is full, <u>or</u> the modem is too slow.

NOTE: You may omit the comma if two clauses connected by a coordinating conjunction are very short: Love it <u>or</u> leave it.

17b Setting Off Items in a Series

Use commas between items in a series of three or more **coordinate elements** (words, phrases, or clauses joined by a coordinating conjunction).

> *Chipmunk, raccoon,* and *Mugwump* are Native American words.

> You may pay <u>by check, with a credit card,</u> or <u>in cash.</u>

> <u>Brazilians speak Portuguese, Colombians speak Spanish,</u> and <u>Haitians speak French and Creole.</u>

NOTE: To avoid ambiguity, always use a comma before the coordinating conjunction that separates the last two items in a series.

Do not use a comma to introduce or to close a series.

> Three important criteria are⌿ fat content, salt content, and taste.

> The provinces Quebec, Ontario, and Alberta⌿ are in Canada.

Use a comma between items in a series of two or more **coordinate adjectives**—adjectives that modify the same word or word group—unless they are joined by a conjunction.

> She brushed her <u>long, shining</u> hair.

> The baby was <u>tired</u> and <u>cranky</u> and <u>wet</u>. (no commas required)

Checklist: Punctuating Adjectives in a Series

☐ If you can reverse the order of the adjectives or insert *and* between the adjectives without changing the meaning, the adjectives are coordinate, and you should use a comma.

She brushed her long, shining hair.

She brushed her shining, long hair.

She brushed her long [and] shining hair.

(continued)

Punctuating with adjectives (continued)

☐ If you cannot, the adjectives are not coordinate, and you should not use a comma.

Ten red balloons fell from the ceiling.

Red ten balloons fell from the ceiling.

Ten [and] red balloons fell from the ceiling.

NOTE: Numbers—such as *ten*—are not coordinate with other adjectives.

17c Setting Off Introductory Elements

An introductory dependent clause, verbal phrase, or prepositional phrase is generally set off from the rest of the sentence by a comma.

> <u>Although the CIA used to call undercover agents *penetration agents*,</u> they now routinely refer to them as *moles*. (dependent clause)

> <u>Pushing onward,</u> Scott struggled toward the South Pole. (verbal phrase)

> <u>During the Depression,</u> movie attendance rose. (prepositional phrase)

If an introductory prepositional phrase is short and no ambiguity is possible, you may omit the comma: <u>After lunch</u> I took a four-hour nap.

See
3b

Close-up: Transitional Words and Phrases

When a <u>transitional word or phrase</u> begins a sentence, it is usually set off with a comma.

> <u>However,</u> any plan that is enacted must be fair.

> <u>In other words,</u> we cannot act hastily.

17d Setting Off Nonessential Material

Use commas to set off nonessential material whether it appears at the beginning, in the middle, or at the end of a sentence.

(1) Nonrestrictive Modifiers

Use commas to set off **nonrestrictive modifiers,** which supply information that is not essential to the meaning of the word or word group they modify. (Do *not* use commas to set off **restrictive modifiers,** which supply information essential to the meaning of the word or word group they modify.)

> **Nonrestrictive** (commas required): Actors, <u>who have inflated egos,</u> are often insecure. (*All* actors—not just those with inflated egos—are insecure.)

> **Restrictive** (no commas): Actors <u>who have inflated egos</u> are often insecure. (Only those actors with inflated egos—not all actors—are insecure.)

In the following examples, commas set off only nonrestrictive modifiers—those that supply nonessential information—but not restrictive modifiers, which supply essential information.

Adjective Clauses

> **Restrictive:** Speaking in public is something <u>that most</u> people fear.

> **Nonrestrictive:** He ran for the bus, <u>which was late as usual</u>.

Prepositional Phrases

> **Restrictive:** The man <u>with the gun</u> demanded their money.

> **Nonrestrictive:** The clerk, <u>with a nod,</u> dismissed me.

Verbal Phrases

> **Restrictive:** The candidates <u>running for mayor</u> have agreed to a debate.

> **Nonrestrictive:** The marathoner, <u>running his fastest,</u> beat his previous record.

Appositives

> **Restrictive:** The film *Citizen Kane* made Orson Welles famous.

> **Nonrestrictive:** *Citizen Kane,* <u>Orson Welles's first film,</u> made him famous.

Checklist: Restrictive and Nonrestrictive Modifiers

To determine whether a modifier is restrictive or non-restrictive, answer these questions:

☐ Is the modifier essential to the meaning of the noun it modifies (*The man with the gun,* not just any man)? If so, it is restrictive and does not take commas.

☐ Is the modifier introduced by *that* (*something that most people fear*)? If so, it is restrictive. *That* cannot introduce a nonrestrictive clause.

☐ Can you delete the relative pronoun without causing ambiguity or confusion (*something [that] most people fear*)? If so, the clause is restrictive.

☐ Is the appositive more specific than the noun that precedes it (*the film Citizen Kane*)? If so, it is restrictive.

Close-up: Using Commas with *That* and *Which*

In general, *that* is used to introduce restrictive clauses, and *which* is used to introduce nonrestrictive clauses. Many writers, however, use *which* with restrictive clauses as well.

Grammar Checker: *That* or *Which*

Your word processor's grammar checker may identify *which* as an error when it introduces a restrictive clause. It will prompt you to add commas, using *which* to introduce a nonrestrictive clause, or to change *which* to *that*. Review the meaning of your sentence, and revise accordingly.

"That" or "Which":
Only the **books which are in the attic** must be moved.

Suggestions:

books, which are in the attic,
———————————— OR ————————————
books that are in the attic

(2) Transitional Words and Phrases

Transitional words and phrases qualify, clarify, and make connections. Because they are not essential to meaning, however, they are always set off by commas when they interrupt a clause or when they begin or end a sentence. See 3b

> The Outward Bound program, for example, is considered safe.
>
> In fact, Outward Bound has an excellent reputation.
>
> Other programs are not so safe, however.

Close-up: Transitional Words and Phrases

When a transitional word or phrase joins two independent clauses, it must be preceded by a semicolon and followed by a comma.

> Laughter is the best medicine; of course, penicillin also comes in handy sometimes.

---

(3) Contradictory Phrases and Absolute Phrases

A phrase that expresses a contradiction is usually set off from the rest of the sentence by one or more commas.

> This medicine is taken after meals, never on an empty stomach.
>
> Mark McGwire, not Sammy Sosa, was the first to break Roger Maris's home-run record.

An **absolute phrase,** which usually consists of a noun plus a participle, is always set off by a comma.

> His fear increasing, he waited to enter the haunted house.

(4) Miscellaneous Nonessential Elements

Other nonessential elements usually set off by commas include tag questions, names in direct address, mild interjections, and *yes* and *no*.

> This is your first day on the job, isn't it?
>
> I wonder, Mr. Honeywell, whether Mr. Albright deserves a raise.
>
> Well, it's about time.
>
> Yes, that's what I thought.

17e Using Commas in Other Conventional Contexts

(1) With Direct Quotations

In most cases, use commas to set off a direct quotation from the **identifying tag** (*he said, she answered,* and so on).

> Emerson said, "I greet you at the beginning of a great career."

> "I greet you at the beginning of a great career," Emerson said.

> "I greet you," Emerson said, "at the beginning of a great career."

When the identifying tag comes between two complete sentences, however, the tag is introduced by a comma but followed by a period.

> "Winning isn't everything," Coach Vince Lombardi once said. "It's the only thing."

(2) With Titles or Degrees Following a Name

> Michael Crichton, MD, wrote *Jurassic Park.*

> Hamlet, Prince of Denmark, is Shakespeare's most famous character.

(3) In Dates and Addresses

> On August 30, 1983, the space shuttle *Challenger* was launched.

> Her address is 600 West End Avenue, New York, NY 10024.

NOTE: When only the month and year are given, do not use a comma to separate the month from the year: May 1968. Do not use a comma to separate the street number from the street or the state name from the zip code.

17f Using Commas to Prevent Misreading

In some cases, a comma is used to prevent ambiguity. For example, consider the following sentence.

> Those who can, sprint the final lap.

Without the comma, *can* appears to be an auxiliary verb ("Those who can sprint. . . ."), and the sentence seems incomplete. The comma tells readers to pause and thereby prevents confusion.

Also use a comma to acknowledge the omission of a repeated word, usually a verb, and to separate words repeated consecutively.

Pam carried the box; Tim, the suitcase.

Everything bad that could have happened, happened.

17g Editing Misused Commas

Do not use commas in the following situations.

(1) To Set Off Restrictive Modifiers

The film, *Malcolm X*, was directed by Spike Lee.

They planned a picnic, in the park.

(2) Between a Subject and Its Predicate

A woman with dark red hair, opened the door.

(3) Between a Verb and an Indirect Quotation or Indirect Question

General Douglas MacArthur vowed, that he would return.

The landlord asked, if we would sign a two-year lease.

(4) In Compounds That Are Not Composed of Independent Clauses

During the 1400s plagues, and pestilence were common. (compound subject)

Many women thirty-five and older are returning to college, and tend to be good students. (compound predicate)

(5) Before a Dependent Clause at the End of a Sentence

Jane Addams founded Hull House, because she wanted to help Chicago's poor.

CHAPTER 18

Using Semicolons

The **semicolon** is used only between items of equal grammatical rank: two independent clauses, two phrases, and so on.

18a Separating Independent Clauses

Use a semicolon between closely related independent clauses that convey parallel or contrasting information but are not joined by a coordinating conjunction.

> Paul Revere's *The Boston Massacre* is an early example of American protest art; Edward Hicks's later "primitive" paintings are socially conscious art with a religious strain.

Close-up: Using Semicolons

Using only a comma or no punctuation at all between independent clauses creates a <u>comma splice</u> or a <u>fused sentence</u>.

See
Ch. 4

Use a semicolon between two independent clauses when the second clause is introduced by a transitional word or phrase (the transitional element is followed by a comma).

> Thomas Jefferson brought two hundred vanilla beans and a recipe for vanilla ice cream back from France; <u>thus</u>, he gave America its all-time favorite ice cream flavor.

18b Separating Items in a Series

Use semicolons between items in a series when one or more of these items include commas.

> Three papers are posted on the bulletin board outside the building: a description of the exams; a list of appeal procedures for students who fail; and an employment ad from an automobile factory, addressed

specifically to candidates whose appeals are turned down. (Andrea Lee, *Russian Journal*)

Laramie, Wyoming; Wyoming, Delaware; and Delaware, Ohio, were three of the places they visited.

18c Editing Misused Semicolons

Do not use semicolons in the following situations.

(1) Between a Dependent and an Independent Clause

Because drugs can now suppress the body's immune reaction; fewer organ transplants are rejected.

(2) To Introduce a List

Despite the presence of CNN and FOX News, the evening news remains a battleground for the three major television networks; CBS, NBC, and ABC.

(3) To Introduce a Direct Quotation

Marie Antoinette may not have said; "Let them eat cake."

Grammar Checker: Editing Misused Semicolons

Your word processor's grammar checker will highlight certain misused semicolons and frequently offer suggestions for revision.

Comma Use:

Although the library is usually open year-round; it will be closed this fall for renovations.

Suggestions:

year-round,

CHAPTER 19

Using Apostrophes

Use an apostrophe to form the possessive case, to indicate omissions in contractions, and to form certain plurals.

19a Forming the Possessive Case

The possessive case indicates ownership. In English, the possessive case of nouns and indefinite pronouns is indicated either with a phrase that includes the word *of* (the hands *of* the clock) or with an apostrophe and, in most cases, an *s* (the clock's hands).

(1) Singular Nouns and Indefinite Pronouns

To form the possessive case of singular nouns and indefinite pronouns, add -'*s*.

"The Monk's Tale" is one of Chaucer's *Canterbury Tales*.

When we would arrive was anyone's guess.

NOTE: With some singular nouns that end in -*s*, pronouncing the possessive ending as a separate syllable can sound awkward. In such cases, it is acceptable to use just an apostrophe: Crispus Attucks' death, Aristophanes' *Lysistrata*.

(2) Plural Nouns

To form the possessive case of regular plural nouns (those that end in -*s* or -*es*), add only an apostrophe.

Laid-off employees received two weeks' severance pay and three months' medical benefits.

The Lopezes' three children are triplets.

To form the possessive case of nouns that have irregular plurals, add -'*s*.

The Children's Hour is a play by Lillian Hellman.

(3) Compound Nouns or Groups of Words

To form the possessive case of compound words or groups of words, add -'*s* to the last word.

The Secretary of State's resignation was accepted under protest.

This is someone else's responsibility.

(4) Two or More Items

To indicate individual ownership of two or more items, add -'s to each item.

Ernest Hemingway's and Gertrude Stein's writing styles have some similarities.

To indicate joint ownership, add -'s only to the last item.

We studied Lewis and Clark's expedition.

> ### Close-up: Apostrophes with Plural Nouns and Personal Pronouns
>
>
>
> Do not use apostrophes with plural nouns that are not possessive.
>
> The Thompson's are out.
>
> These down vest's are very warm.
>
> The Philadelphia Seventy Sixer's have some outstanding players.
>
> Do not use apostrophes to form the possessive case of personal pronouns.
>
> This ticket must be your's or her's.
>
> The next turn is their's.
>
> The doll lost it's right eye.
>
> The next great moment in history is our's.
>
> Be especially careful not to confuse <u>contractions</u> (which always include apostrophes) with the possessive forms of personal pronouns (which never include apostrophes). See 19b
>
> | **Contraction** | **Possessive Form** |
> | --- | --- |
> | <u>Who's</u> on first? | <u>Whose</u> book is this? |
> | <u>They're</u> playing our song. | <u>Their</u> team is winning. |
> | <u>It's</u> raining. | <u>Its</u> paws were muddy. |
> | <u>You're</u> a real pal. | <u>Your</u> résumé is very impressive. |

19b Indicating Omissions in Contractions

Apostrophes replace omitted letters in contractions that combine a pronoun and a verb (*he + will = he'll*) or the elements of a verb phrase (*do + not = don't*).

Frequently Used Contractions	
don't (do not)	they're (they are)
I'm (I am)	we'll (we will)
isn't (is not)	we've (we have)
it's (it is)	won't (will not)
let's (let us)	wouldn't (would not)

Grammar Checker: Revising Contractions

Contractions are generally too informal for use in college writing. If you set your word processor's writing style to Formal or Technical, the grammar checker will highlight contractions and offer suggestions for revision.

Contraction Use:

You'll want to be sure to bring your laptop and external DVD drive.

Suggestions:

You will

Close-up: Indicating Omitted Numbers

In informal writing, an apostrophe may also be used to represent the century in a year: Class of '97, the '60s. In college writing, however, write out the year in full.

19c Forming Plurals

In a few special situations, add -'s to form plurals.

Forming Plurals with Apostrophes

Plurals of Letters
The Italian language has no *j*'s or *k*'s

Plurals of Words Referred to as Words
The supervisor would accept no *if*'s , *and*'s , or *but*'s.

See 24c NOTE: Elements spoken of as themselves (letters, numerals, or words) are set in italic type; the plural ending, however, is not.

CHAPTER 20

Using Quotation Marks

Use quotation marks to set off brief passages of quoted speech or writing, to set off titles, and to set off words used in special ways. Do not use quotation marks when quoting long passages of prose or poetry.

20a Setting Off Quoted Speech or Writing

When you quote a word, phrase, or brief passage of someone's speech or writing, enclose the quoted material in a pair of quotation marks.

Gloria Steinem observed, "We are becoming the men we once hoped to marry."

In an essay about advertising in women's magazines, Gloria Steinem wrote, "When *Ms.* began, we didn't even consider *not* taking ads."

Galsworthy writes that Aunt Juley is "prostrated by the blow" (329). (Note that the end punctuation follows the parenthetical documentation.)

Close-up: Using Quotation Marks with Dialogue

When you record **dialogue** (conversation between two or more people), enclose the quoted words in quotation marks. Begin a new paragraph each time a new speaker is introduced.

When you are quoting several paragraphs of dialogue by one speaker, begin each new paragraph with quotation marks. However, use closing quotation marks only at the end of the entire passage (not at the end of each paragraph).

Special rules govern the punctuation of a quotation when it is used with an **identifying tag**—a phrase (such as *he said*) that identifies the speaker or writer.

(1) Identifying Tag in the Middle of a Quoted Passage

Use a pair of commas to set off an identifying tag that interrupts a quoted passage.

"In the future," pop artist Andy Warhol once said, "everyone will be world famous for fifteen minutes."

If the identifying tag follows a completed sentence but the quoted passage continues, use a period after the tag, and begin the new sentence with a capital letter and quotation marks.

"Be careful," Erin warned. "Reptiles can be tricky."

(2) Identifying Tag at the Beginning of a Quoted Passage

Use a comma after an identifying tag that introduces quoted speech or writing.

The Raven repeated, "Nevermore."

See 21a

Use a colon instead of a comma before a quotation if the identifying tag is a complete sentence.

She gave her final answer: "No."

Grammar Checker: Using Punctuation with Quotation Marks

Your word processor's grammar checker will often highlight missing punctuation in sentences containing quotation marks and offer suggestions for revision.

> Punctuation with Quotations:
> In *The Varieties of Religious Experience*, William James writes "The lustre of the present hour is always borrowed from the background of possibilities it goes with" (141).
> Suggestions:
> writes,

---

(3) Identifying Tag at the End of a Quoted Passage

Use a comma to set off a quotation from an identifying tag that follows it.

"Be careful out there," the sergeant warned.

If the quotation ends with a question mark or an exclamation point, use that punctuation mark instead of the comma. In this situation, the tag begins with a lowercase letter even though it follows end punctuation.

"Is Ankara the capital of Turkey?" she asked.

"Oh boy!" he cried.

NOTE: Commas and periods are always placed inside quotation marks. For information on placement of other punctuation marks with quotation marks, **see 20d.**

Close-up: Quoting Long Prose Passages

Do *not* enclose a **long prose passage** (more than four lines) in quotation marks. Instead, set it off by indenting the entire passage one inch (or ten spaces) from the left-hand margin. Treat the passage like regular text: double-space between lines, and do not add extra space above or below it. Introduce the passage with a colon, and place parenthetical documentation one space *after* the end punctuation.

The following portrait of Aunt Juley illustrates several of the devices Galsworthy uses throughout <u>The Forsyte Saga</u>, such as a journalistic detachment, a sense of the grotesque and an ironic stance:

> Aunt Juley stayed in her room,
> prostrated by the blow. Her face,
> discoloured by tears, was divided into
> compartments by the little ridges of
> pouting flesh which had swollen with
> emotion. . . . Her warm heart could not
> bear the thought that Ann was lying
> there so cold. (329)

Many similar portraits of characters appear throughout the novel.

When quoting a long prose passage that is a single paragraph, do not indent the first line. When quoting two or more paragraphs, however, indent the first line of each paragraph (including the first) *three* additional spaces. If the first sentence of the quoted passage does not begin a paragraph in the source, do not indent it—but do indent the first line of each subsequent paragraph. If the passage you are quoting includes material set in quotation marks, keep those quotation marks.

NOTE: <u>APA guidelines</u> differ from those set forth here, which conform to MLA style.

See
34b

Close-up: Quoting Poetry

Treat one line of poetry like a short prose passage: enclose it in quotation marks and run it into the text. If you quote two or three lines of poetry, separate the lines with <u>slashes</u>, and run the quotation into the text. If you quote more than three lines of poetry, set them off like a long prose passage. (For special emphasis, you may set off fewer lines in this way.) Be sure to reproduce *exactly* the spelling, capitalization, and indentation of the quoted lines.

See 21a

```
Wilfred Owen, a poet who was killed in action in

World War I, expressed the horrors of war with

vivid imagery:

          Bent double, like old beggars under

               sacks.

          Knock-kneed, coughing like hags, we

               cursed through sludge.

          Till on the haunting flares we turned

               our backs

          And towards our distant rest began to

               trudge. (lines 1-4)
```

20b Setting Off Titles

See 24a

<u>Titles</u> of short works and titles of parts of long works are enclosed in quotation marks. Other titles are italicized.

Titles Requiring Quotation Marks

Articles in Magazines, Newspapers, and Professional Journals

"Why Johnny Can't Write" (*Newsweek*)

Essays, Short Stories, Short Poems, and Songs

"Fenimore Cooper's Literary Offenses"

"Flying Home"

"The Road Not Taken"

"The Star-Spangled Banner"

Chapters or Sections of Books

"Miss Sharp Begins to Make Friends" (Chapter 10 of *Vanity Fair*)

Episodes of Radio or Television Series

"Lucy Goes to the Hospital" (*I Love Lucy*)

NOTE: MLA style recommends underlining to indicate italics.

20c Setting Off Words Used in Special Ways

Enclose a word used in a special or unusual way in quotation marks. (If you use *so-called* before the word, do not use quotation marks as well.)

It was clear that adults approved of children who were "readers," but it was not at all clear why this was so. (Annie Dillard)

Also enclose a **coinage**—an invented word—in quotation marks.

After the twins were born, the minivan became a "baby-mobile."

20d Using Quotation Marks with Other Punctuation

Place quotation marks *after* the comma or period at the end of a quotation.

Many, like poet Robert Frost, think about "the road not taken," but not many have taken "the one less traveled by."

Place quotation marks *before* a semicolon or colon at the end of a quotation.

Students who do not pass the test receive "certificates of completion"; those who pass are awarded diplomas.

Taxpayers were pleased with the first of the candidate's promised "sweeping new reforms": a balanced budget.

If a question mark, exclamation point, or dash is part of the quotation, place the quotation marks *after* the punctuation.

"Who's there?" she demanded.

"Stop!" he cried.

"Should we leave now, or—" Vicki paused, unable to continue.

If a question mark, exclamation point, or dash is not part of the quotation, place the quotation marks *before* the punctuation.

Did you finish reading "The Black Cat"?

Whatever you do, don't yell "Uncle"!

The first story—Updike's "*A & P*"—provoked discussion.

Close-up: Quotations within Quotations

Use *single* quotation marks to enclose a quotation within a quotation.

Claire noted, "Liberace always said, 'I cried all the way to the bank.' "

Also use single quotation marks within a quotation to indicate a title that would normally be enclosed in double quotation marks.

I think what she said was, "Play it, Sam. Play 'As Time Goes By.' "

See 20a Use double quotation marks around quotations or titles within a <u>long prose passage</u>.

20e Editing Misused Quotation Marks

Do not use quotation marks to set off indirect quotations (someone else's written or spoken words that are not quoted exactly).

Freud wondered "what women wanted."

Do not use quotation marks to set off slang or technical terms.

Dawn is "into" running.

"Biofeedback" is sometimes used to treat migraines.

Close-up: Titles of Your Own Papers

Do not use quotation marks (or italics) to set off the title of your own paper.

CHAPTER 21

Using Other Punctuation Marks

21a Using Colons

The **colon** is a strong punctuation mark that points readers ahead to the rest of the sentence. When a colon introduces a list or series, explanatory material, or a quotation, it must be preceded by a complete sentence.

(1) Introducing Lists or Series

Use colons to set off lists or series, including those introduced by phrases like *the following* or *as follows*.

Waiting tables requires three skills: memory, speed, and balance.

(2) Introducing Explanatory Material

Use colons to introduce material that explains, exemplifies, or summarizes.

She had one dream: to play professional basketball.

Sometimes a colon separates two independent clauses, the second illustrating or clarifying the first.

The survey presents an interesting finding: Americans do not trust the news media.

Close-up: Using Colons

When a complete sentence follows a colon, the sentence may begin with either a capital or a lowercase letter. However, if the sentence is a quotation, the first word is always capitalized (unless it was not capitalized in the source).

---

(3) Introducing Quotations

When you quote a <u>long prose passage</u>, always introduce it with a colon. Also use a colon before a short quotation when it is introduced by a complete sentence. See 20a

With dignity, Bartleby repeated the words again: "I prefer not to."

Other Conventional Uses of Colons

To Separate Titles from Subtitles
Family Installments: Memories of Growing Up Hispanic

To Separate Minutes from Hours
6:15 a.m.

See 40a **After Salutations in** business letters
Dear Dr. Evans:

See 33a2 **To Separate Place of Publication from Name of Publisher in a** works-cited list
Boston: Wadsworth, 2006.

---

(4) Editing Misused Colons

Do not use colons after expressions such as *namely, for example, such as,* or *that is.*

The Eye Institute treats patients with a wide variety of conditions, such as: myopia, glaucoma, and cataracts.

Do not place colons between verbs and their objects or complements or between prepositions and their objects.

James Michener wrote: *Hawaii, Centennial, Space,* and *Poland.*

Hitler's armies marched through: the Netherlands, Belgium, and France.

21b Using Dashes

(1) Setting Off Nonessential Material

See 17d Like commas, **dashes** can set off nonessential material, but unlike commas, dashes call attention to the material they set off. When you type, you indicate a dash with two unspaced hyphens (which most word-processing programs will convert to a dash).

For emphasis, you may use dashes to set off explanations, qualifications, examples, definitions, and appositives.

Neither of the boys—both nine-year-olds—had any history of violence.

Too many parents learn the dangers of swimming pools the hard way—after their toddler has drowned.

(2) Introducing a Summary

Use a dash to introduce a statement that summarizes a list or series that appears before it.

> "Study hard," "Respect your elders," "Don't talk with your mouth full"—Sharon had often heard her parents say these things.

(3) Indicating an Interruption

In dialogue, a dash may indicate a hesitation or an unfinished thought.

> "I think—no, I know—this is the worst day of my life," Julie sighed.

NOTE: Because too many dashes can make a passage seem disorganized and out of control, dashes should not be overused.

21c Using Parentheses

(1) Setting Off Nonessential Material

Use parentheses to enclose material that is relatively unimportant in a sentence—for example, material that expands, clarifies, illustrates, or supplements.

> In some European countries (notably Sweden and France), superb daycare is offered at little or no cost to parents.

Also use parentheses to set off digressions and afterthoughts.

> Last Sunday we went to the new stadium (it was only half-filled) to see the game.

When a complete sentence set off by parentheses falls within another sentence, it should not begin with a capital letter or end with a period.

> Because the area is so cold (temperatures average in the low twenties), it is virtually uninhabitable.

If the parenthetical sentence does *not* fall within another sentence, however, it must begin with a capital letter and end with appropriate punctuation.

> The region is very cold. (Temperatures average in the low twenties.)

(2) Using Parentheses in Other Situations

Use parentheses around letters and numbers that identify points on a list, dates, cross-references, and documentation.

> All reports must include the following components: (1) an opening summary, (2) a background statement, and (3) a list of conclusions.

> Russia defeated Sweden in the Great Northern War (1700–1721).

> Other scholars also make this point (see p. 54).

> One critic has called the novel "puerile" (Arvin 72).

21d Using Brackets

When one set of parentheses falls within another, use brackets in place of the inner set.

> In her study of American education between 1945 and 1960 (*The Troubled Crusade* [New York: Basic, 1963]), Diane Ravitch addresses issues like progressive education, race, educational reforms, and campus unrest.

Also use brackets within quotations to indicate to readers that the bracketed words are yours and not those of your source. You can bracket an explanation, a clarification, a correction, or an opinion.

> "Even at Princeton he [F. Scott Fitzgerald] felt like an outsider."

If a quotation contains an error, indicate that the error is not yours by following the error with the Latin word *sic* ("thus") in brackets.

> "The octopuss [sic] is a cephalopod mollusk with eight arms."

NOTE: Use brackets to indicate changes that enable you to fit a <u>quotation</u> smoothly into your sentence.

See 31a

21e Using Slashes

(1) Separating One Option from Another

> The either/or fallacy is a common error in logic.

> Writer/director M. Night Shyamalan spoke at the film festival.

Note that there is no space before or after the slash.

(2) Separating Lines of Poetry Run into the Text

The poet James Schevill writes, "I study my defects /
And learn how to perfect them."

In this case, leave one space before and one space after
the slash.

21f Using Ellipses

An **ellipsis**—three *spaced* periods—indicates that you
have omitted words from a prose quotation. Note that an
ellipsis in the middle of a quoted passage can indicate the
omission of a word, a sentence or two, or even a whole
paragraph or more. When deleting material from a quotation, be careful not to change the meaning of the original passage.

Original: "When I was a young man, being anxious
to distinguish myself, I was perpetually starting new
propositions." (Samuel Johnson)

With Omission: "When I was a young man, . . . I
was perpetually starting new propositions."

NOTE: Never begin a quoted passage with an ellipsis.

When you delete words immediately after a punctuation
mark (such as the comma in the above example), the ellipsis always comes *after* the punctuation mark.

Deletion at End of a Sentence: According to hu-
morist Dave Barry, "from outer space Europe appears
to be shaped like a large ketchup stain. . . ." (period
followed by ellipsis)

**Deletion from Middle of One Sentence to End of
Another:** According to Donald Hall, "Everywhere
one meets the idea that reading is an activity desirable
in itself. . . . People surround the idea of reading with
piety and do not take into account the purpose of
reading." (period followed by ellipsis)

**Deletion from Middle of One Sentence to Middle
of Another:** "When I was a young man, . . . I found
that generally what was new was false." (Samuel
Johnson) (comma followed by ellipsis)

NOTE: If a quoted passage already contains ellipses, MLA
recommends that you enclose your own ellipses in brackets

to distinguish them from those that appear in the original quotation.

Close-up: Using Ellipses

If a quotation ending with an ellipsis is followed by parenthetical documentation, the final punctuation *follows* the documentation.

As Jarman argues, "Compromise was impossible . . ." (161).

PART 5

Understanding Spelling and Mechanics

22 Improving Spelling 106
22a Understanding Spelling and Pronunciation 106
22b Learning Spelling Rules 106

23 Knowing When to Capitalize 109
23a Capitalizing Proper Nouns 109
23b Capitalizing Important Words in Titles 111

24 Using Italics 112
24a Setting Off Titles and Names 112
24b Setting Off Foreign Words and Phrases 113
24c Setting Off Elements Spoken of as Themselves and Terms Being Defined 114
24d Using Italics for Emphasis 114

25 Using Hyphens 115
25a Breaking a Word at the End of a Line 115
25b Dividing Compound Words 115

26 Using Abbreviations 117
26a Abbreviating Titles 117
26b Abbreviating Organization Names and Technical Terms 118
26c Abbreviating Dates, Times of Day, Temperatures, and Numbers 118
26d Editing Misused Abbreviations 119

27 Using Numbers 120
27a Spelled-Out Numbers versus Numerals 120
27b Conventional Uses of Numerals 121

CHAPTER 22

Improving Spelling

22a Understanding Spelling and Pronunciation

Because pronunciation in English often provides few clues to spelling, you must memorize the spellings of many words and use a dictionary or spell checker regularly.

(1) Vowels in Unstressed Positions

Many unstressed vowels sound exactly alike. For instance, the unstressed vowels *a*, *e*, and *i* are impossible to distinguish by pronunciation alone in the suffixes -*able* and -*ible*, -*ance* and -*ence*, and -*ant* and -*ent*.

comfort<u>a</u>ble	brilli<u>a</u>nce	serv<u>a</u>nt
compat<u>i</u>ble	excell<u>e</u>nce	independ<u>e</u>nt

(2) Silent Letters

Some English words contain silent letters, such as the *b* in *climb* and the *t* in *mortgage*.

ai<u>s</u>le	depo<u>t</u>
condem<u>n</u>	<u>k</u>night
de<u>s</u>cend	<u>p</u>neumonia

(3) Words That Are Often Pronounced Carelessly

Words like the following are often misspelled because when we pronounce them, we add, omit, or transpose letters.

can<u>d</u>idate	nu<u>c</u>lear	recognize
environ<u>m</u>ent	lib<u>r</u>ary	suppose<u>d</u> to
Feb<u>r</u>uary	quan<u>t</u>ity	use<u>d</u> to

22b Learning Spelling Rules

Memorizing a few reliable spelling rules can help you overcome some of the problems caused by inconsistencies between pronunciation and spelling.

(1) The *ie/ei* Combinations

Use *i* before *e* (*belief*, *chief*) except after *c* (*ceiling*, *receive*) or when pronounced *ay*, as in *neighbor* or *weigh*. **Exceptions:** *either*, *neither*, *foreign*, *leisure*, *weird*, and *seize*. In addition, if the *ie* combination is not pronounced as a unit, the rule does not apply: *atheist*, *science*.

(2) Doubling Final Consonants

The only words that double their consonants before a suffix that begins with a vowel (*-ed* or *-ing*) are those that pass the following three tests:

1. They have one syllable or are stressed on the last syllable.
2. They have only one vowel in the last syllable.
3. They end in a single consonant.

The word *tap* satisfies all three conditions: it has only one syllable, it has only one vowel (*a*), and it ends in a single consonant (*p*). Therefore, the final consonant doubles before a suffix beginning with a vowel (*tapped*, *tapping*).

(3) Silent e before a Suffix

When a suffix that begins with a consonant is added to a word ending in a silent *e*, the *e* is generally kept: *hope/hopeful*. **Exceptions:** *argument*, *truly*, *ninth*, *judgment*, and *abridgment*.

When a suffix that begins with a vowel is added to a word ending in a silent *e*, the *e* is generally dropped: *hope/hoping*. **Exceptions:** *changeable*, *noticeable*, and *courageous*.

(4) y before a Suffix

When a word ends in a consonant plus *y*, the *y* generally changes to an *i* when a suffix is added (*beauty* + *ful* = *beautiful*). The *y* is kept, however, when the suffix *-ing* is added (*tally* + *ing* = *tallying*) and in some one-syllable words (*dry* + *ness* = *dryness*).

When a word ends in a vowel plus *y*, the *y* is kept (*joy* + *ful* = *joyful*). **Exception:** *day* + *ly* = *daily*.

(5) *seed* Endings

Endings with the sound *seed* are nearly always spelled *cede*, as in *precede*. **Exceptions:** *supersede, exceed, proceed,* and *succeed*.

(6) *-able, -ible*

If the root of a word is itself a word, the suffix *-able* is most commonly used (*comfortable, agreeable*). If the root of a word is not a word, the suffix *-ible* is most often used (*compatible, incredible*).

(7) Plurals

Most nouns form plurals by adding *-s*: *tortilla/tortillas, boat/boats*. There are, however, a number of exceptions.

- **Words Ending in *-f* or *-fe*** Some words ending in *-f* or *-fe* form plurals by changing the *f* to *v* and adding *-es* or *-s*: *life/lives, self/selves*. Others add just *-s*: *belief/beliefs, safe/safes*.
- **Words Ending in *-y*** Most words that end in a consonant followed by *y* form plurals by changing the *y* to *i* and adding *-es*: *baby/babies*. **Exceptions:** proper nouns such as *Kennedy* (plural *Kennedys*).
- **Words Ending in *-o*** Most words that end in a consonant followed by *o* add *-es* to form the plural: *tomato/tomatoes, hero/heroes*. **Exceptions:** *silo/silos, piano/pianos, memo/memos, soprano/sopranos*.
- **Words Ending in *-s*, *-ss*, *-sh*, *-ch*, *-x*, and *-z*** Words ending in *-s*, *-ss*, *-sh*, *-ch*, *-x*, and *-z* form plurals by adding *-es*: *Jones/Joneses, kiss/kisses rash/rashes, lunch/lunches, box/boxes, buzz/buzzes*. **Exceptions:** Some one-syllable words that end in *-s* or *-z* double their final consonants when forming plurals: *quiz/quizzes*.
- **Compound Nouns** Hyphenated compound nouns whose first element is more important than the others form the plural with the first element: *sister-in-law/sisters-in-law*.
- **Foreign Plurals** Some words, especially those borrowed from Latin or Greek, keep their foreign plurals.

Singular	**Plural**
criterion	criteria
datum	data
memorandum	memoranda
stimulus	stimuli

> **Computer Tip: Running a Spell Check**
>
> If you use a computer spell checker, remember that it will not identify a word that is spelled correctly but used incorrectly—*then* for *than* or *its* for *it's*, for example— or a typo that creates another word, such as *word* for *work*. Even after you run a spell check, you still need to proofread your papers. For a list of commonly confused words, **see Appendix B.**

CHAPTER 23

Knowing When to Capitalize

In addition to capitalizing the first word of a sentence (including a quoted sentence) and the pronoun *I*, always capitalize proper nouns and important words in titles.

> **Computer Tip: Revising Capitalization Errors**
>
> In *Microsoft Word*, the AutoCorrect tool will automatically capitalize certain words—such as the first word of a sentence or the days of the week. Be sure to proofread your documents after using the AutoCorrect tool, though, since it can actually introduce capitalization errors into your writing.

23a   Capitalizing Proper Nouns

Proper nouns—the names of specific persons, places, or things—are capitalized, and so are adjectives formed from proper nouns.

(1) Specific People's Names

Eleanor Roosevelt   Medgar Evers

Capitalize a title when it precedes a person's name or replaces the name (Senator Barack Obama, Dad). Do not capitalize titles that *follow* names or that refer to the general position, not to the particular person who holds it (Barack Obama, the senator), except for very high-ranking positions: President of the United States. Never capitalize a title denoting a family relationship when it follows an article or a possessive pronoun: an aunt, my uncle.

Capitalize titles or abbreviations of academic degrees, even when they follow a name: Dr. Benjamin Spock, Benjamin Spock, MD.

(2) Names of Particular Structures, Special Events, Monuments, and so on

| the *Titanic* | the World Series |
| the Brooklyn Bridge | Mount Rushmore |

(3) Places and Geographical Regions

| Saturn | the Straits of Magellan |
| Budapest | the Western Hemisphere |

Capitalize *north*, *south*, *east*, and *west* when they denote particular geographical regions (the West), but not when they designate directions (west of town).

(4) Days of the Week, Months, and Holidays

| Saturday | Rosh Hashanah |
| January | Ramadan |

(5) Historical Periods and Events, Documents, and Names of Legal Cases

| the Battle of Gettysburg | Romanticism |
| *Brown* v. *Board of Education* | the Treaty of Versailles |

(6) Races, Ethnic Groups, Nationalities, and Languages

| African American | Korean |
| Latino/Latina | Dutch |

NOTE: When the words *black* and *white* refer to races, they have traditionally not been capitalized. Current usage is divided on whether to capitalize *black*.

(7) Religions and Their Followers; Sacred Books and Figures

Jews	the Talmud	Buddha
Islam	God	the Scriptures

(8) Specific Organizations

the New York Yankees
League of Women Voters
the American Bar Association
the Anti-Defamation League

(9) Businesses, Government Agencies, and Other Institutions

Congress
the Environmental Protection Agency
Lincoln High School
the University of Maryland

(10) Brand Names and Words Formed from Them

Coke	Astroturf	Rollerblades	Post-it

(11) Specific Academic Courses and Departments

Sociology 201   Department of English

NOTE: Do not capitalize a general subject area (sociology, zoology) unless it is the name of a language (French).

(12) Adjectives Formed from Proper Nouns

Keynesian economics	Elizabethan era
Freudian slip	Shakespearean sonnet

When words derived from proper nouns have lost their specialized meanings, do not capitalize them: *china* pattern, *french* fries.

23b   Capitalizing Important Words in Titles

In general, capitalize all words in titles with the exception of articles (*a*, *an*, and *the*), prepositions, coordinating conjunctions, and the *to* in infinitives. If an article, preposition, or coordinating conjunction is the *first* or *last* word in the title, however, do capitalize it.

The Declaration of Independence
Across the River and into the Trees
A Man and a Woman
What Friends Are For

Close-up: Editing Misused Capitals

Do not capitalize the following:
- Seasons (summer, fall, winter, spring)
- Names of centuries (the twenty-first century)
- Names of general historical periods (the automobile age)
- Diseases and other medical terms (unless a proper noun is part of the name): mumps, smallpox, polio

---

ESL Tip

Do not capitalize a word simply because you want to emphasize its importance. If you are not sure whether a word should be capitalized, look it up in a dictionary.

CHAPTER 24

Using Italics

24a Setting Off Titles and Names

See 20b Use italics for the titles and names in the box below. All other titles are set off with <u>quotation marks</u>.

Titles and Names Set in Italics

Books: *David Copperfield, The Bluest Eye*

Newspapers: the *Washington Post,* the *Philadelphia Inquirer* (Articles and names of cities are italicized only when they are part of a title.)

Magazines and Journals: *Rolling Stone, Scientific American, PMLA*

Online Magazines and Journals: *salon.com, theonion.com*

Web Sites or Home Pages: *urbanlegends.com, movie-mistakes.com*

Pamphlets: *Common Sense*

Films: *Casablanca, Citizen Kane*

Television Programs: *Law & Order, 60 Minutes, The Simpsons*

Radio Programs: *All Things Considered, The Tavis Smiley Show*

Long Poems: *John Brown's Body, The Faerie Queen*

Plays: *Macbeth, A Raisin in the Sun*

Long Musical Works: *Rigoletto, Eroica*

Software Programs: *Word, PowerPoint*

Paintings and Sculpture: *Guernica, Pietà*

Ships: *Lusitania*, U.S.S. *Saratoga* (S.S. and U.S.S. are not italicized.)

Trains: *City of New Orleans, The Orient Express*

Aircraft: *The Hindenburg, Enola Gay* (Only particular aircraft, not makes or types such as Piper Cub and Boeing 757, are italicized.)

Spacecraft: *Challenger, Enterprise*

NOTE: Names of sacred books, such as the Bible, and well-known documents, such as the Constitution and the Declaration of Independence, are neither italicized nor placed within quotation marks.

Close-up: Using Italics

MLA style recommends that you underline to indicate italics. However, you may italicize if your instructor prefers. (Note that style guides in other disciplines may require italics.)

24b Setting Off Foreign Words and Phrases

Use italics to set off foreign words and phrases that have not become part of the English language.

"*C'est la vie*," Madeleine said when she saw the long line for basketball tickets.

Spirochaeta plicatilis is a corkscrew-like bacterium.

If you are not sure whether a foreign word has been assimilated into English, consult a dictionary.

24c Setting Off Elements Spoken of as Themselves and Terms Being Defined

Use italics to set off letters, numerals, and words that refer to the letters, numerals, and words themselves.

Is that a *p* or a *g*?

I forget the exact address, but I know it has a *3* in it.

Does *through* rhyme with *cough*?

Italics also set off words and phrases that you go on to define.

A *closet drama* is a play meant to be read, not performed.

NOTE: When you quote a dictionary definition, put the word you are defining in italics and the definition itself in quotation marks.

To *infer* means "to draw a conclusion"; to *imply* means "to suggest."

24d Using Italics for Emphasis

Italics may occasionally be used for emphasis.

Initially, poetry might be defined as a kind of language that says *more* and says it *more intensely* than does ordinary language. (Lawrence Perrine, *Sound and Sense*)

However, overuse of italics is distracting. Instead of italicizing, indicate emphasis with word choice and sentence structure.

CHAPTER 25

Using Hyphens

Hyphens have two conventional uses: to break a word at the end of a line and to link words in certain compounds.

25a Breaking a Word at the End of a Line

A computer never breaks a word at the end of a line; if the full word will not fit, it is brought down to the next line. Sometimes, however, you will want to break a word with a hyphen—for example, to fill in space at the end of a line. When you break a word at the end of a line, divide it only between syllables, consulting a dictionary if necessary. Never divide a word at the end of a page, and never hyphenate a one-syllable word. In addition, never leave a single letter at the end of a line or carry only one or two letters to the next line.

If you divide a <u>compound word</u> at the end of a line, put the hyphen between the elements of the compound (*snow-mobile*, not *snowmo-bile*). _{See 25b}

http://kirsznermandell.wadsworth.com

Computer Tip: Dividing Electronic Addresses (URLs)

Never insert a hyphen to divide an electronic address (URL) at the end of a line. (Readers might think the hyphen is part of the address.) MLA style recommends that you break the URL after a slash. If this is not possible, break it in a logical place—after a period, for example—or avoid the problem altogether by moving the entire URL to the next line.

25b Dividing Compound Words

A **compound word** is composed of two or more words. Some familiar compound words are always hyphenated: *no-hitter, helter-skelter*. Other compounds are always written as one word (*fireplace*) and others as two separate words (*bunk bed*). Your dictionary can tell you whether a particular compound requires a hyphen.

115

> ### Grammar Checker: Hyphenating Compound Words
>
>
>
>   Your word processor's grammar checker will highlight certain compound words with incorrect or missing hyphenation and offer suggestions for revision.
>
>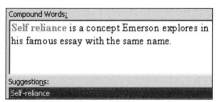
>
> Compound Words:
>
> Self reliance is a concept Emerson explores in his famous essay with the same name.
>
> Suggestions:
>
> Self-reliance

Hyphens are generally used in the following compounds.

(1) In Compound Adjectives

A **compound adjective** is a series of two or more words that function together as an adjective. When a compound adjective comes before the noun it modifies, use hyphens to join its elements.

> The research team tried to use <u>nineteenth-century</u> technology to design a <u>space-age</u> project.

When a compound adjective *follows* the noun it modifies, do not use hyphens to join its elements.

> The three government-operated programs were run smoothly, but the one that was not <u>government operated</u> was short of funds.

NOTE: A compound adjective formed with an adverb ending in *-ly* is not hyphenated even when it precedes the noun: Many <u>upwardly mobile</u> families are on tight budgets.

Use **suspended hyphens**—hyphens followed by a space or by appropriate punctuation and a space—in a series of compounds that have the same principal elements.

> Graduates of <u>two-</u> and <u>four-year</u> colleges were eligible for the grants.

> The exam called for <u>sentence-</u>, <u>paragraph-</u>, and <u>essay-length</u> answers.

(2) With Certain Prefixes or Suffixes

Use a hyphen between a prefix and a proper noun or adjective.

mid-July   pre-Columbian

Use a hyphen to connect the prefixes *all-*, *ex-*, *half-*, *quarter-*, *quasi-*, and *self-* and the suffix *-elect* to a noun.

ex-senator   self-centered
quarter-moon   president-elect

Also hyphenate to avoid certain hard-to-read combinations, such as two *i*'s (*semi-illiterate*) or more than two of the same consonant (*shell-less*).

(3) In Compound Numerals and Fractions

Hyphenate compounds that represent numbers below one hundred, even if they are part of a larger number.

the <u>twenty-first</u> century   three hundred <u>sixty-five</u> days

Also hyphenate the written form of a fraction when it modifies a noun.

a <u>two-thirds</u> share of the business

CHAPTER 26

Using Abbreviations

Generally speaking, **abbreviations** are not appropriate in college writing except in tables, charts, and works-cited lists. Some abbreviations are acceptable only in scientific, technical, or business writing or only in a particular discipline. If you have questions about the appropriateness of a particular abbreviation, consult a style manual in your field.

26a Abbreviating Titles

Titles before and after proper names are usually abbreviated.

Mr. Homer Simpson   Rep. Chaka Fattah
Henry Kissinger, PhD   Dr. Martin Luther King, Jr.

Do not, however, use an abbreviated title without a name.

    doctor
The ~~Dr.~~ diagnosed hepatitis.

26b Abbreviating Organization Names and Technical Terms

Well-known businesses and government, social, and civic organizations are frequently referred to by capitalized initials. These <u>abbreviations</u> fall into two categories: those in which the initials are pronounced as separate units (MTV) and **acronyms,** in which the initials are pronounced as a word (NATO).

See
16a

To save space, you may use accepted abbreviations for complex technical terms that are not well known, but be sure to spell out the full term the first time you mention it, followed by the abbreviation in parentheses.

> Citrus farmers have been using ethylene dibromide (EDB), a chemical pesticide, for more than twenty years. Now, however, EDB has contaminated water supplies.

26c Abbreviating Dates, Times of Day, Temperatures, and Numbers

50 BC (BC follows the date)
3:03 p.m. (lowercase)
AD 432 (AD precedes the date)
180° F (Fahrenheit)

Always capitalize BC and AD. (The alternatives BCE, for "before the Common Era," and CE, for "Common Era," are also capitalized.) The abbreviations a.m. and p.m. are used only when they are accompanied by numbers: *I'll see you in the morning* (not *in the a.m.*).

Avoid the abbreviation *no.* except in technical writing, and then use it only before a specific number: *The unidentified substance was labeled no. 52.*

See
33a2

Close-up: Abbreviations in MLA Documentation

<u>MLA documentation style</u> requires abbreviations of publishers' company names—for example, `Columbia UP` for *Columbia University Press*—in the works-cited list. Do not, however, use such abbreviations in the body of your paper. MLA style also permits the use of abbreviations that designate parts of written works (`ch. 3, sec. 7`)—but

only in the works-cited list and parenthetical documentation. MLA also recommends abbreviating literary works and books of the Bible: <u>Oth</u>. (*Othello*), <tt>Exod</tt>. (Exodus). These words should not be abbreviated in the text of your paper.

26d   Editing Misused Abbreviations

In college writing, abbreviations are not used in the following cases.

(1) Latin Expressions

Poe wrote "The Gold Bug," "The Tell-Tale Heart," ~~etc.~~ *and so on.*

Many musicians (~~e.g.,~~ *for example,* Bruce Springsteen) have been influenced by Bob Dylan.

(2) Names of Days, Months, or Holidays

On ~~Sat., Dec.~~ *Saturday, December* 23, I started my ~~Xmas~~ *Christmas* shopping.

(3) Names of Streets and Places

He lives on Riverside ~~Dr.~~ *Drive* in ~~NYC.~~ *New York City.*

Exceptions: The abbreviations *U.S.* (*U.S. Coast Guard*), *St.* (*St. Albans*), and *Mt.* (*Mt. Etna*) are acceptable, as is *DC* in *Washington, DC.*

(4) Names of Academic Subjects

~~Psych.~~ *Psychology* and English ~~lit.~~ *literature* are required courses.

(5) Units of Measurement

MLA style does not permit abbreviations for units of measurement and requires that you spell out words such as *inches, feet, years, miles, pints, quarts,* and *gallons.*

In technical and business writing, however, some units of measurement are abbreviated when they are preceded by a numeral.

The hurricane had winds of 35 mph.

One new Honda gets over 50 mpg.

(6) Symbols

The symbols =, +, and # are acceptable in technical and scientific writing but not in nontechnical college writing. The symbols % and $ are acceptable only when used _{See 27b} with <u>numerals</u> (15%, $15,000), not when used with spelled-out numbers.

See 27b

CHAPTER 27

Using Numbers

Convention determines when to use a **numeral** (22) and when to spell out a number (twenty-two). Numerals are commonly used in scientific and technical writing and in journalism, but they are used less often in academic or literary writing.

NOTE: The guidelines in this chapter are based on the *MLA Handbook for Writers of Research Papers, 6th ed. (2003)*. <u>APA style</u>, however, requires that all numbers below ten be spelled out if they do not represent specific measurements and that the numbers ten and above be expressed in numerals.

See Ch. 34

27a Spelled-Out Numbers versus Numerals

Unless a number falls into one of the categories listed in **27b,** spell it out *if you can do so in one or two words.*

The Hawaiian alphabet has only <u>twelve</u> letters.

Class size stabilized at <u>twenty-eight</u> students.

The subsidies are expected to total about <u>two million</u> dollars.

Numbers *more than two words* long are expressed in figures.

The dietitian prepared <u>125</u> sample menus.

The developer of the community purchased <u>300,000</u> doorknobs and <u>153,000</u> faucets.

Never begin a sentence with a numeral. If necessary, reword the sentence.

Faulty: 250 students are currently enrolled in World History 106.

Revised: Current enrollment in World History 106 is 250 students.

NOTE: When one number immediately precedes another in a sentence, spell out the first, and use a numeral for the second: *five 3-quart containers.*

Grammar Checker: Spelled-Out Numbers versus Numerals

Your word processor's grammar checker will often highlight numerals in your writing and suggest that you spell them out. Before clicking Change, be sure that the number does not fall into one of the categories listed in **27b.**

> Spell Out Number:
> This essay by Walter Benjamin focuses on 2 groups of people: the victors and the vanquished.
>
> Suggestions:
> two

27b Conventional Uses of Numerals

- **Addresses:** 111 Fifth Avenue, New York, NY 10003
- **Dates:** January 15, 1929   1914–1919
- **Exact Times:** 9:16   10 a.m. or 10:00 a.m. (but spell out times of day when they are used with *o'clock:* ten o'clock)
- **Exact Sums of Money:** $25.11 $6,752.00
- **Divisions of Works:** Act 5   lines 17–28   page 42
- **Percentages and Decimals:** 80% (or eighty percent) 3.14
- **Measurements with Symbols or Abbreviations:** 32°   15 cc
- **Ratios and Statistics:** 20 to 1   a mean of 40
- **Scores:** a lead of 6 to 0
- **Identification Numbers:** Route 66   Track 8 Channel 12

PART 6

Writing with Sources

28 Writing Research Papers
124

28a Choosing a Topic   124
28b Doing Exploratory Research
and Formulating a Research
Question   125
28c Assembling a Working
Bibliography   126
28d Developing a Tentative Thesis
128
28e Doing Focused Research   129
28f Taking Notes   131
28g Fine-Tuning Your Thesis   139
28h Outlining, Drafting, and
Revising   139

29 Using and Evaluating Library
Sources   148

29a Using Library Sources   148
29b Evaluating Library Sources
156

30 Using and Evaluating
Internet Sources   158
30a Using the World Wide Web for
Research   159
30b Using Other Internet Tools
164
30c Evaluating Internet Sites   166

31 Integrating Source Material
into Your Writing   169
31a Integrating Quotations   169
31b Integrating Paraphrases and
Summaries   172

32 Avoiding Plagiarism   173
32a Defining Plagiarism   173
32b Avoiding Unintentional
Plagiarism   173
32c Revising to Eliminate
Plagiarism   174

CHAPTER 28

Writing Research Papers

Research is the systematic investigation of a topic outside your own knowledge and experience. However, doing research means more than just reading about other people's ideas. When you undertake a research project, you become involved in a process that requires you to **think critically**: to evaluate and interpret the ideas explored in your sources and to formulate ideas of your own. Whether you are working with print sources (books, journals, magazines) or electronic resources (online catalogs, databases, the Internet), in the library or at your home computer, your research will be most efficient if you follow a systematic process.

See
29a2

Checklist: The Research Process

- ☐ Choose a topic **(See 28a)**
- ☐ Do exploratory research and formulate a research question **(See 28b)**
- ☐ Assemble a working bibliography **(See 28c)**
- ☐ Develop a tentative thesis **(See 28d)**
- ☐ Do focused research **(See 28e)**
- ☐ Take notes **(See 28f)**
- ☐ Fine-tune your thesis **(See 28g)**
- ☐ Outline your paper **(See 28h1)**
- ☐ Draft your paper **(See 28h2)**
- ☐ Revise your paper **(See 28h3)**

28a Choosing a Topic

The first step in the research process is finding a topic to write about. In many cases, your instructor will help you to choose a topic, either by providing a list of suitable topics or by suggesting a general subject area—for example, a famous trial, an event that happened on the day you were born, a social problem on college campuses, or an issue related to the Internet. Even in these cases, you will still need to choose one of the topics or narrow the subject area—deciding, for example, on one trial, one event, one problem, or one issue.

If your instructor prefers that you select a topic on your own, you should consider a number of possible topics and weigh both their suitability for research and your interest in them. You decide on a topic for your research paper in much the same way in which you decide on a topic for a short essay: you read, brainstorm, talk to people, and ask questions. Specifically, you talk to friends and family members, coworkers, and perhaps your instructor; you read magazines and newspapers; you take stock of your interests; you consider possible topics suggested by your other courses—historical events, scientific developments, and so on; and, of course, you search the Internet. (Your search engine's subject guides can be See 30a3 particularly helpful as you look for a promising topic or narrow a broad subject.)

Checklist: Choosing a Research Topic

As you look for a suitable topic, keep the following guidelines in mind:

☐ **Are you genuinely interested in your research topic?** Be sure the topic you select is one that will hold your interest.

☐ **Is your topic suitable for research?** Be sure your paper will not depend on your personal experiences or value judgments.

☐ **Is your topic too broad? too narrow?** Be sure the boundaries of your research topic are appropriate.

☐ **Can your topic be researched in a library to which you have access?** Be sure that your school library has the sources you need (or that you can access those sources on the Internet).

28b Doing Exploratory Research and Formulating a Research Question

Doing **exploratory research**—searching the Internet and looking through general reference works such as encyclopedias, bibliographies, and specialized dictionaries (either in print or online)—helps you to get an overview of your topic. Your goal is to formulate a **research question,** the question you want your research paper to answer. A research question helps you to decide which sources to seek out, which to examine first, which to examine in depth, and which to skip entirely. (The answer to your research question will be your paper's <u>thesis statement</u>.)

See 2b

28c Assembling a Working Bibliography

As soon as you start your exploratory research, you begin to assemble a **working bibliography** for your paper. (This working bibliography will be the basis for your <u>works-cited list</u>, which will include all the sources you cite in your paper.)

See 33a2

Close-up: Assembling a Working Bibliography

    As you record bibliographic information for your sources, include the following information:

Book   Author(s); title (underlined or in italics); call number (for future reference); city of publication; publisher; date of publication; brief evaluation

Article   Author(s); title of article (in quotation marks); title of journal (underlined or in italics); volume number; date; inclusive page numbers; URL (if applicable); date downloaded (if applicable); brief evaluation

---

As you consider each potential source, keep track of your sources by recording full and accurate bibliographic information—author, title, page numbers, and complete publication information—in a separate computer file designated "Bibliography" or, if you prefer, on individual index cards (see Figures 28.1 and 28.2).

Author —	CBS AP
Title —	"Digital Divide Debated"
Publication —	http://www.cbsnews.com/stories/2002/05/03/tech/
information	main510589.shtml
	May 30, 2002
	Accessed March 2, 2003
Evaluation —	Reports on Bush administration's argument that the digital divide is no longer a significant problem. Cites the findings of the February 2002 Commerce Dept. report.

Figure 28.1 Information for working bibliography in computer file.

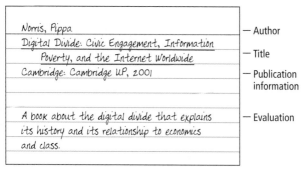

Norris, Pippa	— Author
Digital Divide: Civic Engagement, Information Poverty, and the Internet Worldwide	— Title
Cambridge: Cambridge UP, 2001	— Publication information
A book about the digital divide that explains its history and its relationship to economics and class.	— Evaluation

Figure 28.2 Information for working bibliography on index card.

Keep records of interviews (including telephone and email interviews), meetings, lectures, films, and electronic sources as well as of books and articles. For each source, include not only basic identifying details—such as the date of an interview, the call number of a library book, the electronic address (URL) of an Internet source, or the author of an article accessed from a library's subscription database—but also a brief **evaluation** that includes comments about the kind of information the source contains, the amount of information offered, its relevance to your topic, and its limitations.

As you go about collecting sources and building your working bibliography, monitor the quality and relevance of all the materials you examine. Making informed choices early in the research process will save you a lot of time in the long run. (For more on evaluating library sources, **see 29b;** for guidelines on evaluating Internet sources, **see 30c.**)

Close-up: Preparing an Annotated Bibliography

Some instructors require an **annotated bibliography,** a list of all your sources accompanied by a brief summary and evaluation of each source. The following is an excerpt from an annotated bibliography for a paper on the digital divide.

```
Young, Jeffrey R. "Does 'Digital Divide'
        Rhetoric Do More Harm Than Good?"
```

(*continued*)

Preparing an annotated bibliography (continued)

> <u>Chronicle of Higher Education</u> 9 Nov. 2001.
> 10 Jan. 2005 <http://chronicle.com>. This
> article explains that some scholars feel
> that the focus on the "digital divide"
> among minorities actually promotes the idea
> that they are technologically backwards.
> While programs aimed at closing the
> "digital divide" intend to equalize the
> technological playing field, the rhetoric
> used may actually encourage racist
> stereotypes.
>
> Even though it's a few years old, this
> article really made me reconsider my views
> about the programs that are working to
> bridge the digital divide. Also, it
> supports Henry Louis Gates's argument that
> many minorities are not using the Internet
> because the content does not appeal to
> their interests or needs.

28d Developing a Tentative Thesis

Your **tentative thesis** is a preliminary statement of the main point you think your research will support. This statement, which you will eventually refine into a <u>thesis statement</u>, should be the tentative answer to your research question.

See 28g

Developing a Tentative Thesis

Subject Area
Issue related to the Internet

Topic
Access to the Internet

> **Research Question**
> Do all Americans have equal access to the
> Internet?
>
> **Tentative Thesis**
> Not all Americans have equal access to the
> Internet, and this is a potentially serious
> problem.

Because it suggests the specific direction your research will take as well as the scope and emphasis of your
argument, the tentative thesis you come up with at this
point can help you generate a list of the main ideas you
plan to develop in your paper. This list can help you to
narrow the focus of your research so that you can zero in
on a few specific categories to explore as you read and
take notes.

Listing Your Points

<u>Tentative Thesis:</u> Not all Americans have equal
access to the Internet, and this is a
potentially serious problem.
- Give background about Internet; tell why it's
  important.
- Identify groups that do not have access to
  Internet.
- Explain problems this creates.
- Suggest possible solutions.

28e Doing Focused Research

Once you have decided on a tentative thesis and made a
list of the points you plan to discuss in your paper, you
are ready to begin your focused research. During exploratory research, you look at general reference works
to get an overview of your topic. During **focused research,** however, you look for the specific information—
facts, examples, statistics, definitions, quotations—you
need to support your points.

(1) Reading Sources

As you look for information, try to explore as many
sources, and as many different viewpoints, as possible. It
makes sense to examine more sources than you actually

intend to use. This strategy will enable you to proceed even if one or more of your sources turns out to be biased, outdated, unreliable, superficial, or irrelevant—in other words, not suitable. Exploring different viewpoints is just as important. After all, if you read only those sources that agree on a particular issue, you will have difficulty understanding the full range of opinions about your topic.

As you explore various sources, try to evaluate each source's potential usefulness to you as quickly as possible. For example, if your source is a book, skim the table of contents and the index; if your source is a journal article, read the abstract. Then, if an article or a section of a book seems useful, photocopy it for future reference. Similarly, when you find an online source that looks promising, print it out (or send it to yourself as an email attachment) so that you can evaluate it further later on. (For information on evaluating library sources, **see 29b;** for information on evaluating Internet sources, **see 30c.**)

See Ch. 32 NOTE: Do not paste source material directly into your paper. This strategy can easily lead to unintentional <u>plagiarism</u>.

(2) Balancing Primary and Secondary Sources

In the course of your focused research, you will encounter both **primary sources** (original documents and observations) and **secondary sources** (interpretations of original documents and observations).

Primary and Secondary Sources	
Primary Source	**Secondary Source**
Novel, poem, play, film	Criticism
Diary, autobiography	Biography
Letter, historical document, speech, oral history	Historical analysis
Newspaper article	Editorial
Raw data from questionnaires or interviews	Social science article; case study
Observation/experiment	Scientific article

Primary sources are essential for many research projects, but secondary sources, which provide scholars' insights and interpretations, are also valuable. Remember, though, that the further you get from the primary source, the more likely you are to find inaccuracies introduced by researchers' inadvertent misinterpretations or distortions.

28f Taking Notes

As you locate information in the library and on the Internet, take notes (either by hand or on a computer) to create a record of exactly what you found and where you found it (see Figures 28.3 and 28.4).

(1) Recording Source Information

Each piece of information you record in your notes (whether summarized, paraphrased, or quoted from your sources) should be accompanied by a short descriptive heading that indicates its relevance to one of the points you will develop in your paper. Because you will use these headings to guide you as you organize your notes, you should make them as specific as possible. For example, labeling every note for a paper on the "digital divide" created by the Internet Digital divide or Internet will not prove very helpful later on. More focused headings—for instance, Dangers of digital divide or Government's steps to narrow the gap—will be much more useful.

See 28f3

Also include brief comments that make clear your reasons for recording the information. These comments (enclosed in brackets so you will know they express your own ideas, not those of your source) should establish the purpose of your note—what you think it can explain, support, clarify, describe, or contradict—and perhaps suggest its relationship to other notes or other sources. Any questions you have about the information or its source can also be included in your comments.

Finally, be sure each note accurately identifies the source of the information you are recording. You need not write out the complete citation, but you must include enough information to identify your source. For example, Gates 499 would be enough to send you back to your working bibliography card or file, where you would be able to find the complete documentation for Henry Louis Gates's essay "One Internet, Two Nations." (If you use more than one source by the same author, you need a more complete reference.)

Close-up: Taking Notes

When you take notes, your goal is flexibility: you want to be able to arrange and rearrange information easily and efficiently as your paper takes shape.

- If you take notes **on your computer,** type each individual note (accompanied by source information) under a specific heading rather than listing all information from a single source under the same heading. (Later on, you can move notes around so notes on the same topic are grouped together.)
- If you take notes **by hand,** use the time-tested index-card system, taking care to write on only one side of the card and to use a separate index card for each individual note rather than running several notes together on a single card. (Later, you can enter the information from these notes into your computer file.)

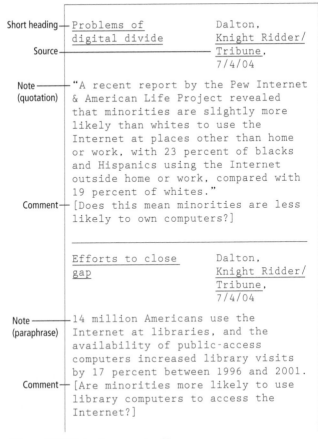

Short heading — Problems of digital divide

Source —

Dalton, Knight Ridder/ Tribune, 7/4/04

Note — (quotation) "A recent report by the Pew Internet & American Life Project revealed that minorities are slightly more likely than whites to use the Internet at places other than home or work, with 23 percent of blacks and Hispanics using the Internet outside home or work, compared with 19 percent of whites."

Comment — [Does this mean minorities are less likely to own computers?]

Efforts to close gap

Dalton, Knight Ridder/ Tribune, 7/4/04

Note — (paraphrase) 14 million Americans use the Internet at libraries, and the availability of public-access computers increased library visits by 17 percent between 1996 and 2001.

Comment — [Are minorities more likely to use library computers to access the Internet?]

Figure 28.3 Notes in computer file.

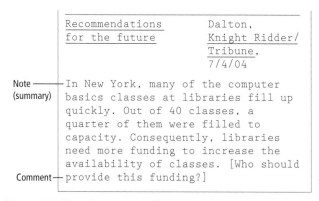

> Recommendations | Dalton,
> for the future | Knight Ridder/
> | Tribune,
> | 7/4/04

Note (summary) — In New York, many of the computer basics classes at libraries fill up quickly. Out of 40 classes, a quarter of them were filled to capacity. Consequently, libraries need more funding to increase the availability of classes. [Who should

Comment — provide this funding?]

Figure 28.3 Notes in computer file (*continued*).

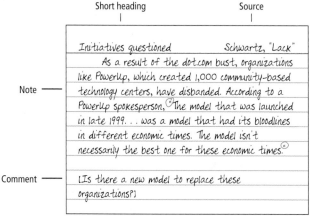

Short heading   Source

> Initiatives questioned   Schwartz, "Lack"
>
> As a result of the dot.com bust, organizations like PowerUp, which created 1,000 community-based technology centers, have disbanded. According to a PowerUp spokesperson, "The model that was launched in late 1999. . . was a model that had its bloodlines in different economic times. The model isn't necessarily the best one for these economic times."
>
> [Is there a new model to replace these organizations?]

Note — (center section)
Comment — (bottom section)

Figure 28.4 Notes on index card.

Checklist: Taking Notes

☐ **Identify the source of each piece of information.**

☐ **Include everything now that you will need later** to understand your note—names, dates, places, connections with other notes—and to remember why you recorded it.

☐ **Distinguish quotations from paraphrases and summaries and your own ideas from those of your sources.** If you copy a source's words, place them in quotation marks. (If you take notes by hand, circle the quotation marks; if you type your notes, boldface quotation marks.) If you write down your own ideas,

(continued)

Taking notes (continued)

See
Ch. 32

enclose them in brackets—and, if you are typing, italicize them as well. These techniques will help you avoid accidental plagiarism in your paper.

☐ **Put a writer's comments into your own words whenever possible,** summarizing and paraphrasing material as well as adding your own observations and analyses.

☐ **Copy a writer's comments accurately if you quote a source,** using the exact words, spelling, punctuation marks, and capitalization.

ESL Tip

If you take notes in English (rather than in your native language), you will probably find it easier to transfer the notes into a draft of your paper. However, you may find it faster and more effective to use your native language when writing your own comments about each note.

---

(2) Managing Photocopies and Printouts

Much of the information you gather will be in the form of photocopies (of articles, book sections, and so on) and material downloaded or printed out from electronic sources. Learning to manage this source information efficiently will save you a lot of time.

First, be careful not to allow the ease of copying and downloading to encourage you to postpone decisions about the usefulness of your sources. Remember, you can easily accumulate so many pages that it will be almost impossible for you to keep track of all your information.

You should also keep in mind that photocopies and printouts are just raw information, not information that has already been interpreted and evaluated. Making copies of sources is only the first step in the process of taking thorough, careful notes. You still have to paraphrase and summarize your source's ideas and make connections among them.

Also, keep in mind that photocopies and printouts do not have much flexibility. For example, a single page of text may include information that should be earmarked for several different sections of your paper. This lack of flexibility makes it difficult for you to arrange source material into any meaningful order. Just as you would with any source, you have to transcribe your notes into your computer or onto index cards. These notes will give you the flexibility you need to write your paper.

Remember, you should approach photocopies and material you download or print out just as you approach any other source: as material that you will read, highlight, annotate, and then take notes about.

Close-up: Avoiding Plagiarism

To avoid the possibility of accidental plagiarism, be sure to keep all downloaded material in a separate file—not in your notes file. After you read this material and decide how to use it, you can move the notes you take into your notes file (along with full source information).

See Ch. 32

Checklist: Working with Photocopies and Computer Printouts

☐ Record full and accurate source information, including the inclusive page numbers, electronic address (URL), and any other relevant information, on the first page of each copy.

☐ Clip or staple together consecutive pages of a single source.

☐ Do not copy a source without reminding yourself—*in writing*—why you are doing so. In pencil or on removable self-stick notes, record your initial responses to the source's ideas, jot down cross-references to other works or notes, and highlight important sections.

☐ Photocopying can be time-consuming and expensive, so try to avoid copying material that is only marginally relevant to your paper.

☐ Keep photocopies and printouts in a separate file so you will be able to find them when you need them.

---

(3) Summarizing, Paraphrasing, and Quoting

Summarizing Sources A **summary** is a brief restatement *in your own words* of a source's main idea. When you summarize a source, you condense the author's ideas into a few concise sentences. You do *not* include your own opinions or interpretations of the writer's ideas. If you think it is necessary to include a distinctive word or phrase from your source, place it in quotation marks; otherwise, you will be committing plagiarism.

See Ch. 32

Original Source:

Today, the First Amendment faces challenges from groups who seek to limit expressions of racism and bigotry. A growing number of legislatures have passed rules against "hate speech"—[speech] that is offensive on the basis of race, ethnicity, gender, or sexual orientation. The rules are intended to promote respect for all people and protect the targets of hurtful words, gestures, or actions.

Legal experts fear these rules may wind up diminishing the rights of all citizens. "The bedrock principle [of our society] is that government may never suppress free speech simply because it goes against what the community would like to hear," says Nadine Strossen, president of the American Civil Liberties Union and professor of constitutional law at New York University Law School. In recent years, for example, the courts have upheld the right of neo-Nazis to march in Jewish neighborhoods; protected cross-burning as a form of free expression; and allowed protesters to burn the American flag. The offensive, ugly, distasteful, or repugnant nature of expression is not reason enough to ban it, courts have said.

But advocates of limits on hate speech note that certain kinds of expression fall outside of First Amendment protection. Courts have ruled that "fighting words"—words intended to provoke immediate violence—or speech that creates a clear and present danger are not protected forms of expression. As the classic argument goes, freedom of speech does not give you the right to yell "Fire!" in a crowded theater. (Sudo, Phil. "Freedom of Hate Speech?" *Scholastic Update* 124.14 [1992]: 17–20.)

Summary: The right to freedom of speech, guaranteed by the First Amendment, is becoming more difficult to defend. Some people think stronger laws against the use of "hate speech" weaken the First Amendment, but others argue that some kinds of speech remain exempt from this protection (Sudo 17).

Close-up: Summaries

- **Summaries are original.** They should use your own language and phrasing, not the language and phrasing of your source.

- **Summaries are concise.** They should always be much shorter than the original.
- **Summaries are accurate.** They should precisely express the main idea of your source.
- **Summaries are objective.** They should not include your opinions.
- **Summaries are complete.** They should reflect the entire source, not just one part of it.

Paraphrasing Sources A summary conveys just the main idea of a source; a **paraphrase** is a *detailed* restatement, in your own words, of all a source's important ideas—but not your opinions or interpretations of those ideas. In a paraphrase, you indicate not only the source's main points but also its order, tone, and emphasis. Consequently, a paraphrase can sometimes be as long as the source itself.

Compare the following paraphrase with the summary of the same source on page 136.

Paraphrase:

Many groups want to limit the right of free speech guaranteed by the First Amendment to the Constitution. They believe this is necessary to protect certain groups of people from "hate speech." Women, people of color, and gay men and lesbians, for example, may find that hate speech is used to intimidate them. Legal scholars are afraid that even though the rules against hate speech are well intentioned, such rules undermine our freedom of speech. As Nadine Strossen, president of the American Civil Liberties Union, says, "The bedrock principle [of our society] is that government may never suppress free speech simply because it goes against what the community would like to hear" (qtd. in Sudo 17). People who support speech codes point out, however, that certain types of speech are not protected by the First Amendment—for example, words that create a "clear and present danger" or that would lead directly to violence (Sudo 17).

Close-up: Paraphrases

- **Paraphrases are original.** They should use your original language and phrasing, not the language and phrasing of your source.

(continued)

Paraphrases (continued)

- **Paraphrases are accurate.** They should precisely reflect both the ideas and the emphasis of your source.
- **Paraphrases are objective.** They should not include your own opinions or interpretations.
- **Paraphrases are complete.** They should include all the important ideas in your source.

ESL Tip

If you find yourself imitating a writer's sentence structure and vocabulary, try reading the passage you want to paraphrase and then putting it aside and thinking about it. Then, try to write down the ideas you remember without looking back at the original text.

Quoting Sources When you **quote,** you copy a writer's statements exactly as they appear in a source, word for word and punctuation mark for punctuation mark, enclosing the borrowed words in quotation marks. As a rule, you should not quote extensively in a research paper. The use of numerous quotations interrupts the flow of your discussion and gives readers the impression that your paper is just an unassimilated collection of other people's ideas.

Checklist: When to Quote

- ☐ Quote when a source's wording or phrasing is so distinctive that a summary or paraphrase would diminish its impact.
- ☐ Quote when a source's words—particularly those of a recognized expert on your subject—will lend authority to your paper.
- ☐ Quote when paraphrasing would create a long, clumsy, or incoherent phrase or would change the meaning of the original.
- ☐ Quote when you plan to disagree with a source. Using a source's exact words helps to show readers that you are being fair.

28g   Fine-Tuning Your Thesis

After you have finished your focused research and note-taking, you are ready to refine your tentative thesis into a carefully worded statement that expresses a conclusion that your research can support. This <u>thesis statement</u> should be more detailed than your tentative thesis, accurately conveying the direction, emphasis, and scope of your paper.

See 2b

Fine-Tuning Your Thesis

Tentative Thesis

Not all Americans have equal access to the Internet, and this is a potentially serious problem.

Thesis Statement

Although the Internet has changed our lives for the better, it threatens to leave many people behind, creating two distinct classes—those who have access and those who do not.

28h   Outlining, Drafting, and Revising

Keeping your thesis in mind, you are now ready to outline your supporting points and draft your paper.

(1) Outlining

Before you write your rough draft, you should make an outline. At this point, you need to make some sense out of all the notes you have accumulated, and you do this by sorting and organizing them. By identifying categories and subcategories of information, you begin to see your paper take shape and are able to construct an outline that reflects this shape. A **formal outline** indicates not only the exact order in which you will present your ideas but also the relationship between main ideas and supporting details.

NOTE: The outline you construct at this stage is only a guide for you to follow as you draft your paper; it is likely to change as you draft and revise.

Checklist: Constructing a Formal Outline

☐ Write your thesis statement at the top of the page.

☐ Review your notes to make sure that each note expresses only one general idea. If this is not the case, recopy any unrelated information, creating a separate note.

☐ Check that the heading for each note specifically characterizes the note's information. If it does not, change the heading.

☐ Sort your notes by their headings, keeping a miscellaneous pile for notes that do not seem to fit into any category. Irrelevant notes—those unrelated to your paper's thesis—should be set aside (but not discarded).

☐ Check your categories for balance. If most of your notes fall into one or two categories, change some of your headings to create narrower, more focused categories. If you have only one or two notes in a category, you will need to do additional research or treat that topic only briefly (or not at all).

☐ Organize the individual notes within each group, adding more specific subheads as needed. Arrange your notes in an order that highlights the most important points and subordinates lesser ones.

☐ Decide on a logical order in which to discuss your paper's major points.

☐ Construct your formal outline, using divisions and subdivisions that correspond to your headings. (Outline only the body of your paper, not your introduction and conclusion.) Be sure each heading has at least two subheadings; if one does not, combine it with another heading. Follow outline format strictly:

    I. First major point of your paper
       A. First subpoint
       B. Next subpoint
          1. First supporting example
          2. Next supporting example
             a. First specific detail
             b. Next specific detail
   II. Second major point

☐ Review your completed outline to make sure you have not placed too much emphasis on a relatively unimportant idea, ordered ideas illogically, or created sections that overlap with others.

Computer Tip: Outlining

Before you begin writing, create a separate file for each major section of your outline. Then, copy your notes into these files in the order in which you intend to use them. You can print out each file as you need it and use it as a guide as you write.

(2) Drafting

When you write your <u>rough draft</u>, follow your outline, using your notes as needed. As you draft, jot down questions to yourself, and identify points that need further clarification (you can bracket those ideas or print them in boldface on your draft, or you can write them on self-stick notes). Leave space for material you plan to add, and bracket phrases or whole sections that you think you may later decide to move or delete. In other words, lay the groundwork for a major revision. See 2c1

As your draft takes shape, you will need to supply transitions between sentences and paragraphs to show how your points are related. Be careful to copy source information fully and accurately on this and every subsequent draft, placing documentation as close as possible to the material it identifies.

Computer Tip: Drafting

You can use a split screen or multiple windows to view your notes as you draft your paper. You can also copy the material that you need from your notes and then insert it into the text of your paper. (As you copy, be especially careful that you do not unintentionally commit <u>plagiarism</u>.) See 32b

Shaping the Parts of Your Paper Like any other essay, a research paper has an introduction, a body, and a conclusion. In your rough draft, as in your outline, you focus on the body of your paper. You should not spend time planning an introduction or a conclusion at the drafting stage; your ideas will change as you write, and you will want to develop your opening and closing paragraphs later to reflect those changes.

See 3d1 In your **introduction,** you identify your topic and establish how you will approach it. Your introduction also includes your thesis statement, which expresses the position you will support in the rest of the paper. In your rough draft, however, an undeveloped introduction is perfectly acceptable; in fact, your thesis statement alone can serve as a placeholder for the more polished introduction that you will write later.

See 3a As you draft the **body** of your paper, indicate its direction with strong topic sentences that correspond to the divisions of your outline.

```
       In the late 1990s, many argued that the
Internet had ushered in a new age, one in which
instant communication would bring people closer
together and eventually eliminate national
boundaries.
```

See 38b You can also use headings if they are a convention of the discipline in which you are writing.

```
Responses to Digital Divide

       In response, the government, corporations,
nonprofit organizations, and public libraries made
efforts to bridge the gap between the "haves" and
the "have-nots."
```

Even in your rough draft, carefully worded topic sentences and headings and will help you keep your discussion under control.

See 3d2 The **conclusion** of a research paper often restates the thesis. This is especially important in a long paper, because by the time your readers get to the end, they may have lost sight of your paper's main idea. Your conclusion can also include a summary of your key points, a call for action, or perhaps an apt quotation. In your rough draft, however, your concluding paragraph is usually very brief.

Working Source Material into Your Paper In the body of your paper, you use source material to support your points. In the process, you evaluate and interpret your sources, comparing different ideas and assessing conflicting points of view. As a writer, your job is to draw your own conclusions, blending information from various sources into a paper that coherently and forcefully presents your own original viewpoint to your readers.

Be sure to <u>integrate source material</u> smoothly into your paper, clearly and accurately identifying the relationships among various sources (and between those sources' ideas and your own). If two sources present conflicting interpretations, you should be especially careful to use precise language and accurate transitions to make the contrast apparent (for instance, "`Although the Bush administration remains optimistic, some studies suggest . . .`"). When two sources agree, you should make this clear (for example, "`Like Young, McPherson believes . . .`" or "`Department of Commerce statistics confirm Gates's point`"). Such phrasing will provide a context for your own comments and conclusions. If different sources present complementary information about a subject, blend materials from the sources *carefully*, keeping track of which ideas come from which source.

See Ch. 31

(3) Revising

A good way to start revising is to check to see that your thesis statement still accurately expresses your paper's central focus. Then, make an outline of your draft, and compare it with the outline you made before you began the draft. If you find significant differences, you will have to revise your thesis statement or rewrite sections of your paper. The checklists in **2c2** can guide your revision of your paper's overall structure and its individual paragraphs, sentences, and words.

Of course, you should pay particular attention to your instructor's revision suggestions, which can come orally (in a conference) or in handwritten comments on your paper. Alternatively, your instructor may use *Microsoft Word*'s Comment tool to make comments electronically on your draft (see Figure 28.5). When you revise, you can incorporate these suggestions (see Figure 28.6).

|The| Bill and Melinda Gates Foundation has provided libraries across the country with funding

Comment: You need a transition sentence before this one to show that this paragraph is about a new idea. See 3b.

Figure 28.5 Rough draft with instructor's comments (excerpt).

that allows them to purchase computers and
connect them to the Internet (Egan). Nonprofit
organizations also sponsor Web sites, such as The
Digital Divide Network, a site that posts stories
about the digital divide from a variety of
perspectives. |By posting information on the Web
site that they created|, the   **Comment:** Wordy. See
                                        11a.
site's sponsor hopes to raise
awareness of the problems that the digital divide
causes.

**Figure 28.5 Rough draft with instructor's comments (excerpt)
(*continued*).**

Nonprofit organizations also worked to bridge
the digital divide. The Bill and Melinda Gates
Foundation, for example, has provided libraries
across the country with funding that allows them
to purchase computers and connect to the Internet
(Egan). Nonprofit organizations also sponsor Web
sites, such as The Digital Divide Network, a site
that posts stories about the digital divide from a
variety of perspectives. By posting information,
the site's sponsor hopes to raise awareness of the
problems that the digital divide causes.

Figure 28.6 Revision incorporating instructor's suggestions.

Feedback you get from **peer review**—other students'
comments, handwritten or electronic—can also help you
revise (see Figure 28.7). As you incorporate your classmates' suggestions, as well as your own changes and any
suggested by your instructor, you can use *Microsoft Word*'s
Track Changes tool to help you keep track of the revi-
sions you make on your draft (see Figure 28.8).

‖A recent article│observes that many African-American and other minority groups argue that digital divide rhetoric might actually stereotype minorities. The article says that digital divide rhetoric "could discourage businesses or academics from creating content or services tailored for minority communities—ultimately making the digital divide a self-fulfilling prophecy."│Many scholars and leaders in the African-American community fear that a focus on the digital divide will lead to its being seen as a fact to be accepted rather than as a problem to be solved. Tara L. McPherson │says│that "the idea of challenging the digital divide is not about denying it's existence. But it is to ensure that the focus on the digital divide doesn't naturalize a kind of exclusion of investment│."

Comment: You need a transition sentence here!

Comment: Ditto, this is really awk. ☺

Comment: Tell us the name and where this came from.

Comment: Do you need a p. #?

Comment: Use a stronger word—*asserts, claims,* etc. Wilson doesn't like us to keep using "says." ☺

Comment: I think you're supposed to have the author's last name here.

Figure 28.7 Rough draft with peer reviewers' comments (excerpt).

In other cases, the groups targeted by digital divide programs argue that they might do more harm than good. A recent article in the Chronicle of Higher Education observes that many African-American and other minority groups argue that digital divide rhetoric might actually stereotype minorities. The article says that digital divide rhetoric "could discourage businesses or academics from creating content or

Figure 28.8 Revision with Track Changes.

```
services tailored for minority communities—
ultimately making the digital divide a self-
fulfilling prophecy" (Young). Many scholars and
leaders in the African-American community fear
that a focus on the digital divide will lead to
its being seen as a fact to be accepted rather
than as a problem to be solved. Tara L.
McPherson ~~says~~ agrees, arguing that "the idea
of challenging the digital divide is not about
denying its existence. But it is to ensure that
the focus on the digital divide doesn't
naturalize a kind of exclusion of investment~~.~~"
(qtd. in Young).
```

Figure 28.8 Revision with Track Changes (*continued*).

Checklist: Revising a Research Paper

- ☐ Should you do more research to find support for certain points?
- ☐ Do you need to reorder the major sections of your paper?
- ☐ Should you rearrange the order in which you present your points within those sections?
- ☐ Do you need to add topic sentences? section headings? transitional paragraphs?
- ☐ Have you integrated your notes smoothly into your paper?
- ☐ Do you introduce source material with identifying tags?
- ☐ Are quotations blended with paraphrase, summary, and your own observations and reactions?
- ☐ Have you avoided plagiarism by carefully documenting all borrowed ideas?
- ☐ Have you analyzed and interpreted the ideas of others rather than simply stringing those ideas together?
- ☐ Do your own ideas—not those of your sources—dominate your discussion?

See
Ch. 31

See
31a

See
Ch. 32

http://kirsznermandell.wadsworth.com

Computer Tip: Revising

When you finish revising your paper, copy the file that contains your working bibliography, and insert it at the end of your paper. Delete any irrelevant entries, and then compile your works-cited list. (Make sure that the format of the entries on your works-cited list conforms to the documentation style you are using.)

Close-up: Preparing a Final Draft

Before you print out the final version of your paper, <u>edit and proofread</u> a hard copy of your works-cited list as well as the paper itself. Next, consider (or reconsider) your paper's **title.** It should be descriptive enough to tell your readers what your paper is about, and it should create interest in your subject. Your title should also be consistent with the <u>purpose</u> and tone of your paper. (You would hardly want a humorous title for a paper about the death penalty or world hunger.) Finally, your title should be engaging and to the point—and perhaps even provocative. Often a quotation from one of your sources will suggest a likely title.

When you are satisfied with your title, read your paper through one last time, proofreading for any grammar, spelling, or typing errors you may have missed. Pay particular attention to parenthetical documentation and works-cited entries. (Remember that every error undermines your credibility.) Finally, make sure your paper's format conforms to your instructor's guidelines. Once you are satisfied that your paper is as accurate as you can make it, print out a final copy. Then, fasten the pages with a paper clip (do not staple the pages or fold the corners together), and hand it in.

See
2d

See
1a

CHAPTER 29

Using and Evaluating Library Sources

29a Using Library Sources

Even though the Internet has changed the nature of research, the library is still the best place to begin a research project. With its wide variety of print and electronic resources—some suitable for <u>exploratory research</u>, others for <u>focused research</u>—the library gives you access to material that you cannot get anywhere else.

See 28b

See 28e

Close-up: Advantages of Using the Library

- Many important and useful publications are available only in print or through the library's subscription databases and not on the Internet.
- The information in your college library will almost always be more focused and more useful than much of what you will find on the Internet. An Internet search often yields far more information (most of it irrelevant to your topic) than you can reasonably handle or properly evaluate.
- The information you see on an Internet site—unlike information in your library's subscription databases—may not be there when you try to access it at a later time. (For this reason, <u>MLA</u> recommends that you print out all Internet documents you plan to use in your research.)
- Anyone can publish on the Internet, so sites can vary greatly in quality. Because librarians screen the material in your college library, it will usually meet academic standards of reliability. (Even so, you still have to <u>evaluate</u> any information before you use it in a paper.)
- The authorship and affiliation of Internet documents can often be difficult or impossible to determine, but this is not usually the case with the sources in your college library.

See Ch. 33

See 30c

---

(1) Using the Online Catalog

Most college and other libraries have abandoned print catalog systems in favor of **online catalogs**—computer databases that list all the books, journals, and other materials held by the library.

You access the online catalog (as well as the other electronic resources of the library) by using computer terminals located throughout the library. Typing in specific words or phrases enables you to find the information you need. When you search an online catalog for information about a topic, you can conduct either a *keyword search* or a *subject search*.

Conducting a Keyword Search When you carry out a **keyword search,** you enter into the online catalog a word or words associated with your topic. The computer then retrieves catalog entries that contain those words. The more precise your keywords, the more specific and useful the information you will receive. (Combining search terms with AND, OR, and NOT enables you to narrow or broaden your search. This technique is called conducting a <u>Boolean search</u>.)

See 30a2

Conducting a Subject Search When you carry out a **subject search,** you enter specific subject headings into the online catalog. The subject headings in the library are most often arranged according to headings listed in the five-volume manual *Library of Congress Subject Headings*, which is held at the reference desk of your library. Although it may be possible to guess at a subject heading, your search will be more successful if you consult these volumes to identify the exact words you need.

Checklist: Keyword Dos and Don'ts

When conducting a keyword search, remember the following hints:

- ☐ Use precise, specific keywords to distinguish your topic from similar topics.
- ☐ Enter both singular and plural keywords where appropriate—*printing press* and *printing presses*, for example.
- ☐ Enter both abbreviations and their full-word equivalents (for example, *US* and *United States*).
- ☐ Try variant spellings (for example, *color* and *colour*).
- ☐ Don't use too long a string of keywords. (If you do, you will retrieve large amounts of irrelevant material.)

(2) Using Electronic Resources

Today's libraries have electronic resources that enable you to find a wide variety of sources. The same computer terminals that enable you to access the online catalog may also enable you to access this source material.

Online databases are collections of digital information—citations of books; reports; and journal, magazine, and newspaper articles (and sometimes the articles themselves)—arranged for easy access and retrieval by computer. Different libraries offer different databases and make them available in different ways. Most libraries have implemented Web-based systems that make it easy for users to access databases (and online catalogs) from outside the library. One of your first tasks should be to determine what your library has to offer. Visit your library's Web site, or ask a reference librarian for more information.

Once you have searched the databases and found useful information, you can print out or download bibliographic citations, **abstracts** (short summaries), or even full text.

General and Specialized Subscription Databases The databases available in your college library are likely to be **subscription databases,** which means that the library must subscribe to them in order to make them available to students and faculty. Licensing and copyright agreements restrict the use of these subscription databases; they are not available from outside the library to those who are not affiliated with the school.

Some library subscription databases for articles cover many subject areas (*Expanded Academic ASAP* or *Lexis-Nexis Academic Universe,* for example); others cover one subject area in great detail (*PsycINFO* or *Sociological Abstracts,* for example). Assuming that your library offers a variety of databases (some libraries subscribe to hundreds), how do you know which ones will be best for your research topic? One strategy is to begin by searching a general database that includes full-text articles and then move on to a more specialized database that covers your subject in more detail. The specialized databases are more likely to include scholarly and professional journal articles, but they are also less likely to include the full text.

Searching Databases There are two ways to search library subscription databases for information on a topic: by subject headings and by keyword(s). When you search by **subject headings,** you choose a heading from a list of terms recognized by that database.

The other option is **keyword searching,** which allows you to type in any significant term likely to be found in the title, subject headings, abstract, or (if the full text is available) text of an article. Keyword searching also allows you to link terms using **boolean operators** (AND, OR, NOT). For example, *elderly* AND *abuse* would retrieve only articles that mention both elderly people and abuse; *elderly* OR *aged* OR *senior citizens* would retrieve articles that mention any of these terms. Keyword searching is particularly helpful when you need to narrow or expand the focus of your search.

Both subject heading and keyword searches are useful ways to find articles on your topic. The most important thing is to be persistent. One good article often leads to another because abstracts and text may suggest other terms you can use.

(3) Consulting General Reference Works

During your **exploratory research,** general reference works can provide a broad overview of a particular subject. The following reference works, available in electronic form as well as in print, are useful for exploratory research.

General Encyclopedias General multivolume encyclopedias are available both in electronic format and in print. For example, *The New Encyclopaedia Britannica* is available on CD-ROM and DVD, as well as on the World Wide Web at <http://www.britannica.com>.

Specialized Encyclopedias, Dictionaries, and Bibliographies These specialized reference works contain in-depth articles focusing on a single subject area.

General Bibliographies General bibliographies list books available in a wide variety of fields.

> *Books in Print.* An index of authors and titles of books in print in the United States. The *Subject Guide to Books in Print* indexes books according to subject area.

The Bibliographic Index. A tool for locating bibliographies.

Biographical References Biographical reference books provide information about people's lives as well as bibliographic listings.

Living Persons

Who's Who in America. Gives concise biographical information about prominent Americans.

Who's Who. Collects concise biographical facts about notable British men and women.

Current Biography. Includes articles on people of many nationalities.

Deceased Persons

Dictionary of American Biography. Considered the best of American biographical dictionaries. Includes articles on over 13,000 Americans.

Dictionary of National Biography. The most important reference work for British biography.

Webster's Biographical Dictionary. Perhaps the most widely used biographical reference work. Includes people from all periods and places.

(4) Consulting Specialized Reference Works

More specialized reference works can help you find the facts, examples, statistics, definitions, and quotations that you will need for your **focused research.** The following reference works—many of which are available on CD-ROM, on DVD, or online as well as in print versions— are most useful for focused research.

Unabridged Dictionaries Unabridged dictionaries, such as the *Oxford English Dictionary,* are comprehensive works that give detailed information about words.

Special Dictionaries These dictionaries focus on such topics as usage, synonyms, slang and idioms, etymologies, and foreign terms; some focus on specific disciplines, such as accounting or law.

Yearbooks and Almanacs A **yearbook** is an annual publication that updates factual and statistical information already published in a reference source. An **almanac** provides lists, charts, and statistics about a wide variety of subjects.

World Almanac. Includes statistics about government, population, sports, and many other subjects. Published annually since 1868.

Information Please Almanac. Includes information unavailable in the *World Almanac.* Published annually since 1947.

Facts on File. Covering 1940 to the present, this work offers digests of important news stories from metropolitan newspapers.

Editorials on File. Reprints important editorials from American and Canadian newspapers.

Atlases An **atlas** contains maps and charts as well as historical, cultural, political, and economic information.

National Geographic Society. *National Geographic Atlas of the World.* The most up-to-date atlas available.

Rand McNally Cosmopolitan World Atlas. A modern and extremely legible medium-sized atlas.

We the People: An Atlas of America's Ethnic Diversity. Presents information about specific ethnic groups. Maps show immigration routes and settlement patterns.

Quotation Books A **quotation book** contains numerous quotations on a wide variety of subjects. Such quotations can be especially useful for your paper's introductory and concluding paragraphs.

Bartlett's Familiar Quotations. Quotations are arranged chronologically by author.

The Home Book of Quotations. Quotations are arranged by subject. An author index and a keyword index are also included.

(5) Finding Books

The online catalog gives you the call numbers you need for locating specific titles. A **call number** is like a book's address in the library: it tells you exactly where to find the book you are looking for. (Figure 29.1 shows an online catalog entry for a book.)

(6) Finding Articles

A **periodical** is a newspaper, magazine, scholarly journal, or other publication that is published at regular intervals

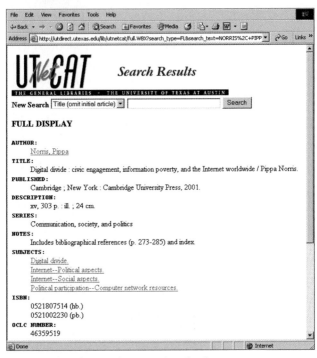

File Edit View Favorites Tools Help

Address http://utdirect.utexas.edu/lib/utnetcat/full.WBX?search_type=FL&search_text=NORRIS%2C+PIPP

UTNetCAT — *Search Results*

THE GENERAL LIBRARIES · THE UNIVERSITY OF TEXAS AT AUSTIN

New Search | Title (omit initial article) ▾ | | Search |

FULL DISPLAY

AUTHOR:
    Norris, Pippa
TITLE:
    Digital divide : civic engagement, information poverty, and the Internet worldwide / Pippa Norris
PUBLISHED:
    Cambridge ; New York : Cambridge University Press, 2001.
DESCRIPTION:
    xv, 303 p. : ill. ; 24 cm.
SERIES:
    Communication, society, and politics
NOTES:
    Includes bibliographical references (p. 273-285) and index.
SUBJECTS:
    Digital divide.
    Internet--Political aspects.
    Internet--Social aspects.
    Political participation--Computer network resources.
ISBN:
    0521807514 (hb.)
    0521002230 (pb.)
OCLC NUMBER:
    46359519

Figure 29.1 Online catalog entry for a book.

(weekly, monthly, or quarterly). **Periodical indexes** list articles from a selected group of magazines, newspapers, or scholarly journals. These indexes may be available in your library in bound volumes, on microfilm or microfiche, on CD-ROM or DVD, or in one of the library's subscription databases. Choosing the right index for your research saves you time and energy by allowing you to easily find articles written about your subject.

NOTE: Articles in scholarly journals provide current information and are written by experts in the field. Because these journals focus on a particular subject area, they can provide in-depth analysis.

Close-up: Frequently Used Subscription Databases

    The following subscription databases are found in most academic libraries. (Be sure to check your library's Web site or ask a librarian about those available to you.)

General Indexes	Description
Ebscohost	Database system for thousands of periodical articles on many subjects
Expanded Academic ASAP	A largely full-text database covering all subjects in thousands of magazines and scholarly journals
FirstSearch	Full-text articles from many popular and scholarly periodicals
LexisNexis Academic Universe	Includes full-text articles from national, international, and local newspapers. Also includes large legal and business sections.
Readers' Guide to Periodical Literature	Index to popular periodicals.

Specialized Indexes	Description
Dow Jones Interactive	Full text of articles from US newspapers and trade journals
ERIC	Largest database of education-related journal articles and reports in the world
General BusinessFile ASAP	A full-text database covering business topics
PubMed (MEDLINE)	Covers articles in medical journals. Some may be available in full text.
PsycINFO	Covers psychology and related fields
Sociological Abstracts	Covers the social sciences

Microfilm and Microfiche Extremely small images of pages of a periodical may be stored on microfilm. (You need a microfilm scanner to read or photocopy the pages.) Microfiche is similar to microfilm, but images are on a 5-by-7-inch sheet of film and are scanned with a microfiche reader.

(7) Using Special Library Services

As you do focused research, consult a librarian if you plan to use any of the following special services.

Close-up: Special Library Services

- **Interlibrary Loans** Your library may be part of a library system that allows loans of books from one location to another. Check with your librarian.
- **Special Collections** Your library may house special collections of books, manuscripts, or documents.
- **Government Documents** A large university library may have a separate government documents area with its own catalog or index. A good Web site for locating government publications is <http://www.firstgov.gov>.
- **Vertical File** The vertical file includes pamphlets from a variety of organizations and interest groups, newspaper clippings, and other material collected by librarians.

29b Evaluating Library Sources

Whenever you find information in the library (print or electronic), you should take the time to **evaluate** it—to assess its usefulness and its reliability. To determine the usefulness of a library source, you should ask yourself the following questions:

- *Does the Source Treat Your Topic in Enough Detail?* To be useful, your source should treat your topic in detail. Skim the book's table of contents and index for references to your topic. To be of any real help, a book should include a section or chapter on your topic, not simply a footnote of brief reference. For articles, read the abstract, or skim the entire article for key facts, looking closely at section headings, information set in boldface type, and topic sentences. An article should have your topic as its central subject, or at least one of its main concerns.
- *Is the Source Current?* The date of publication tells you whether the information in a book or article is up-to-date. A source's currency is particularly important for scientific and technological subjects. But even in the humanities, new discoveries and new ways of thinking lead scholars to reevaluate and modify their ideas. Be sure to check with your instructor to see if he or she prefers sources that have been published after a particular date.
- *Is the Source Respected?* A contemporary review of a source can help you make this assessment. *Book Review Digest*, available in the reference section of your li-

brary, lists popular books that have been reviewed in at least three newspapers or magazines and includes excerpts from representative reviews. Book reviews are also available from the *New York Times Book Review's* Web site <http://www.nytimes.com/books>, which includes text of book reviews the newspaper has published since 1980.

- *Is the Source Reliable?* Is the source largely fact or unsubstantiated opinion? Does the writer support his or her conclusions? Does the writer include documentation? Is the supporting information balanced? Is the writer objective, or does he or she have a particular agenda to advance? Is the writer associated with a special interest group that may affect his or her view of the issue?

- *Is the Source a Scholarly or Popular Publication?* In general, **scholarly publications**—books and journals aimed at an audience of expert readers—are more respected and reliable than **popular publications**—books, magazines, and newspapers aimed at an audience of general readers. Assuming they are current and written by reputable authors, however, articles from popular publications may be appropriate for your research. But remember that most popular publications do not have the same rigorous standards as scholarly publications. For example, although some popular periodicals (such as *Atlantic Monthly* and *Harper's*) generally contain articles that are reliable and carefully researched, other periodicals do not. For this reason, before you use information from popular sources such as *Newsweek* or *Sports Illustrated*, check with your instructor.

Scholarly and Popular Publications

Scholarly Publications	**Popular Publications**
Scholarly publications report the results of research.	Popular publications entertain and inform.
Scholarly publications are frequently published by a university press or have some connection with a university or academic organization.	Popular publications are published by commercial presses.

(continued)

Scholarly and popular publications (continued)

Scholarly Publications	Popular Publications
Scholarly publications are **refereed;** that is, an editorial board or group of expert reviewers determines what will be published.	Popular publications are usually not refereed.
Scholarly publications are usually written by someone who is a recognized authority in the field about which he or she is writing.	Popular publications may be written by experts in a particular field, but more often they are written by staff or freelance writers.
Scholarly publications are written for a scholarly audience, so they often contain a highly technical vocabulary and challenging content.	Popular publications are written for general readers, so they tend to use accessible language and do not have very challenging content.
Scholarly publications nearly always contain extensive documentation as well as a bibliography of works consulted.	Popular publications rarely cite sources or use documentation.
Scholarly publications are published primarily because they make a contribution to a particular field of study.	Popular publications are published primarily to make a profit.

CHAPTER 30

Using and Evaluating Internet Sources

The **Internet** is a vast system of networks that links millions of computers. Because of its size and diversity, the Internet allows people from all over the world to communicate quickly and easily. Furthermore, because it is inexpensive to publish text, pictures, and sound online (via the Internet), businesses, government agencies, libraries, and universities are able to make available vast amounts of information.

30a Using the World Wide Web for Research

When most people refer to the Internet, they actually mean the **World Wide Web,** which is just a part of the Internet. (**See 30b** for other components of the Internet that you can use in your research.) The Web relies on **hypertext links,** key words highlighted in blue. By clicking your mouse on these links, you can move easily from one part of a document to another or from one Web site to another.

The Web enables you to connect to a vast number of documents. For example, you can call up a **home page** or **Web page** (an individual document), or a **Web site** (a collection of Web pages). Government agencies, businesses, universities, libraries, newspapers and magazines, journals, and public interest groups, as well as individuals, all operate their own Web sites. Each of these sites contains hypertext links that can take you to other relevant sites.

Close-up: Limitations of Internet Research

Even with all its advantages, the Internet does not give you access to all the high-quality print and electronic resources found in a typical college library. For this reason, you should consider the Internet to be a supplement to your library research, not a substitute for it. See **29a** for information about library sources.

To carry out a Web search, you need a **Web browser,** a tool that enables you to find information on the Web. Two of the most popular browsers—*Netscape Navigator* and *Microsoft Internet Explorer*—display the full range of text, photos, sound, and video available in Web documents. (Most new computers come with one of these browsers already installed.)

Most colleges and universities provide Internet access to students free of charge. Once you are connected to the Internet, you have to use your browser to connect to a **search engine,** a program that helps you retrieve information by searching the documents that are available on the Internet.

Close-up: Popular Search Engines

AllTheWeb <www.alltheweb.com>: This excellent search engine provides comprehensive coverage of the Web. Many users think that this search engine is as good as *Google*. In addition to generating Web page results, *AllTheWeb* has the ability to search for news stories, pictures, video clips, MP3s, and FTP files.

AltaVista <www.altavista.com>: Good, precise engine for focused searches. Fast and easy to use.

Ask Jeeves <www.ask.com>: Good beginner's site. Allows you to narrow your search by asking questions, such as *Are dogs smarter than pigs?*

Excite <www.excite.com>: Good for general topics. Because it searches over 250 million Web sites, you often get more information than you need.

Go <http://infoseek.go.com>: Enables you to access information in a directory of reviewed sites, news stories, and Usenet groups.

Google <www.google.com>: Arguably the best search engine available. Accesses a large database that enables you to carry out an image search as well as a Web page search. *Google* is easy to navigate, and searches usually yield a high percentage of useful hits.

HotBot <www.hotbot.com>: Excellent, fast search engine for locating specific information. Good search options allow you to fine-tune your searches.

Lycos <www.lycos.com>: Enables you to search for specific media (graphics, for example). A somewhat small index of Web pages.

Teoma <www.teoma.com>: Teoma is a search engine owned by *Ask Jeeves*. Although it has a smaller index of the Web than *Google* and *AllTheWeb*, it is very effective when it comes to answering questions. It contains a Refine feature that offers suggested topics to explore after you do a search. It also has a Resources section of results that will point you to linked resources about various topics.

WebCrawler <www.webcrawler.com>: Good for beginners. Easy to use.

Yahoo! <www.yahoo.com>: Good for exploratory research. Enables you to search using either subject headings or keywords. Searches its own indexes as well as the Web.

> **Computer Tip: Specialized Search Engines**
>
> *Voice of the Shuttle* (humanities search engine)
>   <http://vos.ucsb.edu/>
> *Pilot-Search.com* (literary search engine)
>   <http://www.pilot-search.com/>
> *FedWorld* (US government database and report search engine)
>   <http://www.fedworld.gov/>
> *HealthFinder* (health, nutrition, and diseases information
>   for consumers)
>   <http://www.healthfinder.gov/default.htm>
> *The Internet Movie Database* (search engine and database
>   for film facts, reviews, and so on)
>   <http://www.imdb.com>
> *SportQuest* (sports search engine)
>   <http://www.sportquest.com/>
> *FindLaw* (legal search engine)
>   <http://www.findlaw.com/>

Because even the best search engines search only a fraction of what is on the Web, you should also carry out a metasearch using a **metacrawler,** a search engine that searches several search engines simultaneously. *Dogpile* <www.dogpile.com>, *Metacrawler* <www.metacrawler.com>, and *Zworks* <www.zworks.com> are useful tools for discovering the full range of online sources.

There are three ways to use search engines to find the information you want: entering an electronic address, doing a keyword search, and using subject guides.

(1) Entering an Electronic Address

The most basic way to access information on the Web is to go directly to a specific electronic address, called a **URL.** Search engines and Web browsers display a dialog box that enables you to enter the electronic address of a specific Web site (see Figure 30.1). Once you type in an address and click on *search* (or hit *enter* or the return key), you will be connected to the Web site you want. Make sure that you type the electronic address exactly as it appears, without adding spaces or adding or deleting punctuation marks. Remember that omitting just a single letter or punctuation mark will send you to the wrong site—or to no site at all.

(2) Doing a Keyword Search

Search engines also enable you to do a keyword search. On the first page (home page) of the search engine that you have chosen, you will find a box in which you can enter a keyword or keywords (see Figure 30.1). When you hit *enter* or the return key, the search engine retrieves and displays all the Web pages that contain your keywords.

Keep in mind that a search engine identifies any site in which the keyword or keywords that you have typed appear. (These sites are called **hits.**) Thus, a general keyword such as *Baltimore* could result in over a million hits. Because examining all these sites would be impossible, you need to focus your search, just as you would with your library's online catalog. By carrying out a **Boolean search,** combining keywords with AND, OR, or NOT (typed in capital letters), you can eliminate irrelevant hits from your search. For example, to find Web pages that have to do with Baltimore's economy, type *Baltimore* AND *economy.* Some search engines allow you to search using three or four keywords—*Baltimore* AND *economy* NOT *agriculture,* for example. Focusing your searches in this way will enable you to retrieve information quickly and easily.

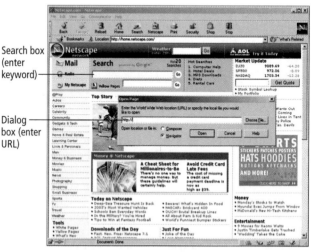

Search box (enter keyword)

Dialog box (enter URL)

Figure 30.1 Home page of *Netscape Navigator.*

(3) Using Subject Guides

Some search engines, such as *Yahoo!, About.com,* and *Look Smart,* contain a **subject guide**—a list of general categories (*The Humanities, The Arts, Entertainment, Business,* and so on) from which you can choose (see Figure 30.2). Each of these categories will lead you to more specific lists of categories and subcategories, until eventually you get to the topic you want. For example, clicking on *The Humanities* would lead you to *History*, which in turn would lead you to *American History* and eventually to *Vietnam War.* Although this is a time-consuming strategy for finding specific information, it can be an excellent tool for finding or narrowing a topic.

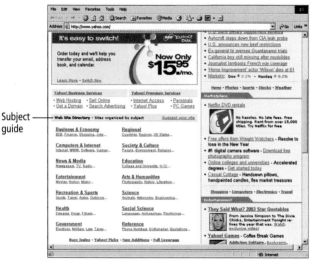

Figure 30.2 *Yahoo!* home page with subject guide.

Checklist: Tips for Effective Web Searches

☐ **Choose the right search engine.** No one all-purpose search engine exists. Use a subject guide, such as the one available on *Yahoo!*, for exploratory research, and use a search engine, such as *Google* (or a metasearch engine, such as *Dogpile*), for more focused research.

☐ **Choose your keywords carefully.** A search engine is only as good as the keywords you use. Choose key-words carefully.

☐ **Narrow your search.** Carry out a Boolean search to make your searches more productive.

(continued)

Tips for effective Web searches (continued)

☐ **Check your spelling.** If your search does not yield the results you expect, check to make sure you have spelled your search terms correctly. Even a one-letter mistake can cause a search engine to retrieve the wrong information—or no information at all.

☐ **Include enough terms.** If you are looking for information on housing, for example, search for several variations of your keyword: *housing, houses, home buyer, buying houses, residential real estate,* and so on.

☐ **Consult the Help screen.** Most search engines have a help screen. If you have trouble with your search, do not hesitate to consult it. A little time spent here can save you a lot of time later.

☐ **Add useful sites to your Bookmark or Favorites list.** Whenever you find a particularly useful Web site, **bookmark** it by selecting this option on the menu bar of your browser (with some browsers, such as *Microsoft Explorer,* this option is called Favorites). When you add a site to your bookmark list, you can return to the site whenever you want to by opening the bookmark menu and selecting it.

30b Using Other Internet Tools

In addition to the World Wide Web, the Internet contains a number of other components that you can use to gather information for your research.

(1) Using Email

Email can be very useful to you as you do research because it enables you to exchange ideas with classmates, ask questions of your instructors, and even conduct long-distance interviews. You can follow email links in Web documents, and you can transfer word-processing documents or other files (as email attachments) from one computer to another.

(2) Using Listservs

Listservs, (sometimes called **discussion lists**), electronic mailing lists to which you must subscribe, enable you to communicate with groups of people interested in particular topics. (Many schools, and even individual courses, have their own listservs.) Individuals in a listserv send emails to a main email address, and these messages are routed to all members in the group. Some listserv subscribers may be experts who can answer your queries. Keep in mind, however, that anyone can join a listserv, so make sure you <u>evaluate</u> the information you get before you use it in your research. See 30c

(3) Using Newsgroups

Like listservs, **newsgroups** are discussion groups. Unlike listserv messages, which are sent to you as email, newsgroup messages are collected on the **Usenet** system, a global collection of news servers, where anyone who subscribes can access them. In a sense, newsgroups function as gigantic bulletin boards where users post messages that others can read and respond to. Thus, newsgroups can be a source of specific information as well as suggestions about where to look for further information. Just as you would with a listserv, you should evaluate information you get from a newsgroup before you use it.

(4) Using FTP and Telnet

At one time, you needed special software to access telnet and FTP. Now they can be accessed with most programs that access the Web.

FTP (file transfer protocol) enables you to transfer documents at high speed from one computer on the Internet to another. With FTP, you can get full text of books and articles as well as pictures. The most common use for FTP is for downloading updates from computer software manufacturers.

Telnet is a program that enables you to make a connection via telephone to another computer on the Internet. With telnet you can download anything from another host computer.

(5) Using MUDS, MOOS, IRCS, and Instant Messaging

With emails and listservs, there is a delay between the time a message is sent and the time it is received. **MUDS, MOOS, IRCS,** and **instant messaging** enable you to send and receive messages in real time. Communication is **synchronous;** that is, messages are sent and received as they are typed. Synchronous communication programs are being used more and more in college settings—for class discussions, online workshops, and collaborative projects.

30c   Evaluating Internet Sites

Web sites vary greatly in reliability. Because anyone can operate a Web site and thereby publish anything, regardless of quality, critical evaluation of Web-based material is even more important than evaluation of more traditional sources of information, such as books and journal articles.

Determining the quality of a Web site is crucial if you plan to use it as a source for your research. If you are using a Web site for personal information or entertainment, it is probably enough just to be aware of what is legal and what is illegal (for example, you should not download copyrighted material, such as software or music, illegally posted on a Web site). However, if you are using the Internet to locate appropriate sources for a research project, you need to be much more careful. For this reason, you should evaluate the content of any Web site for *accuracy*, *credibility*, *objectivity* or *reasonableness*, *currency*, *coverage* or *scope*, and *stability*.

Accuracy   **Accuracy** refers to the reliability of the material itself and to the use of proper documentation. Factual errors—especially errors in facts that are central to the main point of the source—should cause you to question the reliability of the material you are reading.

- Is the text free of basic grammatical and mechanical errors?
- Does the site contain factual errors?
- Does the site provide a list of references?
- Are links available to other references?
- Can information be verified with print or other resources?

Credibility   **Credibility** refers to the credentials of the person or organization responsible for the site. Web sites operated by well-known institutions (the Smithsonian or the U.S. Department of Health and Human Services, for example) have a high degree of credibility. Those operated by individuals (private Web pages or **blogs**—Web logs—for example) are often less reliable.

- Does the site list an author? Are credentials (for example, professional or academic affiliations) provided for the author or authors?
- Is the author a recognized authority in his or her field?
- Is the site **refereed?** That is, does an editorial board or a group of experts determine what material appears on the Web site?
- Does the organization sponsoring the Web site exist apart from its Web presence?
- Can you determine how long the Web site has existed?

Checklist: Determining the Legitimacy of an Anonymous or Questionable Web Source

When a Web source is anonymous (or has an author whose name is not familiar to you), you have to take special measures to determine its legitimacy.

☐ **Post a query.** If you subscribe to a newsgroup or list-serv, ask others in the group what they know about the source and its author.

☐ **Follow the links.** Follow the hypertext links in a document to other documents. If the links take you to legitimate sources, you know that the author is aware of these sources of information.

☐ **Do a keyword search.** Do a search using the name of the sponsoring organization or the author as keywords. Other documents (or citations in other works) may identify the author.

☐ **Look at the URL.** The last part of a Web site's URL can tell you whether the site is sponsored by a commercial entity (*.com*), a nonprofit organization (*.org*), an educational institution (*.edu*), the military (*.mil*), or a government agency (*.gov*). Knowing this information can tell you whether an organization is trying to sell you something (*.com*) or just providing information (*.edu* or *.org*).

Objectivity or Reasonableness **Objectivity** or **reasonableness** refers to the degree of bias that a Web site exhibits. Some Web sites make no secret of their biases. They openly advocate a particular point of view or action, or they are clearly trying to sell something. Other Web sites may hide their biases. For example, a Web site may present itself as a source of factual information when it is actually advocating a political point of view.

- Does advertising appear in the text?
- Does a business, a political organization, or a special interest group sponsor the site?
- Does the site express a particular viewpoint?
- Does the site contain links to other sites that express a particular viewpoint?

Currency **Currency** refers to how up-to-date the Web site is. The easiest way to assess a site's currency is to determine when it was last updated. Keep in mind, however, that even if the date on the site is current, the information that the site contains may not be.

- Is the most recent update displayed?
- Are all the links to other sites still functioning?
- Is the actual information on the page up-to-date?
- Does the site clearly identify the date it was created?

Coverage or Scope **Coverage** or **scope** refers to the comprehensiveness of the information on a Web site. More is not necessarily better, but some sites may be incomplete. Others may provide information that is no more than common knowledge. Still others may present discussions that may not be suitable for college-level research.

- Does the site provide in-depth coverage?
- Does the site provide information that is not available elsewhere?
- Does the site identify a target audience? Does this target audience suggest the site is appropriate for your research needs?

Stability **Stability** refers to whether or not the site is being maintained. A stable site will be around when you want to access it again. Web sites that are here today and gone tomorrow make it difficult for readers to check your sources or for you to obtain updated information.

- Has the site been active for a long period of time?
- Is the site updated regularly?
- Is the site maintained by a well-known, reliable organization, committed to financing the site?

CHAPTER 31

Integrating Source Material into Your Writing

Weave paraphrases, summaries, and quotations of source material smoothly into your paper, adding your own analysis or explanation to increase coherence and to show the relevance of your sources to the points you are making.

31a Integrating Quotations

Quotations should never be awkwardly dropped into your paper, leaving the exact relationship between the quotation and your point unclear. Instead, use a brief introductory remark to provide a context for the quotation, and quote only those words you need to make your point.

Acceptable: For the Amish, the public school system is a problem because it represents "the threat of absorption into mass society" (Hostetler 193).

Unacceptable: For the Amish, the public school system represents a problem. "A serious problem confronting Amish society from the viewpoint of the Amish themselves is the threat of absorption into mass society through the values promoted in the public school system" (Hostetler 193).

Whenever possible, use an **identifying tag** (a phrase that identifies the source) to introduce the quotation.

Identifying Tag: As John Hostetler points out, the Amish see the public school system as a problem because it represents "the threat of absorption into mass society" (193).

Close-up: Integrating Source Material into Your Writing

To make sure all your sentences do not sound the same, experiment with different methods of integrating source material into your paper.

(continued)

169

Integrating source material into your writing (continued)

- Vary the verbs you use to introduce a source's words or ideas (instead of repeating *says*).

acknowledges	discloses	observes
admits	explains	predicts
affirms	finds	proposes
believes	illustrates	reports
claims	implies	speculates
comments	indicates	suggests
concludes	insists	summarizes
concurs	notes	warns

- Vary the placement of the identifying tag, putting it sometimes in the middle or at the end of the quoted material instead of always at the beginning.

Quotation with Identifying Tag in Middle:
"A serious problem confronting Amish society from the viewpoint of the Amish themselves," <u>observes Hostetler</u>, "is the threat of absorption into mass society through the values promoted in the public school system" (193).

Paraphrase with Identifying Tag at End: The Amish are also concerned about their children's exposure to the public school system's values, <u>notes Hostetler</u> (193).

Close-up: Punctuating Identifying Tags

Whether or not you use a comma with an identifying tag depends on where you place it in the sentence. If the identifying tag immediately precedes a quotation, use a comma.

<u>As Hostetler points out</u>, "The Amish are successful in maintaining group identity" (56).

If the identifying tag does not immediately precede a quotation, do not use a comma.

<u>Hostetler points out</u> that the Amish frequently "use severe sanctions to preserve their values" (56).

NOTE: Never use a comma after *that*.

<u>Hostetler also points out</u> that͵ Amish society is "defined by religion" (76).

Substitutions or Additions within Quotations When you make changes or additions to make a quotation fit into your paper, acknowledge your changes by enclosing them in brackets.

> **Original Quotation:** "Immediately after her wedding, she and her husband followed tradition and went to visit almost everyone who attended the wedding" (Hostetler 122).

> **Quotation Revised to Make Verb Tenses Consistent:** Nowhere is the Amish dedication to tradition more obvious than in the events surrounding marriage. Right after the wedding celebration, the Amish bride and groom "visit almost everyone who [has] attended the wedding" (Hostetler 122).

> **Quotation Revised to Supply an Antecedent for a Pronoun:** "Immediately after her wedding, [Sarah] and her husband followed tradition and went to visit almost everyone who attended the wedding" (Hostetler 122).

> **Quotation Revised to Change a Capital to a Lowercase Letter:** The strength of the Amish community is illustrated by the fact that "[i]mmediately after her wedding, she and her husband followed tradition and went to visit almost everyone who attended the wedding" (Hostetler 122).

Omissions within Quotations When you delete unnecessary or irrelevant words, substitute an <u>ellipsis</u> (three spaced periods) for the deleted words. _{See 21f}

> **Original:** "Not only have the Amish built and staffed their own elementary and vocational schools, but they have gradually organized on local, state, and national levels to cope with the task of educating their children" (Hostetler 206).

> **Quotation Revised to Eliminate Unnecessary Words:** "Not only have the Amish built and staffed their own elementary and vocational schools, but they have gradually organized . . . to cope with the task of educating their children" (Hostetler 206).

NOTE: If the passage you are quoting already contains ellipses, MLA style recommends that you place brackets around any ellipses you add.

Close-up: Omissions within Quotations

Be sure that you do not misrepresent quoted material when you delete words from it. For example, do not say, "the Amish have managed to maintain . . . their culture" when the original quotation is "the Amish have managed to maintain *parts of* their culture."

NOTE: For information on integrating long quotations into your papers, **see 20a.**

31b Integrating Paraphrases and Summaries

Introduce paraphrases and summaries with identifying tags, and end them with appropriate documentation. Doing so allows readers to differentiate your ideas from the ideas of your sources.

Misleading (Ideas of Source Blend with Ideas of Writer): Art can be used to uncover many problems that children have at home, in school, or with their friends. For this reason, many therapists use art therapy extensively. Children's views of themselves in society are often reflected by their art style. For example, a cramped, crowded art style using only a portion of the paper shows their limited role (Alschuler 260).

Correct (Identifying Tag Differentiates Ideas of Source from Ideas of Writer): Art can be used to uncover many problems that children have at home, in school, or with their friends. For this reason, many therapists use art therapy extensively. According to William Alschuler in Art and Self-Image, children's views of themselves in society are often reflected by their art style. For example, a cramped, crowded art style using only a portion of the paper shows their limited role (260).

CHAPTER 32

Avoiding Plagiarism

32a Defining Plagiarism

Plagiarism is presenting another person's ideas or words as if they were your own. Most plagiarism that occurs is **unintentional plagiarism**—for example, inadvertently pasting a quoted passage from a downloaded file directly into a paper and forgetting to include the quotation marks and documentation. However, there is a difference between an honest mistake and **intentional plagiarism**—for example, copying sentences from a journal article or submitting a paper that someone else has written. The penalties for unintentional plagiarism may sometimes be severe, but intentional plagiarism is almost always dealt with harshly: students who intentionally plagiarize can receive a failing grade for the paper (or the course) or even be expelled from school.

The availability on the Web of information that can be downloaded and copied has increased the likelihood of accidental plagiarism. In fact, the freewheeling appropriation and circulation of information that routinely takes place on the Web may give the false impression that this material does not need to be documented. Whether they appear in print or in electronic form, however, the words, ideas, and images of others (including photographs, graphs, charts, and statistics) must be properly documented.

32b Avoiding Unintentional Plagiarism

The most common cause of unintentional plagiarism is sloppy research habits. To avoid this problem, start your research paper early. Do not cut and paste text from a Web site or full-text database directly into your paper. Never use sources that you have not actually read or invent sources that do not exist. If you paraphrase, do so correctly by following the examples in **28f3;** changing a few words here and there is not enough.

> **ESL Tip**
>
> Because writing in a second language can be dif-
> ficult, you may be tempted to closely follow the syntax and
> word choice of your sources. Be aware, however, that this
> constitutes plagiarism.

See
Pt. 7 In addition to taking careful notes and distinguishing
between your ideas and those of your sources, you must
also use proper <u>documentation</u>. In general, you must
document any words, ideas, and images that you borrow
from your sources (whether print or electronic). Of
course, certain items need not be documented: **common
knowledge** (information most readers probably know),
facts available from a variety of reference sources, familiar sayings and well-known quotations, and your own
original research (interviews and surveys, for example).
Information that is another writer's original contribution, however, must be acknowledged. So, although you
do not have to document the fact that John F. Kennedy
graduated from Harvard in 1940 or that he was elected
president in 1960, you do have to document a historian's
evaluation of his presidency.

32c Revising to Eliminate Plagiarism

You can avoid plagiarism by using documentation wher-
ever it is required and by following these guidelines.

(1) Enclose Borrowed Words in Quotation Marks

> **Original:** DNA profiling begins with the established
> theory that no two people, except identical twins, have
> the same genetic makeup. Each cell in the body con-
> tains a complete set of genes. (Tucker, William. "DNA
> in Court." *The American Spectator* Nov. 1994: 26)

> **Plagiarism:** William Tucker points out that
> DNA profiling is based on the premise that
> genetic makeup differs from person to person
> and that <u>each cell in the body contains a
> complete set of genes</u> (26).

Even though the student writer does document the
source of his information, he uses the source's exact
words without placing them in quotation marks.

Correct (Borrowed Words in Quotation Marks):
William Tucker points out that DNA profiling
is based on the premise that genetic makeup
differs from person to person and that
"[e]ach cell in the body contains a complete
set of genes" (26).

Correct (Paraphrase): William Tucker points out
that DNA profiling is based on the accepted
premise that genetic makeup differs from
person to person and that every cell includes
a full set of an individual's genes (26).

(2) Do Not Imitate a Source's Syntax and Phrasing

Original: If there is a garbage crisis, it is that we are
treating garbage as an environmental threat and not
what it is: a manageable—though admittedly complex—civic issue. (Poore, Patricia. "America's
'Garbage Crisis.'" *Harper's* Mar. 1994: 39)

Plagiarism: If a garbage crisis does exist, it
is that people see garbage as a menace to the
environment and not what it actually is: a
controllable—if obviously complicated—public
problem (Poore 39).

Although this student does not use the exact words of her
source, she closely imitates the original's syntax and
phrasing, simply substituting synonyms for the author's
words.

**Correct (Paraphrase in Writer's Own Words; One
Distinctive Phrase Placed in Quotation Marks):**
Patricia Poore argues that America's
"garbage crisis" is exaggerated; rather than
viewing garbage as a serious environmental
hazard, she says, we should look at garbage
as a public problem that may be complicated
but that can be solved (39).

(3) Document Statistics Obtained from a Source

Although many people assume that statistics are common knowledge, statistics are usually the result of original research and must therefore be documented.

Correct (Documentation Provided): According
to one study of 303 accidents recorded,
almost one-half took place before the
drivers were legally allowed to drive at
eighteen (Schuman et al. 1027).

Computer Tip: Plagiarism and
Internet Sources

Any time you download text from the Internet, you risk committing plagiarism. To avoid the possibility of plagiarism, follow these guidelines:

- Download information into individual files so that you can keep track of your sources.
- Do not simply cut and paste blocks of downloaded text into your paper; summarize or paraphrase this material first.
- If you do record the exact words of your source, enclose them in quotation marks.
- Whether your information is from emails, online discussion groups, listservs, or World Wide Web sites, give proper credit by providing appropriate documentation.

---

(4) Differentiate Your Words and Ideas from Those of Your Source

Original: At some colleges and universities traditional survey courses of world and English literature . . . have been scrapped or diluted. . . . What replaces them is sometimes a mere option of electives, sometimes "multicultural" courses introducing material from Third World cultures and thinning out an already thin sampling of Western writings, and sometimes courses geared especially to issues of class, race, and gender. (Howe, Irving. "The Value of the Canon." *The New Republic* 2 Feb. 1991: 40–47).

Plagiarism: At many universities the Western literature survey courses have been edged out by courses that emphasize minority concerns. These courses are "thinning out an already thin sampling of Western writings" in favor of courses geared especially to issues of "class, race, and gender" (Howe 40).

Because the student writer does not differentiate his ideas from those of his source, it appears that only the quotation in the last sentence is borrowed when, in fact, the first sentence also owes a debt to the original. The student should have clearly identified the boundaries of the borrowed material by introducing it with an identifying tag and ending with documentation. (Note that a quotation always requires its own documentation.)

Correct: According to critic Irving Howe, at many universities the Western literature survey courses have been edged out by courses that emphasize minority concerns (41). These courses, says Howe, are "thinning out an already thin sampling of Western writings" in favor of "courses geared especially to issues of class, race, and gender" (40).

Checklist: Avoiding Plagiarism

☐ **Take careful notes.** Be sure you have recorded information from your sources carefully and accurately.

☐ **In your notes, clearly identify borrowed material.** In handwritten notes, put all words borrowed from your sources inside circled quotation marks, and enclose your own comments within brackets. If you are taking notes on a computer, boldface all quotation marks.

☐ **In your paper, differentiate your ideas from those of your sources** by clearly introducing borrowed material with an identifying tag and by following it with documentation.

☐ **Enclose all direct quotations** used in your paper within quotation marks.

☐ **Review all paraphrases and summaries** in your paper to make certain they are in your own words and that any distinctive words and phrases from a source are quoted.

☐ **Document all quoted material and all paraphrases and summaries** of your sources.

☐ **Document all information** that is open to dispute or that is not common knowledge.

☐ **Document all opinions, conclusions, figures, tables, statistics, graphs, and charts** taken from a source.

☐ **Never submit the work of another person as your own.** Do not buy a paper from an online paper mill or use a paper given to you by a friend. In addition, never include in your paper passages that have been written by a friend, relative, or writing tutor.

PART 7

Documenting Sources

33 MLA Documentation Style 183

33a Using MLA Style   184
33b MLA-Style Manuscript
      Guidelines   211
33c Sample MLA-Style Research
      Paper   213

34 APA Documentation Style 232

34a Using APA Style   232
34b APA-Style Manuscript
      Guidelines   244
34c Sample APA-Style Research
      Paper   246

35 Chicago Documentation
      Style   261

35a Using Chicago Style   261
35b Chicago-Style Manuscript
      Guidelines   274
35c Sample Chicago-Style Research
      Paper (Excerpts)   276

36 CSE (Formerly CBE) and
      Other Documentation Styles
      283

36a Using CSE Style   283
36b CSE-Style Manuscript
      Guidelines   289
36c Sample CSE-Style Research
      Paper (Excerpts)   290
36d Using Other Documentation
      Styles   294

DIRECTORY OF MLA PARENTHETICAL REFERENCES

1. A work by a single author (p. 185)
2. A work by two or three authors (p. 185)
3. A work by more than three authors (p. 186)
4. A work in multiple volumes (p. 186)
5. A work without a listed author (p. 186)
6. A work that is one page long (p. 186)
7. An indirect source (p. 186)
8. More than one work (p. 187)
9. A literary work (p. 187)
10. The Bible (p. 188)
11. An entire work (p. 188)
12. Two or more authors with the same last name (p. 188)
13. A government document or a corporate author (p. 188)
14. A legal source (p. 189)
15. An electronic source (p. 189)

DIRECTORY OF MLA WORKS-CITED LIST ENTRIES

 ### Print Sources

Entries for Books

Authors

1. A book by one author (p. 191)
2. A book by two or three authors (p. 191)
3. A book by more than three authors (p. 191)
4. Two or more books by the same author (p. 191)
5. A book by a corporate author (p. 192)

Editions, Multivolume Works, Forewords, Translations, Sacred Works

6. An edited book (p. 192)
7. A subsequent edition of a book (p. 192)
8. A republished book (p. 193)
9. A book in a series (p. 193)
10. A multivolume work (p. 193)
11. The foreword, preface, or afterword of a book (p. 193)
12. A book with a title within its title (p. 194)
13. A translation (p. 194)
14. The Bible (p. 194)

Parts of Books

15. A short story, play, or poem in an anthology (p. 194)
16. A short story, play, poem, or essay in a collection of an author's work (p. 195)
17. An essay in an anthology (p. 195)
18. More than one work from the same anthology (p. 195)
19. An article in a reference book (signed/unsigned) (p. 195)

Dissertations, Pamphlets, Government Publications, Legal Sources

20. A dissertation (published/unpublished) (p. 196)
21. A pamphlet (p. 196)
22. A government publication (p. 196)
23. A legal source (p. 197)

Entries for Articles

Scholarly Journals

24. An article in a scholarly journal with continuous pagination through an annual volume (p. 198)
25. An article in a scholarly journal with separate pagination in each issue (p. 198)

Magazines and Newspapers

26. An article in a weekly magazine (signed/unsigned) (p. 198)
27. An article in a monthly magazine (p. 199)
28. An article that does not appear on consecutive pages (p. 199)
29. An article in a newspaper (signed/unsigned) (p. 199)
30. An editorial in a newspaper (p. 199)
31. A letter to the editor of a newspaper (p. 199)
32. A book review in a newspaper (p. 199)
33. An article with a title within its title (p. 200)

Entries for Miscellaneous Print and Nonprint Sources

Lectures and Interviews

34. A lecture (p. 200)
35. A personal interview (p. 200)
36. A published interview (p. 200)

Letters

37. A personal letter (p. 200)
38. A letter published in a collection (p. 200)

39. A letter in a library's archives (p. 201)

Films, Videotapes, Radio and Television Programs, Recordings

40. A film (p. 201)
41. A videotape, DVD, or laser disc (p. 201)
42. A radio or television program (p. 201)
43. A recording (p. 201)

Paintings, Photographs, Cartoons, Advertisements

44. A painting (p. 202)
45. A photograph (p. 202)
46. A cartoon or comic strip (p. 202)
47. An advertisement (p. 202)

Electronic Sources
Search

Entries from Internet Sites

Internet-Specific Sources

48. An entire Web site (p. 203)
49. A document within a Web site (p. 203)
50. A home page for a course (p. 203)
51. A personal home page (p. 204)
52. A radio program accessed from an Internet archive (p. 204)
53. An email (p. 204)
54. An online posting (newsgroup or online forum) (p. 204)
55. A synchronous communication (MOO or MUD) (p. 204)

Books, Articles, Reviews, Letters, and Reference Works on the Internet

56. A book (p. 205)
57. An article in a scholarly journal (p. 205)
58. An article in a magazine (p. 205)
59. An article in a newspaper (p. 205)
60. An article in a newsletter (p. 205)
61. A review (p. 205)
62. A letter to the editor (p. 206)
63. An article in an encyclopedia (p. 206)
64. A government publication (p. 206)

Paintings, Photographs, Cartoons, and Maps on the Internet

65. A painting (p. 206)
66. A photograph (p. 206)

67. A cartoon (p. 207)
68. A map (p. 207)

Entries from Subscription Services

Journal Articles, Magazine Articles, and News Services from Subscription Services

69. A scholarly journal article with separate pagination in each issue (p. 208)
70. A scholarly journal article with continuous pagination throughout an annual volume (p. 209)
71. A monthly magazine article (p. 209)
72. A news service (p. 209)
73. A newspaper article (p. 209)

Other Electronic Sources

DVDs and CD-ROMs

74. A nonperiodical publication on DVD, CD-ROM, or diskette database (p. 210)
75. A periodical publication on a DVD or CD-ROM database (p. 210)

CHAPTER 33

MLA Documentation Style

Documentation is the formal acknowledgment of the sources you use in your paper. This chapter explains and illustrates the documentation style recommended by the Modern Language Association (MLA). Chapter 34 discusses the documentation style of the American Psychological Association (APA), Chapter 35 gives an overview of the format recommended by *The Chicago Manual of Style*, and Chapter 36 presents the formats recommended by the Council of Science Editors (CSE) and organizations in other disciplines.

33a Using MLA Style

MLA style* is required by many instructors of English and other languages as well as instructors in other humanities disciplines. MLA documentation has three parts: *parenthetical references in the body of the paper (also known as in-text citations), a works-cited list, and content notes.*

(1) Parenthetical References

MLA documentation uses parenthetical references in the body of the paper keyed to a works-cited list at the end of the paper. A typical parenthetical reference consists of the author's last name and a page number.

```
The colony appealed to many idealists in Europe

(Kelley 132).
```

If you state the author's name or the title of the work in your discussion, do not include it in the parenthetical reference.

```
Penn's political motivation is discussed by Joseph

J. Kelley in Pennsylvania, The Colonial Years,

1681-1776 (44).
```

To distinguish two or more sources by the same author, include the title after the author's name. If the title is long, use an abbreviated version. When you shorten a title, begin with the word by which the work is alphabetized in the list of works cited.

```
Penn emphasized his religious motivation (Kelley,

Pennsylvania 116).
```

Close-up: Punctuating with MLA Parenthetical References

Paraphrases and Summaries Parenthetical references are placed *before* the sentence's end punctuation.

```
Penn's writings epitomize seventeenth-century

religious thought (Dengler and Curtis 72).
```

---

*MLA documentation format follows the guidelines set in the *MLA Handbook for Writers of Research Papers*, 6th ed. New York, MLA, 2003.

Quotations Run In with the Text Parenthetical references are placed *after* the quotation but *before* the end punctuation.

```
As Ross says, "Penn followed his conscience in
all matters" (127).
```

```
According to Williams, "Penn's utopian vision
was informed by his Quaker beliefs . . . " (72).
```

Quotations Set Off from the Text When you quote more than four lines of <u>prose</u> or more than three lines of <u>poetry</u>, parenthetical references are placed one space *after* the end punctuation.

See 20a

```
According to Arthur Smith, William Penn
envisioned a state based on his religious
principles:
            Pennsylvania would be a commonwealth
            in which all individuals would follow
            God's truth and develop according to
            God's law. For Penn, this concept of
            government was self-evident. It would
            be a mistake to see Pennsylvania as
            anything but an expression of Penn's
            religious beliefs. (314)
```

SAMPLE MLA PARENTHETICAL REFERENCES

1. A Work by a Single Author

```
Fairy tales reflect the emotions and fears of
children (Bettelheim 23).
```

2. A Work by Two or Three Authors

```
The historian's main job is to search for clues
and solve mysteries (Davidson and Lytle 6).
```

```
With the advent of behaviorism, psychology began a
new phase of inquiry (Cowen, Barbo, and Crum 31-34).
```

3. A Work by More Than Three Authors
List only the first author, followed by et al. ("and others"), or list the last names of all authors in the order in which they appear on the work's title page.

> Helping each family reach its goals for healthy
>
> child development and overall family well-being
>
> was the primary approach of Project EAGLE (Bartle
>
> et al. 35).

> or

> Helping each family reach its goals for healthy
>
> child development and overall family well-being
>
> was the primary approach of Project EAGLE (Bartle,
>
> Couchonnal, Canda, and Staker 35).

4. A Work in Multiple Volumes
If you list more than one volume of a multivolume work in your works-cited list, include the appropriate volume and page number (separated by a colon followed by a space).

> Gurney is incorrect when he says that a twelve-
>
> hour limit is negotiable (6: 128).

5. A Work without a Listed Author
Use the full title (if brief) or a shortened version of the title (if long), beginning with the word by which it is alphabetized in the works-cited list.

> The group issued an apology a short time later
>
> ("Satire Lost" 22).

6. A Work That Is One Page Long
Do not include a page reference for a one-page article.

> Sixty percent of Arab Americans work in white-
>
> collar jobs (El-Badru).

7. An Indirect Source
If you use a statement by one author that is quoted in the work of another author, indicate that the material is from an indirect source with the abbreviation qtd. in ("quoted in").

> According to Valli and Lucas, "the form of the
>
> symbol is an icon or picture of some aspect of

```
the thing or activity being symbolized" (qtd. in

Wilcox 120).
```

8. More Than One Work

Cite each work as you normally would, separating one citation from the other with a semicolon.

```
The Brooklyn Bridge has been used as a subject by

many American artists (McCullough 144; Tashjian

58).
```

NOTE: Long parenthetical references distract readers. Whenever possible, present them as <u>content notes</u>.

See 33a3

9. A Literary Work

When citing a work of **fiction,** it is often helpful to include more than the author's name and the page number in the parenthetical citation. Follow the page number with a semicolon, and then add any additional information that might be helpful.

```
In Moby-Dick, Melville refers to a whaling

expedition funded by Louis XIV of France (151;

ch. 24).
```

Parenthetical references to **poetry** do not include page numbers. In parenthetical references to long poems, cite division and line numbers, separating them with a period.

```
In the Aeneid, Virgil describes the ships as

cleaving the "green woods reflected in the calm

water" (8.124).
```

(In this citation, the reference is to book 8, line 124 of the *Aeneid*.)

When citing short poems, identify the poet and the poem in the text of the paper and use line numbers in the citation.

```
In "A Song in the Front Yard," Brooks's speaker

says, "I've stayed in the front yard all my

life / I want a peek at the back" (lines 1-2).
```

NOTE: When citing lines of a poem, include the word line (or lines) in the first parenthetical reference; use just numbers in subsequent references.

In citing a **play,** include the act, scene, and line numbers (in arabic numerals), separated by periods; titles of well-known literary works (such as Shakespeare's plays) are often abbreviated (<u>Mac</u>. 2.2.14-16).

10. The Bible

MLA style requires that a biblical citation include the version of the Bible (underlined) and the book (abbreviated if longer than four letters, but not underlined or enclosed in quotation marks), followed by the chapter and verse numbers (separated by a period).

> The cynicism of the speaker is apparent when he
>
> says, "All things are wearisome; no man can speak
>
> of them all" (<u>New English Bible</u>, Eccles. 1.8).

NOTE: The first time you use a biblical citation, include the version in your parenthetical reference; after that, only include the book. If you are using more than one version of the Bible, however, include the version in each in-text citation.

11. An Entire Work

When citing an entire work, include the author's name and the work's title in the text of your paper rather than in a parenthetical reference.

> Lois Lowry's <u>Gathering Blue</u> is set in a
>
> technologically backward village.

12. Two or More Authors with the Same Last Name

To distinguish authors with the same last name, include their initials in your parenthetical references.

> Recent increases in crime have caused thousands
>
> of urban homeowners to install alarms (L. Cooper,
>
> 115). Some of these alarms use sophisticated
>
> sensors that were developed by the army (D.
>
> Cooper, 76).

13. A Government Document or a Corporate Author

Cite such works using the organization's name followed by the page number (American Automobile Association 34). You can avoid long parenthetical references by working the organization's name into your paper.

> According to the President's Commission for the
>
> Study of Ethical Problems in Medicine and

Biomedical and Behavioral Research, the issues

relating to euthanasia are complicated (76).

14. A Legal Source

Acts or laws that appear in the text of your paper or in the works-cited list should not be underlined or enclosed in quotation marks. In the parenthetical reference, titles are usually abbreviated, and the act or law is referred to by sections. Include the USC (United States Code) and the year (if relevant) the act or law was passed.

Such research should include investigations into

the cause, diagnosis, early detection,

prevention, control, and treatment of autism (42

USC 284q, 2000).

Names of legal cases are usually abbreviated (Roe v. Wade). They are underlined in the text of your paper but not in the works-cited list.

In <u>Goodridge v. Department of Public Health</u>, the

court ruled that the Commonwealth of

Massachusetts has not adequately provided a

reasonable constitutional cause for barring

homosexual couples from civil marriages (2003).

15. An Electronic Source

If a reference to an electronic source includes paragraph numbers rather than page numbers, use the abbreviation par. or pars. followed by the paragraph number or numbers.

The earliest type of movie censorship came in the

form of licensing fees, and in Deer River,

Minnesota, "a licensing fee of $200 was deemed

not excessive for a town of 1000" (Ernst, par.

20).

If the electronic source has no page or paragraph numbers, try to cite the work in your discussion rather than in a parenthetical reference. By consulting your works-cited list, readers will be able to determine that the source is electronic and may therefore not have page numbers.

```
In her article "Limited Horizons," Lynne Cheney
says that schools do best when students read
literature not for practical information but for
its insights into the human condition.
```

(2) Works-Cited List

The **works-cited list,** which appears at the end of your paper, is an alphabetical listing of all the research materials you cite. Double-space within and between entries on the list, and indent the second and subsequent lines of each entry one-half inch (five spaces). (**See 33b** for full manuscript guidelines.)

SAMPLE MLA WORKS-CITED LIST ENTRIES

 Print Sources

Entries for Books

Book citations include the author's name; book title (underlined); and publication information (place, publisher, date). Capitalize all major words of the title except articles, coordinating conjunctions, prepositions, and the *to* of an infinitive (unless such a word is the first or last word of the title or subtitle). Do not underline the period that follows a book's title.

Close-up: Publishers' Names

MLA requires that you use abbreviated forms of publishers' names in the list of works cited. In general, omit articles; abbreviations, such as *Inc.* and *Corp.*; and words such as *Publishers, Books,* and *Press*. If the publisher's name includes a person's name, use the last name only. Finally, use standard abbreviations whenever you can—*UP* for University Press and *P* for Press, for example.

Name	Abbreviation
Basic Books	Basic
Government Printing Office	GPO
The Modern Language Association of America	MLA
Oxford University Press	Oxford UP
Alfred A. Knopf, Inc.	Knopf
Random House, Inc.	Random
University of Chicago Press	U of Chicago P

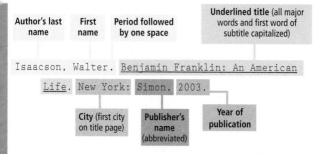

Author's last name | First name | Period followed by one space | Underlined title (all major words and first word of subtitle capitalized)

Isaacson, Walter. <u>Benjamin Franklin: An American
    Life</u>. New York: Simon, 2003.

City (first city on title page) | Publisher's name (abbreviated) | Year of publication

Authors

1. A Book by One Author

Bettelheim, Bruno. <u>The Uses of Enchantment: The
    Meaning and Importance of Fairy Tales</u>. New
    York: Knopf, 1976.

2. A Book by Two or Three Authors

List the first author with last name first. List subsequent authors with first name first in the order in which they appear on the title page.

Peters, Michael A., and Nicholas C. Burbules.
    <u>Poststructuralism and Educational Research</u>.
    Lanham: Rowman, 2004.

3. A Book by More Than Three Authors

Either list the first author only, followed by et al. ("and others"), or include all the authors in the order in which they appear on the title pages.

Moffett, Marian, et al. <u>A World History of
    Architecture</u>. Boston: McGraw, 2004.

or

Moffett, Marian, Michael Fazio, and Lawrence
    Wodehouse. <u>A World History of Architecture</u>.
    Boston: McGraw, 2004.

4. Two or More Books by the Same Author

List books by the same author in alphabetical order by title. After the first entry, use three unspaced hyphens followed by a period in place of the author's name.

Ede, Lisa. <u>Situating Composition: Composition
    Studies and the Politics of Location</u>.
    Carbondale: Southern Illinois UP, 2004.

```
---. Work in Progress. 6th ed. Boston: Bedford,
     2004.
```

NOTE: If the author is the editor or translator of the second entry, place a comma and the appropriate abbreviation after the hyphens (---, ed.). See entry 6 for more on edited books and entry 13 for more on translated books.

5. A Book by a Corporate Author
A book is cited by its corporate author when individual members of the association, commission, or committee that produced it are not identified on the title page.

```
American Automobile Association. Western Canada
     and Alaska. Heathrow: AAA, 2004.
```

Editions, Multivolume Works, Forewords, Translations, Sacred Works

6. An Edited Book
An edited book is a work prepared for publication by a person other than the author. If your focus is on the *author's* work, begin your citation with the author's name. After the title, include the abbreviation Ed. ("Edited by") followed by the editor or editors.

```
Twain, Mark. Adventures of Huckleberry Finn. Ed.
     Michael Patrick Hearn. New York: Norton,
     2001.
```

If your focus is on the *editor's* work, begin your citation with the editor's name followed by the abbreviation ed. ("editor") if there is one editor or eds. ("editors") if there is more than one. After the title, give the author's name preceded by the word By.

```
Hearn, Michael Patrick, ed. Adventures of
     Huckleberry Finn. By Mark Twain. New York:
     Norton, 2001.
```

7. A Subsequent Edition of a Book
When citing an edition other than the first, include the edition number that appears on the work's title page.

```
Wilson, Charles Banks. Search for the Native
     American Purebloods. 3rd ed. Norman: U of
     Oklahoma P, 2000.
```

8. A Republished Book

Include the original publication date after the title of a republished book—for example, a paperback version of a hardcover book.

> Wharton, Edith. <u>The House of Mirth</u>. 1905. New
>
>   York: Scribner's, 1975.

9. A Book in a Series

If the title page indicates that the book is a part of a series, include the series name, neither underlined nor enclosed in quotation marks, and the series number, followed by a period, before the publication information.

> Davis, Bertram H. <u>Thomas Percy</u>. Twayne's English
>
>   Authors Ser. 313. Boston: Twayne, 1981.

10. A Multivolume Work

When all volumes of a multivolume work have the same title, include the number of the volume you are using.

> Fisch, Max H., ed. <u>Writings of Charles S. Peirce:</u>
>
>   <u>A Chronological Edition</u>. Vol. 4. Bloomington:
>
>   Indiana UP, 2000.

When you use two or more volumes, cite the entire work.

> Fisch, Max H., ed. <u>Writings of Charles S. Peirce:</u>
>
>   <u>A Chronological Edition</u>. 6 vols. Bloomington:
>
>   Indiana UP, 2000.

If the volume you are using has an individual title, you may cite the title without mentioning any other volumes.

> Mares, Milan. <u>Fuzzy Cooperative Games:</u>
>
>   <u>Cooperation with Vague Expectations</u>. New
>
>   York: Psysica-Verlag, 2001.

If you wish, however, you may include supplemental information, such as the number of the volume, the title of the entire work, the total number of volumes, or the inclusive publication dates.

11. The Foreword, Preface, or Afterword of a Book

> Campbell, Richard. Preface. <u>Media and Culture: An</u>
>
>   <u>Introduction to Mass Communication</u>. By
>
>   Bettina Fabos. Boston: Bedford, 2005. vi-xi.

12. A Book with a Title within Its Title

If the book you are citing contains a title that is normally underlined to indicate italics (a novel, play, or long poem, for example), do not underline the interior title.

```
Fulton, Joe B. Mark Twain in the Margins: The

        Quarry Farm Marginalia and A Connecticut

        Yankee in King Arthur's Court. Tuscaloosa: U

        of Alabama P, 2000.
```

If the book you are citing contains a title that is normally enclosed in quotation marks, keep the quotation marks.

```
Hawkins, Hunt, and Brian W. Shaffer, eds.

        Approaches to Teaching Conrad's "Heart of

        Darkness" and "The Secret Sharer." New York:

        MLA, 2002.
```

13. A Translation

```
García Márquez, Gabriel. One Hundred Years of

        Solitude. Trans. Gregory Rabassa. New York:

        Avon, 1991.
```

14. The Bible

Underline the title, and give full publication information.

```
The New English Bible with the Apocrypha: Oxford

        Study Edition. New York: Oxford UP, 1976.
```

Parts of Books

15. A Short Story, Play, or Poem in an Anthology

```
Chopin, Kate. "The Storm." Literature: Reading,

        Reacting, Writing. Ed. Laurie G. Kirszner

        and Stephen R. Mandell. 5th ed. Boston:

        Wadsworth, 2004. 176-79.

Shakespeare, William. Othello, The Moor of

        Venice. Shakespeare: Six Plays and the

        Sonnets. Ed. Thomas Marc Parrott and Edward

        Hubler. New York: Scribner's, 1956. 145-91.
```

See entry 18 for information on how to cite more than one work from the same anthology.

16. A Short Story, Play, Poem, or Essay in a Collection of an Author's Work

```
Bukowski, Charles. "lonely hearts." The Flash of

    Lightning behind the Mountain: New Poems.

    New York: Ecco, 2004. 115-16.
```

NOTE: The title of the poem is not capitalized because it appears in lowercase letters in the original.

17. An Essay in an Anthology

Even if you cite only one page of the essay in your paper, supply inclusive page numbers for the entire essay.

```
Crevel, Rene. "From Babylon." Surrealist Painters

    and Poets: An Anthology. Ed. Mary Ann Caws.

    Cambridge: MIT P, 2001. 175-77.
```

18. More Than One Work from the Same Anthology

List each work from the same anthology separately, followed by a cross-reference to the entire anthology. Also list complete publication information for the anthology itself.

```
Agar, Eileen. "Am I a Surrealist?" Caws 3-7.

Caws, Mary Ann, ed. Surrealist Painters and

    Poets: An Anthology. Cambridge: MIT P, 2001.

Crevel, Rene. "From Babylon." Caws 175-77.
```

19. An Article in a Reference Book (Signed/Unsigned)

For a signed article, begin with the author's name. For unfamiliar reference books, include full publication information.

```
Drabble, Margaret. "Expressionism." The Oxford

    Companion to English Literature. 6th ed. New

    York: Oxford UP, 2000.
```

If the article is unsigned, begin with the title. For familiar reference books, do not include publication information.

```
"Cubism." The Encyclopedia Americana. 2004 ed.
```

NOTE: You may omit page numbers if the reference book lists entries alphabetically. If you are listing one definition among several from a dictionary, include the abbreviation Def. ("Definition") along with the letter or number that corresponds to the definition.

    "Justice." Def. 2b. The Concise Oxford

        Dictionary. 10th ed. 1999.

Dissertations, Pamphlets, Government Publications, Legal Sources

20. A Dissertation (Published/Unpublished)

Cite a published dissertation the same way you would cite a book, but add relevant dissertation information before the publication information. For dissertations published by University Microfilms International (UMI), include the order number at the end of the entry.

    Rodriguez, Jason Anthony. Bureaucracy and

        Altruism: Managing the Contradictions

        of Teaching. Diss. U of Texas at

        Arlington, 2003. Arlington: UMI, 2004.

        ATT 1416857.

NOTE: University Microfilms, which publishes most of the dissertations in the United States, also publishes in CD-ROM. For the proper format for citing CD-ROMs, see entries 74 and 75.

Use quotation marks for the title of an unpublished dissertation.

    Bon Tempo, Carl Joseph. "Americans at the Gate:

        The Politics of American Refugee Policy."

        Diss. U of Virginia, 2004.

21. A Pamphlet

Cite a pamphlet as you would a book. If no author is listed, begin with the title (underlined).

    Choosing the Right Digital Camera. Rochester:

        Kodak, 2004.

22. A Government Publication

If the publication has no listed author, begin with the name of the government, followed by the name of the agency; you may use an abbreviation if its meaning is clear: United States. Cong. Senate.

```
United States. Office of Consumer Affairs. 2003

     Consumer's Resource Handbook. Washington:

     GPO, 2003.
```

When citing two or more publications by the same government, use three unspaced hyphens in place of the name for the second and subsequent entries. If you also cite more than one work from the same agency of that government, use an additional set of unspaced hyphens in place of the agency name.

```
United States. FAA. Passenger Airline Safety in

     the Twenty-First Century. Washington: GPO,

     2003.

---. ---. Recycled Air in Passenger Airline

     Cabins. Washington: GPO, 2002.
```

23. A Legal Source

In general, you do not need a works-cited entry for familiar historical documents or acts with USC (United States Code) numbers. Parenthetical references in the text are sufficient—(US Const., art. 3, sec. 2) or (15 USC 111g, 2003), for example. If you do cite an act in the works-cited list, include the name of the act, its Public Law (Pub. L.) number, its enactment date, and its Statutes at Large (Stat.) cataloging number.

```
Children's Health Act. Pub. L. 106-310. 17 Oct.

     2000. Stat. 114.1101.
```

In works-cited entries for legal cases, abbreviate names of cases, but spell out the first important word of each party's name. Include the case number, the name of the deciding court, and the decision date. Do not underline the case name in the works-cited list.

```
Goodridge v. Department of Public Health. No.

     SJC-08860. Supreme Ct. of Mass. 18 Nov.

     2003.
```

Entries for Articles

Article citations include the author's name; the title of the article (in quotation marks); the title of the periodical (underlined); the month (abbreviated except for May, June, and July) and the year; and the pages on which the full article appears, without the abbreviations *p.* or *pp.*

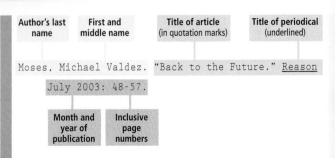

Author's last name | First and middle name | Title of article (in quotation marks) | Title of periodical (underlined)

Moses, Michael Valdez. "Back to the Future." Reason
      July 2003: 48-57.

Month and year of publication | Inclusive page numbers

Scholarly Journals

24. An Article in a Scholarly Journal with Continuous Pagination through an Annual Volume

For an article in a journal with continuous pagination—for example, one in which an issue ends on page 172 and the next issue begins with page 173—include the volume number, followed by the date of publication (in parentheses). Follow the publication date with a colon, a space, and the inclusive page numbers.

    Siderits, Mark. "Perceiving Particulars: A
        Buddhist Defense." Philosophy East and West
        54 (2004): 367-83.

25. An Article in a Scholarly Journal with Separate Pagination in Each Issue

For a journal in which each issue begins with page 1, include the volume number, a period, and the issue number.

    Hayes, B. Grant. "Group Counseling in Schools:
        Effective or Not?" The International Journal
        of Sociology and Social Policy 21.3 (2001):
        12-21.

Magazines and Newspapers

26. An Article in a Weekly Magazine (Signed/Unsigned)

For signed articles, start with the author, last name first. In dates, the day precedes the month.

    Corliss, Richard. "His Days in Hollywood." Time
        14 June 2004: 56-62.

For unsigned articles, start with the title of the article.

"Ronald Reagan." <u>National Review</u> 28 June 2004:

    14-17.

27. An Article in a Monthly Magazine

Thomas, Evan. "John Paul Jones." <u>American History</u>

    Aug. 2003: 22-25.

28. An Article That Does Not Appear on Consecutive Pages

When, for example, an article begins on page 120 and then skips to page 186, include only the first page number, followed by a plus sign.

Di Giovanni, Janine. "The Shiites of Iraq."

    <u>National Geographic</u> June 2004: 2+.

29. An Article in a Newspaper (Signed/Unsigned)

Krantz, Matt. "Stock Success Not Exactly

    Unparalleled." <u>Wall Street Journal</u> 11 June

    2004: B1+.

"A Steadfast Friend on 9/11 Is Buried." <u>New York</u>

    <u>Times</u> 6 June 2002: B8.

NOTE: Omit the article *the* from the title of a newspaper even if the newspaper's actual title includes the article.

30. An Editorial in a Newspaper

Brooks, David. "Living in the Age of Political

    Segregation." Editorial. <u>Dayton Daily News</u> 1

    July 2004, final ed.: A12.

31. A Letter to the Editor of a Newspaper

Chang, Paula. Letter. <u>Philadelphia Inquirer</u> 10

    Dec. 2003, suburban ed.: A17.

32. A Book Review in a Newspaper

Straw, Deborah. "Thinking about Tomorrow." Rev.

    of <u>Planning for the 21st Century: A Guide</u>

    <u>for Community Colleges</u>, by William A.

    Wojciechowski and Dedra Manes. <u>Community</u>

    <u>College Week</u> 7 June 2004: 15.

33. An Article with a Title within Its Title

If the article you are citing contains a title that is normally enclosed within quotation marks, use single quotation marks for the interior title.

```
Zimmerman, Brett. "Frantic Forensic Oratory:
     Poe's 'The Tell-Tale Heart.'" Style 35
     (2001): 34-50.
```

If the article you are citing contains a title that is normally underlined to indicate italics, underline it in your works-cited entry.

```
Lingo, Marci. "Forbidden Fruit: The Banning of
     The Grapes of Wrath in the Kern County Free
     Library." Libraries and Culture 38 (2003):
     351-78.
```

Entries for Miscellaneous Print and Nonprint Sources

Lectures and Interviews

34. A Lecture

```
Grimm, Mary. "An Afternoon with Mary Grimm."
     Visiting Writers Program, Dept. of English.
     Wright State U. 16 Apr. 2004.
```

35. A Personal Interview

```
West, Cornel. Personal interview. 28 Dec. 2002.
Tannen, Deborah. Telephone interview. 8 June
     2003.
```

36. A Published Interview

```
Huston, John. "The Outlook for Raising Money: An
     Investment Banker's Viewpoint." NJBIZ 30
     Sept. 2002: 2-3.
```

Letters

37. A Personal Letter

```
Tan, Amy. Letter to the author. 7 Apr. 2001.
```

38. A Letter Published in a Collection

```
Joyce, James. "Letter to Louis Gillet." 20 Aug.
     1931. James Joyce. By Richard Ellmann. New
     York: Oxford UP, 1965. 631.
```

39. A Letter in a Library's Archives

```
Stieglitz, Alfred. Letter to Paul Rosenberg. 5

    Sept. 1923. Stieglitz Archive. Yale U Arts

    Lib., New Haven.
```

Films, Videotapes, Radio and Television Programs, Recordings

40. A Film

Include the title of the film (underlined), the distributor, and the date, along with other information that may be useful to readers, such as the names of the performers, the director, and the writer.

```
Citizen Kane. Dir. Orson Welles. Perf. Welles,

    Joseph Cotten, Dorothy Comingore, and Agnes

    Moorehead. RKO, 1941.
```

If you are focusing on the contribution of a particular person, begin with that person's name.

```
Welles, Orson, dir. Citizen Kane. Perf. Welles,

    Joseph Cotten, Dorothy Comingore, and Agnes

    Moorehead. RKO, 1941.
```

41. A Videotape, DVD, or Laser Disc

Cite a videotape, DVD, or laser disc as you would cite a film, but include the medium before the name of the distributor.

```
Bowling for Columbine. Dir. Michael Moore. 2002.

    DVD. United Artists and Alliance Atlantis,

    2003.
```

42. A Radio or Television Program

```
"War Feels Like War." P.O.V. Dir. Esteban Uyarra.

    PBS. WPTD, Dayton. 6 July 2004.
```

43. A Recording

List the composer, conductor, or performer (whichever you are focusing on), followed by the title (and, when citing jacket notes, a description of the material), manufacturer, and year of issue.

```
Boubill, Alain, and Claude-Michel Schönberg. Miss

    Saigon. Perf. Lea Salonga, Claire Moore, and

    Jonathan Pryce. Cond. Martin Koch. Geffen,

    1989.
```

```
Marley, Bob. "Crisis." Lyrics. Bob Marley and the
     Wailers. Kava Island Records, 1978.
```

Paintings, Photographs, Cartoons, Advertisements

44. A Painting

```
Hopper, Edward. Railroad Sunset. 1929. Whitney
     Museum of American Art, New York.
```

45. A Photograph
Cite a photograph in a museum's collection in the same way you cite a painting.

```
Stieglitz, Alfred. The Steerage. 1907. Los
     Angeles County Museum of Art.
```

To cite a personal photograph, begin with a descriptive title (neither underlined nor set in quotation marks), followed by the place the photograph was taken, the photographer, and the date.

```
Rittenhouse Square, Philadelphia. Personal
     photograph by author. 6 May 2003.
```

46. A Cartoon or Comic Strip

```
Trudeau, Garry. "Doonesbury." Comic strip.
     Philadelphia Inquirer 15 Sept. 2003, late
     ed.: E13.
```

47. An Advertisement

```
Microsoft. Advertisement. National Review 8 June
     2004: 17.
```

[Search] Electronic Sources

Entries from Internet Sites

The documentation style for Internet sources presented here conforms to the most recent guidelines published in the *MLA Handbook for Writers of Research Papers* (6th ed.) and found online at <http://www.mla.org>.

MLA style recognizes that full source information for Internet sources is not always available. Include in your citation whatever information you can reasonably obtain: the title of the Internet site (underlined); the editor of the site (if available); the version number of the source (if applicable); the date of electronic publication (or update); the number or range of pages, paragraphs, or sections (if available); the name of any institution or sponsor; the date of access to the source; and the URL.

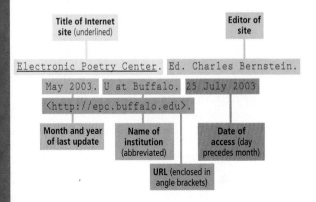

MLA requires that you enclose the electronic address (URL) within angle brackets to distinguish the address from the punctuation in the rest of the citation. If a URL will not fit on a line, the computer will carry the entire URL over to the next line. If you prefer to divide the URL, divide it after a slash. (Do not insert a hyphen.) If it is excessively long, give just the URL of the site's search page. Readers can then access the document by entering the author's name or the source's title.

Internet-Specific Sources

48. An Entire Web Site

Philadelphia Writers Project. Ed. Miriam Kotzen
       Green. May 1998. Drexel U. 12 June 2001
       <http://www.Drexel.edu/letrs/wwp>.

49. A Document within a Web Site

"D Day: June 7th, 1944." The History Channel
       Online. 1999. History Channel. 7 June 2002
       <http://historychannel.com/thisday/today/
       997690.html>.

50. A Home Page for a Course

Mulry, David. Composition and Literature. Course
       home page. Jan. 2003-Apr. 2003. Dept. of
       English, Odessa College. 6 Apr. 2003

```
<http://www.odessa.edu/dept/english/
dmulryEnglish_1302.html>.
```

51. A Personal Home Page

```
Gainor, Charles. Home page. 22 July 2003. 10 Nov.
      2003 <http://www.chass.utoronto.ca:9094/
      ~char>.
```

52. A Radio Program Accessed from an Internet Archive

```
Edwards, Bob. "Country Music's First Family."
      Morning Edition. 16 July 2002. NPR Archives.
      2 Oct. 2002 <http://www.npr.org/programs/
      morning/index.html>.
```

53. An Email

```
Smith, Karen. Email to the author. 28 June 2004.
```

54. An Online Posting (Newsgroup or Online Forum)

```
Gilford, Mary. "Dog Heroes in Children's
      Literature." Online posting. 17 Mar. 1999.
      12 Apr. 1999 <news:alt.animals.dogs>.
Schiller, Stephen. "Paper Cost and Publishing
      Costs." Online posting. 24 Apr. 2002. 11 May
      2002. Book Forum. 17 May 2002 <www.nytimes.com/
      webin/webx?13A^41356.ee765e/0>.
```

55. A Synchronous Communication (MOO or MUD)

MOOs (multiuser domain, object oriented) and MUDs (multiuser domain) are Internet programs that enable users to communicate in real time. To cite a communication posted in a MOO or a MUD, give the name (or names) of the writer(s), a description of the event, the date of the event, the forum (LinguaMOO, for example), the date of access, and the URL (starting with telnet://).

```
Guitar, Gwen. Online discussion of Cathy in Emily
      Brontë's Wuthering Heights. 17 Mar. 2002.
      LinguaMOO. 17 Mar. 2002 <telnet://
      lingua.utdallas.edu:8888>.
```

Books, Articles, Reviews, Letters, and Reference Works on the Internet

56. A Book

> Douglass, Frederick. <u>My Bondage and My Freedom</u>.
>
>   Boston, 1855. 8 June 2000 <gopher://
>
>   gopher.vt.edu:10024/22/178/3>.

57. An Article in a Scholarly Journal

When you cite information from an electronic source that has a print version, include the publication information for the printed source, the number of pages or paragraphs (if available), and the date you accessed it.

> Dekoven, Marianne. "Utopias Limited: Post-Sixties
>
>   and Postmodern American Fiction." <u>Modern</u>
>
>   <u>Fiction Studies</u> 41.1 (1995): 13 pp. 17 Mar.
>
>   1999 <http://muse.jhu.edu/journals/mfs.v041/
>
>   41.1dwkovwn.html>.

58. An Article in a Magazine

> Weiser, Jay. "The Tyranny of Informality." <u>Time</u>
>
>   26 Feb. 1996. 1 Mar. 2002 <http://
>
>   www.enews.com/magazines.tnr/current/
>
>   022696.3.html>.

59. An Article in a Newspaper

> Lohr, Steve. "Microsoft Goes to Court." <u>New York</u>
>
>   <u>Times on the Web</u> 19 Oct. 1998. 29 Apr. 1999
>
>   <http://www.nytimes.com/web/docroot/
>
>   library.ciber/week/1019business.html>.

60. An Article in a Newsletter

> "Unprecedented Cutbacks in History of Science
>
>   Funding." <u>AIP Center for History of Physics</u>
>
>   27.2 (Fall 1995). 26 Feb. 1996 <http://
>
>   www.aip.org/history/fall95.html>.

61. A Review

> Ebert, Roger. Rev. of <u>Star Wars: Episode I—The</u>
>
>   <u>Phantom Menace</u>, dir. George Lucas. <u>Chicago</u>
>
>   <u>Sun-Times Online</u> 8 June 2000. 22 June 2000

<http://www.suntimes.com/output/ebert1/
          08show.html>.

62. A Letter to the Editor

Chen-Cheng, Henry H. Letter. <u>New York Times on
          the Web</u> 19 July 1999. 19 July 1999 <http://
          www.nytimes.com/hr/mo/day/letters/
          ichen-cheng.html>.

63. An Article in an Encyclopedia

Include the article's title, the title of the database (underlined), the version number (if available), the date of electronic publication, the sponsor, and the date of access as
well as the URL.

"Hawthorne, Nathaniel." <u>Encyclopaedia Britannica
          Online</u>. 2002. Encyclopaedia Britannica. 16
          May 2002 <http://www.search.eb.com>.

64. A Government Publication

Cite an online government publication as you would cite
a print version; end with the information required for an
electronic source.

United States. Dept. of Justice. Bureau of
          Justice Statistics. <u>Violence against Women:
          Estimates from the Redesigned National Crime
          Victimization Survey</u>. Jan. 1995. 10 July
          2003 <http://www.ojp.usdoj.gov/bjs/
          020131.pdf>.

Paintings, Photographs, Cartoons, and Maps on the Internet

65. A Painting

Seurat, Georges-Pierre. <u>Evening, Honfleur</u>. 1886.
          Museum of Mod. Art, New York. 8 Jan. 2004
          <http://www.moma.org/collection/depts/
          paint_sculpt/blowups/paint_sculpt_002.html>.

66. A Photograph

Brady, Mathew. <u>Ulysses S. Grant 1822-1885</u>. <u>Mathew
          Brady's National Portrait Gallery</u>. 2 Oct.
          2002 <http://www.npg.si.edu/exh/brady/
          gallery/56gal.html>.

67. A Cartoon

Stossel, Sage. "Star Wars: The Next Generation."

Cartoon. <u>Atlantic Unbound</u> 2 Oct. 2002. 14

Nov. 2002 <http://www.theatlantic.com/

unbound/sage/ss990519.htm>.

68. A Map

"Philadelphia, Pennsylvania." Map. <u>U.S.

Gazetteer</u>. US Census Bureau. 17 July 2000

<http://www.census.gov/cgi-bin/gazetteer>.

Entries from Subscription Services

Subscription services can be divided into those to which you subscribe (**personal subscription services**), such as America Online, and those to which your library subscribes (**library subscription services**), such as Gale Group Databases, LexisNexis, and ProQuest Direct.

To cite information from a **personal subscription service,** include the name of the database (underlined) as well as the name of the subscription service. If the personal subscription service provides a URL for a specific document, follow the examples in entries 48–55. Personal subscription services usually supply information without a URL, however. If the subscription service enables you to use a **keyword** to access material, type Keyword followed by a colon and the keyword (after the date of access).

"Kafka, Franz." <u>Compton's Encyclopedia Online</u>.

Vers. 3.1. 2000. America Online. 8 June

2003. Keyword: Compton's.

If instead of using a keyword you follow a series of **topic labels,** type the word Path followed by a colon and then the sequence of topics (separated by semicolons) you followed to get to the material.

"Elizabeth Adams." <u>History Resources</u>. 11 Nov.

2002. America Online. 28 Apr. 2002. Path:

Research; Biography; Women in Science;

Biographies.

To cite information from a **library subscription service,** supply the publication information (including page numbers, if available) followed by the name of the database (underlined), the name of the subscription service, the library at which you accessed the database, the date of access, and the URL of the service's home page.

> Luckenbill, Trent. "Environmental Litigation:
>
>   Down the Endless Corridor." <u>Environment</u> 8
>
>   June 2001: 34-42. <u>ABI/INFORM Global</u>.
>
>   ProQuest Direct. Drexel U Lib.,
>
>   Philadelphia, PA. 12 Oct. 2001
>
>   <http://www.umi.com/proquest>.

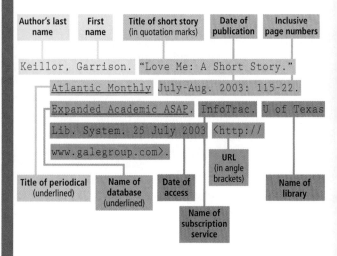

Journal Articles, Magazine Articles, and News Services from Subscription Services

69. A Scholarly Journal Article with Separate Pagination in Each Issue

> Schaefer, Richard J. "Editing Strategies in
>
>   Television News Documentaries." <u>Journal of</u>
>
>   <u>Communication</u> 47.4 (1997): 69-89. <u>InfoTrac</u>
>
>   <u>OneFile Plus</u>. Gale Group Databases. Augusta
>
>   R. Kolwyck Lib., Chattanooga, TN. 2 Oct.
>
>   2002 <http://www.galegroup.com>.

NOTE: Along with the name of the library, you may include the city and state if you think they would be helpful.

70. A Scholarly Journal Article with Continuous Pagination throughout an Annual Volume

Hudson, Nicholas. "Samuel Johnson, Urban Culture,

and the Geography of Postfire London."

Studies in English Literature 42 (2002):

557-80. MasterFILE Premier. EBSCOhost.

Augusta R. Kolwyck Lib., Chattanooga, TN. 15

Sept. 2003 <http://www.epnet.com>.

71. A Monthly Magazine Article

Livermore, Beth. "Meteorites on Ice." Astronomy

July 1993: 54-58. Expanded Academic ASAP

Plus. Gale Group Databases. Augusta R.

Kolwyck Lib., Chattanooga, TN. 12 Nov. 2003

<http://www.galegroup.com>.

Wright, Karen. "The Clot Thickens." Discover Dec.

1999. MasterFILE Premier. EBSCOhost. Augusta

R. Kolwyck Lib., Chattanooga, TN. 10 Oct.

2003 <http://www.epnet.com>.

72. A News Service

Ryan, Desmond. "Some Background on the Battle of

Gettysburg." Knight Ridder/Tribune News

Service 7 Oct. 1993. InfoTrac OneFile Plus.

Gale Group Databases. Augusta R. Kolwyck

Lib., Chattanooga, TN. 16 Nov. 2003

<http://www.galegroup.com>.

73. A Newspaper Article

Meyer, Greg. "Answering Questions about the West

Nile Virus." Dayton Daily News 11 July 2002:

Z3-7. Academic Universe News. LexisNexis.

Augusta R. Kolwyck Lib., Chattanooga, TN. 17

Feb. 2003 <http://web.lexis-nexis.com>.

Other Electronic Sources

DVDs and CD-ROMs

74. A Nonperiodical Publication on DVD, CD-ROM, or Diskette Database
Cite a nonperiodical publication on DVD, CD-ROM, or diskette the same way you would cite a book, but also include a description of the medium of publication.

"Windhover." The Oxford English Dictionary. 2nd

ed. DVD. Oxford: Oxford UP, 2001.

"Whitman, Walt." DiskLit: American Authors. CD-

ROM. Boston: Hall, 2000.

75. A Periodical Publication on a DVD or CD-ROM Database

Zurbach, Kate. "The Linguistic Roots of Three

Terms." Linguistic Quarterly 37 (1994): 12-

47. InfoTrac: Magazine Index Plus. CD-ROM.

Information Access. Jan. 2001.

(3) Content Notes

Content notes—multiple bibliographical citations or other material that does not fit smoothly into the text—are indicated by a **superscript** (raised numeral) in the paper. Notes can appear either as footnotes at the bottom of the page or as endnotes on a separate sheet entitled Notes, placed after the last page of the paper and before the works-cited list. Content notes are double-spaced within and between entries. The first line is indented one-half inch (five spaces), and subsequent lines are typed flush left.

For Multiple Citations
In the Paper

Many researchers emphasize the necessity of having

dying patients share their experiences.[1]

In the Note

[1]Kübler-Ross 27; Stinnette 43; Poston 70; Cohen

and Cohen 31-34; Burke 1:91-95.

For Other Material

In the Paper

The massacre during World War I is an event the
survivors could not easily forget.[2]

In the Note

[2]For a firsthand account of these events, see
Bedoukian 178-81.

33b MLA-Style Manuscript Guidelines

Although MLA papers do not usually include abstracts,
internal headings, tables, or graphs, this situation is
changing. Be sure you know what your instructor expects.

The following guidelines are based on the latest version of the *MLA Handbook for Writers of Research Papers*.

Checklist: Typing Your Paper

When typing your paper, use the student paper
in **33c** as your model.

☐ Type your paper with a one-inch margin at the top
and bottom and on both sides. Double-space your
paper throughout.

☐ Type your name, your instructor's name, the course
title, and the date on separate lines flush with the
upper-left margin. Double-space, center, and type the
title. Double-space again, and begin typing the text of
the paper.

☐ Capitalize all important words in your title, but not
prepositions, articles, coordinating conjunctions, or
the *to* in infinitives (unless they begin or end the title
or subtitle). Do not underline your title or enclose it
in quotation marks. Never put a period after the title,
even if it is a sentence.

☐ Set off more than four lines of prose or more than
three lines of poetry by indenting the whole quotation one inch (or ten spaces). If you quote a single
paragraph or part of a paragraph, do not indent the
first line beyond one inch. If you quote two or more
paragraphs, however, indent the first line of each
paragraph an additional quarter inch. (If the first sentence does not begin a paragraph, do not indent it.
Indent the first line only in successive paragraphs.)

(continued)

Typing your paper (continued)

See
33a

☐ Number all pages of your paper consecutively—including the first—in the upper right-hand corner, one-half inch from the top, flush right. Type your name followed by a space before the page number on every page.

☐ If you use source material in your paper, follow <u>MLA documentation style</u>.

Checklist: Using Visuals

See
38d

☐ Insert <u>visuals</u> into the text as close as possible to where they are discussed.

☐ Label each table with the word Table followed by an arabic numeral (for instance, Table 1). Double-space, and type a descriptive caption, with the first line flush with the left-hand margin; indent subsequent lines one-quarter inch. Capitalize the caption as if it were a title. (Both the table number and the descriptive caption should appear above the table.) Below the table, type the word Source, followed by a colon and all source information. Type the first line of the source information flush with the left-hand margin; indent subsequent lines one-quarter inch.

☐ Label other types of visual material—graphs, charts, photographs, clip art, drawings, and so on—Fig. (Figure) followed by an arabic numeral (for example, Fig. 2). Type each label and a title or caption on the same line, followed by source information, directly below the visual. Type all lines flush with the left-hand margin.

☐ Do not include the source of the visual in the works-cited list unless you use other material from that source elsewhere in the paper.

Checklist: Preparing the MLA Works-Cited List

See
33a3

☐ Begin the works-cited list on a new page after the last page of text or <u>content notes</u>, numbered as the next page of the paper.

☐ Center the title Works Cited one inch from the top of the page. Double-space between the title and the first entry.

- ☐ Each entry on the works-cited list has three divisions: author, title, and publication information. Separate divisions with a period and one space.
- ☐ List entries alphabetically, with last name first. Use the author's full name as it appears on the title page. If a source has no listed author, alphabetize it by the first word of the title (not counting the article).
- ☐ Type the first line of each entry flush with the left-hand margin; indent subsequent lines one-half inch (or five spaces).
- ☐ Double-space within and between entries.
- ☐ Enclose URLs in angle brackets. If a URL carries over to the next line, break the URL after a slash; do not insert a hyphen. If your word-processing program automatically converts URLs to hotlinks, turn off this feature. (You can do this with *Microsoft Word* by opening the AutoCorrect function under the Tools menu, and then selecting AutoFormat.)

33c Sample MLA-Style Research Paper

The following student paper, "The Great Digital Divide," uses MLA documentation style. It includes MLA-style in-text citations, a notes page, a works-cited list, and a bar graph.

Student's
last name
and page
number on
every page
(including
the first)

1″

↑ ½″
Romney 1

Kimberly Romney

Professor Wilson

English 102

20 April 2004

The Great Digital Divide   ← Center title

Indent ½″⟶
(or five spaces)

Today, a basic understanding of   ← Double-space

computers and how to use them is necessary
1″

1″   for success. For this reason, those who are

unfamiliar with modern digital technology

find themselves at a great disadvantage

when it comes to education and employment.

One of the most exciting digital

technologies available is the information

superhighway, better known as the

Internet. The Internet, with its

accompanying software and services, is

rapidly changing the way we access and see

information. Clearly, the Internet offers

great promise, but some argue that it is

Thesis
statement

creating many problems as well. Although

the Internet has changed our lives for the

better, it threatens to leave many people

behind, creating two distinct classes—

those who have access and those who do not.

In the late 1990s, many argued that

the Internet had ushered in a new age, one

in which instant communication would bring

people closer together and eventually

Quotations
from Inter-
net source,
introduced
by author's
name, are

eliminate national boundaries. In

"Building a Global Community," former Vice

President Al Gore took this optimistic

↑
1″
↓

Romney 2

view, seeing the Internet as a means "to   not followed
deepen and extend our oldest and most   by a para-
                                             graph or
cherished global values: rising standards   page number
of living and literacy, an ever-widening   because this
                                             information
circle of freedom, and individual   was not pro-
                                             vided in the
empowerment." Gore went on to say that he   electronic
could envision the day when we would   text
"extend our knowledge and our prosperity
to our most isolated inner cities, to the
barrios, the favelas, the colonias, and
our most remote rural villages."

    Others, however, argued that for many
people, the benefits of the Internet were
not nearly this obvious or far-reaching.
They maintained that the Internet was
creating what many have called a "digital   Parenthetical
                                             documenta-
divide" (<u>Digital Divide Network</u>), which tion refers to
excludes a large percentage of the poor,   material ac-
                                             cessed from
elderly, disabled, and members of many   a Web site
minority groups from current technological
advancements.

    A survey conducted by the US
Department of Commerce in 2002 showed that
white people and those with higher annual
incomes were more likely to own computers
than minorities and people from low-income
households. In households where the
average income was $75,000 and over, 89%
had access to a computer. In households
earning $10,000-$14,999, only 25% had
access to a computer. Moreover, although

Romney 3

61% of the white households had access to a
computer, only 37.1% of African-American
and 40% of Hispanic households had home
computers.

¶ synthe-
sizes infor-
mation
from a
Commerce
Depart-
ment
study and
a news-
paper
article

Super-
script
number
identifies
content
note

    While the Department of Commerce
study suggested that financial
circumstances were largely responsible for
the "digital divide," the gap in computer
ownership across incomes indicated that
other factors might also be contributing
to the disparity. For example, in a 1999
New York Times op-ed article, Henry Louis
Gates Jr. argued that bridging the digital
divide would "require more than cheap
PC's"; it would "involve content" (500).[1]
African Americans were not interested in
the Internet, Gates wrote, because the
content rarely appealed to them. Gates
compared the lack of interest in the
Internet with the history of African
Americans' relationship to the recording
industry. According to Gates, blacks began
to buy records "only when mainstream
companies . . . introduced so-called race
records, blues and jazz discs aimed at a
nascent African American market" (501).
Gates believed that Web sites that address
the needs of African Americans could play
the same role that race records did for the
music industry. Ignoring the race problem,
Gates warned, would lead to a form of

Romney 4

cyber-segregation that would devastate the
African-American community (501).

It was clear to many that people
without Internet access had difficulty at
school, trouble obtaining jobs, and fewer
opportunities to save money and time as
consumers. They also lacked access to
educational materials and to jobs posted on
the Internet. With access to only a portion
of available goods and services, people who
were offline did not have the advantages
that people who were online could routinely
get. The Internet was clearly widening the
economic and social divide that already
separated people in this country.

Student's original conclusions; no documentation necessary

In response, the government,
corporations, nonprofit organizations, and
public libraries made efforts to bridge
the gap between the "haves" and "have-
nots." For example, the Education
Department's Community Technology Centers
Program (CTC) helped finance computer
activity centers for students and adults.
Also, the Department of Commerce's
Technology Opportunities Program (TOP)
provided money and services to
organizations that needed more technology
to operate efficiently. One recipient was
America's Second Harvest, which used the
funds to track donations to its national
network of food banks (Schwartz, "Report").

Parenthetical documentation includes abbreviated title when two or more works by the same author are cited

Romney 5

Nonprofit organizations also worked to bridge the digital divide. The Bill and Melinda Gates Foundation, for example, has provided libraries across the country with funding that allows them to purchase computers and connect to the Internet (Egan). Nonprofit organizations also sponsor Web sites, such as <u>The Digital Divide Network</u>, a site that posts stories about the digital divide from a variety of perspectives. By posting information, the site's sponsor hopes to raise awareness of the problems that the digital divide causes.

Recently, however, some people have begun to question the need for many of these initiatives. In fact, as illustrated in fig. 1, computer use by young people between the ages of three and twenty-four rose dramatically between 1998 and 2001.

Several recent studies seem to support this view. For example, a 2004 study by the Pew Research Center found that nearly 66% of whites and Hispanics and 61% of African Americans use the Internet (Nelson). Another study conducted by the University of Texas at Dallas also found that the digital divide seems to be closing. According to Professor Donald Hicks, research shows that "broadband

Romney 6

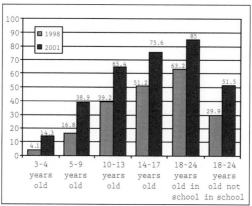

Fig. 1. United States, Dept. of Commerce, Economics and Statistics Admin., Natl. Telecommunications and Information Admin., <u>A Nation Online: How Americans Are Expanding Their Use of the Internet</u> (Washington: GPO, 2002) 43, 20 Jan. 2005 <http://www.ntia.doc.gov/ntiahome/dn/nation_online.pdf>.

Internet is more readily available in minority neighborhoods than in areas that are home to more whites" (Nelson). Even earlier, a 2002 report by the US Department of Commerce, using the most recent census data then available, concluded that Internet access in homes had increased significantly between 1999 and 2001, even among minorities.

Arguing that significant strides have been made to bridge the digital divide, the Bush administration believes that programs

(Margin note:) Graph summarizes relevant data. Source information is typed directly below the figure

Romney 7

like CTC and TOP are no longer needed ("Digital Divide Debated"). At the same time, as the result of the dot.com bust, private industry has withdrawn some support for efforts to bridge the digital divide. One organization, called PowerUp, worked with corporations to create community-based technology centers. In places like Austin, Texas, PowerUp worked to establish a computer center in the city's impoverished neighborhood by collaborating with AOL Time Warner and the Austin Urban League (Doggett). Despite its initial success, the organization was hard hit by an economic downturn. According to a PowerUp spokesperson, "The model that was launched in late 1999 . . . was a model that had its bloodlines in different economic times. The model isn't necessarily the best one for these economic times" (Schwartz, "Lack"). In 2002, PowerUp closed its offices, leaving the community centers they created to find funding on their own.

In other cases, the groups targeted by digital divide programs argue that such programs might do more harm than good. A recent article in the <u>Chronicle of Higher Education</u> observes that many African-American and other minority groups argue that digital divide rhetoric might

---

Ellipsis indicates that the student has deleted words from the quotation

actually stereotype minorities. The
article says that digital divide rhetoric
"could discourage businesses or academics
from creating content or services tailored
for minority communities—ultimately making
the digital divide a self-fulfilling
prophecy" (Young). Many scholars and
leaders in the African-American community
fear that a focus on the digital divide
will lead to its being seen as a fact to be
accepted rather than as a problem to be
solved. Tara L. McPherson agrees, arguing
that "the idea of challenging the digital
divide is not about denying its existence.
But it is to ensure that the focus on the
digital divide doesn't naturalize a kind
of exclusion of investment" (qtd. in
Young).

Qtd. in indicates that McPherson's comments were quoted in Young's article

However, despite the appearance that
the digital divide is closing and the claims
that digital divide rhetoric may actually
be harmful, many public officials and
private interest groups continue to voice
their concerns that gaps in technological
literacy and availability remain a problem
among many populations and communities. In
fact, a 2002 report published by the Benton
Foundation disagrees with the US
Department of Commerce's findings. This
report contends that federal funding is
key in continuing to bring more people into

Romney 9

the digital age. While the Department of
Commerce report maintains that most people
have access to computers in their homes,
the Benton Foundation's report uses the
same statistics to argue that many people
continue to have difficulty accessing the
Internet. The Benton report found that 75%
of people with household incomes less than
$15,000 and 66% with incomes between
$15,000 and $35,000 are not yet using the
Internet. Wealthier Americans, however,
have significantly greater access to the
Internet. Of the Americans with incomes of
$50,000-$75,000 a year, 67.3% use the
Internet. Thus, the Benton Foundation
strongly disagrees with the Bush
administration's recommendation to
cut programs like the Department of
Commerce's Technology Opportunities
Program and the Community Technology
Centers Program:

Quotation of
more than
four lines is
typed as
a block,
indented 1"
(or ten
spaces), and
double-
spaced, with
no quotation
marks

> TOP and CTC are important
> engines of digital opportunity.
> They are emblematic of the
> importance of federal leadership
> in the effort to bridge the
> digital divide. Federal
> leadership brings the power of
> information to underserved
> communities. A federal retreat
> from that leadership role would

Romney 10

undermine innovative efforts to
bring digital opportunity to
underserved communities and
jeopardize many successful
community programs. Rather than
walking away from the
investment, the federal
government should build upon
the success of these programs
to bring digital opportunity to
the entire nation. (Benton
Foundation)

The success of programs offered by
the public library system also challenges
the wisdom of the federal government's
desire to cut funding for programs that
increase computer literacy. According to a
recent article published in the <u>Knight
Ridder/Tribune Business News</u>, the New York
public library system's computer literacy
courses drew over eighteen thousand
people in 2003. The demand for these
classes is so high that many classes fill
up, leaving people frustrated and
disappointed (Dalton). The clear
conclusion is that although the gap
between the haves and have-nots may be
closing, continued success depends on
continued financial support of successful
programs.[2]

Parenthetical documentation is placed one space after end punctuation

Superscript number identifies content note

Romney 11

It is not only minorities and the impoverished who are affected by the digital divide. Many people know that children in inner-city schools lack access to computer technology and to the Internet, but few know that children attending schools in rural areas are also at risk. Vicky Wellborn, a high school English teacher in a small town, reports that her school only recently instituted a computer literacy program. As they ordered computers, the instructors realized that one of their biggest challenges would be training themselves. Although the computer literacy program has been helpful to many students, the difficulties of teaching an unfamiliar subject continue to challenge teachers at the school (Wellborn).

Conclusion recommends solutions for problem of "digital divide"

Although many strides have been made in closing the gap between those who have access to the Internet and technology and those who do not, problems and new challenges remain. Steps must be taken to solve these problems. First, we must continue efforts to make the Internet available to the widest possible audience. We must also ensure that the rhetoric surrounding the term digital divide is used to close this gap, not to create a new one by establishing or reinforcing stereotypes about minorities. A broader

Romney 12

definition of what the digital divide is might help us to see that it has the potential to marginalize many groups of people—the poor, the elderly, the disabled, and rural schoolchildren, for example—not just members of minority groups. On a practical level, the federal government should continue to fund programs that increase access to computer technology in general, and to the Internet in particular. Unless we take steps to make these resources available to all, we will quickly become two separate and unequal societies: one "plugged-in" and privileged and one "unplugged" and marginalized.

Because concluding ¶ introduces no new material (it summarizes material already discussed and presents student's original conclusions), no documentation is necessary

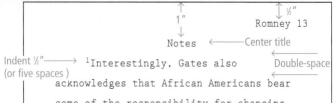

Notes ←——Center title

Indent ½"——→ ¹Interestingly, Gates also
(or five spaces)
acknowledges that African Americans bear
some of the responsibility for changing
the situation.

² Other evidence suggests that the
digital divide is a problem not only of
Internet access, but also of access to
technology in general. For example, in
areas where punch-card voting machines
were used, voters were seven times more
likely to have their ballots discarded
than in areas that used other types of
ballots. When minority voters had access
to better technology, however, their votes
were more likely to register (Kennard).

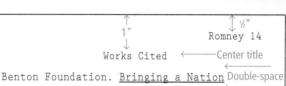

Romney 14

Works Cited ←—— Center title

Benton Foundation. <u>Bringing a Nation</u>
Online: The Importance of Federal
Leadership. By Norris Dickard,
et al. July 2002. 7 Feb. 2005
⟨http://www.benton.org/publibrary/
nationonline⟩.

Dalton, Richard J. Jr. "New York Libraries
Try to Close Minorities' Digital
Divide." <u>Knight Ridder/Tribune
Business News</u> 4 July 2004. <u>Expanded
Academic ASAP</u>. Gale Group Databases.
U of Texas Lib. System. 20 Jan. 2005
⟨http://www.galegroup.com⟩.

"Digital Divide Debated." <u>CBS News.com</u> 30
May 2002. 2 Jan. 2005 ⟨http://
www.cbsnews.com/stories/2002/
05/30/tech/main510589.shtml⟩.

<u>The Digital Divide Network</u>. 2 Feb. 2005
⟨http://www.digitaldividenetwork.org/
content/sections/index.cfm⟩.

Doggett, Shelley. "'E-Team' Provides Local
Youth with Lessons in Technology."
<u>The Daily Texan Online</u> 14 Feb. 2001.
3 Jan. 2005 ⟨http://
www.dailytexanonline.com⟩.

Egan, Timothy. "Bill Gates Views What He's
Sown in Libraries." <u>New York Times</u> 6
Nov. 2002: A18.

Indent ½"
(or five
spaces)

Report by a
corporate
author

Article
from an
online
news
service

Entry for
an entire
Web site

Article
from a
news-
paper

Romney 15

Essay in an anthology

Gates, Henry Louis Jr. "One Internet, Two
      Nations." <u>The Blair Reader</u>. 4th ed.
      Ed. Laurie G. Kirszner and Stephen R.
      Mandell. Upper Saddle River: Prentice,
      2002. 499-501.

Speech accessed from an Internet site

Gore, Al. "Building a Global Community."
      <u>Remarks Prepared for the 15th
      International ITU Conference</u>. 12 Oct.
      1998. 12 Jan. 2005 <http://
      clinton3.nara.gov/WH/EOP/OVP/speeches/
      itu.html>.

Newspaper article accessed from a library subscription database

Kennard, William E. "Democracy's Digital
      Divide." <u>Christian Science Monitor</u> 7
      Mar. 2002. <u>Academic Universe: News</u>.
      LexisNexis. U of Texas Lib. System. 17
      Jan. 2005 <http://web.lexis-nexis.com>.

Nelson, Colleen McCain. "Ethnic Gap on
      Internet Narrowing, Study Says."
      <u>Knight Ridder/Tribune Business News</u> 10
      June 2004. <u>Expanded Academic ASAP</u>.
      Gale Group Databases. U of Texas Lib.
      System. 20 Jan. 2005 <http://
      www.galegroup.com>.

Schwartz, John. "A Lack of Money Forces
      Computer Initiative to Close." <u>New
      York Times</u> 30 Oct. 2002. <u>Expanded
      Academic ASAP</u>. Gale Group Databases. U
      of Texas Lib. System. 20 Jan. 2005
      <http://www.galegroup.com>.

Romney 16

---. "Report Disputes Bush Approach to
    Bridging 'Digital Divide.'" <u>New York
    Times</u> 11 July 2002. <u>Expanded Academic
    ASAP</u>. Gale Group Databases. U of Texas
    Lib. System. 19 Jan. 2005 <http://
    www.galegroup.com>.

United States. Dept. of Commerce. Economics
    and Statistics Admin., Natl.
    Telecommunications and Information
    Admin. <u>A Nation Online: How Americans
    Are Expanding Their Use of the
    Internet</u>. Washington: GPO, 2002. 20
    Jan. 2005 <http://www.ntia.doc.gov/
    ntiahome/dn/Nation_Online.pdf>.

Wellborn, Vicky. "Re: Computer Literacy."
    Email to the author. 23 Sept. 2004.

Young, Jeffrey. R. "Does 'Digital Divide'
    Rhetoric Do More Harm Than Good?"
    <u>Chronicle of Higher Education</u> 9 Nov.
    2001. 10 Jan. 2005 <http://
    chronicle.com>.

Three
unspaced
hyphens
used in-
stead of
repeating
author's
name

Govern-
ment
docu-
ment
accessed
from the
Internet

DIRECTORY OF APA IN-TEXT CITATIONS

1. A work by a single author (p. 233)
2. A work by two authors (p. 233)
3. A work by three to five authors (p. 233)
4. A work by six or more authors (p. 233)
5. Works by authors with the same last name (p. 234)
6. A work by a corporate author (p. 234)
7. A work with no listed author (p. 234)
8. A personal communication (p. 234)
9. An indirect source (p. 234)
10. A specific part of a source (p. 234)
11. An electronic source (p. 235)
12. Two or more works within the same parenthetical reference (p. 235)
13. A table (p. 235)

DIRECTORY OF APA REFERENCE LIST ENTRIES

 ### Print Sources

Entries for Books

Authors

1. A book with one author (p. 236)
2. A book with more than one author (p. 237)
3. A book with no listed author or editor (p. 237)
4. A book with a corporate author (p. 237)

Editions, Multivolume Works, Forewords

5. An edited book (p. 237)
6. A work in several volumes (p. 237)
7. The foreword, preface, or afterword of a book (p. 237)

Parts of Books

8. A selection from an anthology (p. 237)
9. An article in a reference book (p. 238)

Government Reports

10. A government report (p. 238)

Entries for Articles

Scholarly Journals

11. An article in a scholarly journal with continuous pagination through an annual volume (p. 239)

12. An article in a scholarly journal with separate pagination in each issue (p. 239)

Magazines and Newspapers

13. A magazine article (p. 239)
14. A newspaper article (p. 239)
15. A letter to the editor of a newspaper (p. 239)

Entries for Miscellaneous Print Sources

Letters

16. A personal letter (p. 240)
17. A published letter (p. 240)

Entries for Other Sources

Television Broadcasts, Films, CDs, Audiocassette Recordings, Computer Software

18. A television broadcast (p. 240)
19. A television series (p. 240)
20. A film (p. 240)
21. A CD recording (p. 240)
22. An audiocassette recording (p. 240)
23. Computer software (p. 241)

earch **Electronic Sources**

Entries from Internet Sites

Internet-Specific Sources

24. An Internet article based on a print source (p. 241)
25. An article in an Internet-only journal (p. 242)
26. A document from a university Web site (p. 242)
27. A Web document (no author identified, no date) (p. 242)
28. An email (p. 242)
29. A message posted to a newsgroup (p. 242)
30. A searchable database (p. 243)

Abstracts, Newspaper Articles

31. An abstract (p. 243)
32. An article in a daily newspaper (p. 243)

CHAPTER 34

APA Documentation Style

34a Using APA Style

APA style[*] is used extensively in the social sciences. APA documentation has three parts: *parenthetical references in the body of the paper*, a *reference list*, and optional *content footnotes*.

(1) Parenthetical References

APA documentation uses short parenthetical references in the body of the paper keyed to an alphabetical list of references that follows the paper. A typical parenthetical reference consists of the author's last name (followed by a comma) and the year of publication.

Many people exhibit symptoms of depression after the death of a pet (Russo, 2000).

If the author's name appears in the introductory phrase, include the year of publication there as well.

According to Russo (2000), many people exhibit symptoms of depression after the death of a pet.

Note that you may include the author's name and the date either in the introductory phrase or in parentheses at the end of the borrowed material.

When quoting directly, include the page number in parentheses after the quotation.

According to Weston (1996), children from one-parent homes read at "a significantly lower level than those from two-parent homes" (p. 58).

NOTE: A long quotation (forty words or more) is not set in quotation marks. It is set as a block, and the entire quotation is double-spaced and indented one-half inch (or five to seven spaces) from the left margin. Parenthetical documentation is placed one space after the final punctuation.

---

[*]APA documentation format follows the guidelines set in the *Publication Manual of the American Psychological Association*, 5th ed. Washington, DC: APA, 2001.

SAMPLE APA IN-TEXT CITATIONS

1. A Work by a Single Author

```
Many college students suffer from sleep
deprivation (Anton, 1999).
```

2. A Work by Two Authors

```
There is growing concern over the use of
psychological testing in elementary schools
(Albright & Glennon, 1982).
```

3. A Work by Three to Five Authors

If a work has more than two but fewer than six authors, mention all names in the first reference; in subsequent references in the same paragraph, cite only the first author followed by `et al.` ("and others"). When the reference appears in later paragraphs, include the year.

First Reference

```
(Sparks, Wilson, & Hewitt, 2001)
```

Subsequent References in the Same Paragraph

```
(Sparks et al.)
```

Reference in Later Paragraphs

```
(Sparks et al., 2001)
```

4. A Work by Six or More Authors

When a work has six or more authors, cite the name of the first author followed by `et al.` and the year in all references.

```
(Miller et al., 1995)
```

> ### Close-up: Citing Works by Multiple Authors
>
> When referring to multiple authors in your discussion, join the last two names with `and`.
>
> ```
> According to Rosen, Wolfe, and Ziff
> (1988). . . .
> ```
>
> In-text citations, however, require an **ampersand.**
>
> ```
> (Rosen, Wolfe, & Ziff, 1988)
> ```

5. Works by Authors with the Same Last Name
If your reference list includes works by two or more authors with the same last name, use each author's initials in all in-text citations.

    F. Bor (2001) and S. D. Bor (2000) concluded
    that no further study is needed.

6. A Work by a Corporate Author
If the name of a corporate author is long, abbreviate it after the first citation.

First Reference

    (National Institute of Mental Health [NIMH],
    2001)

Subsequent Reference

    (NIMH, 2001)

7. A Work with No Listed Author
If a work has no listed author, cite just the first two or three words of the title and the year. Use quotation marks around titles of periodical articles and chapters of books; use italics for titles of books, periodicals, brochures, reports, and the like.

    ("New Immigration," 2000)

8. A Personal Communication
Cite letters, memos, telephone conversations, personal interviews, emails, messages from electronic bulletin boards, and so on only in the text—*not* in the reference list.

    (R. Takaki, personal communication, October 17,
    2001)

9. An Indirect Source

    Cogan and Howe offer very different
    interpretations of the problem (cited in
    Swenson, 2000).

10. A Specific Part of a Source
Use abbreviations for the words *page* (p.), *pages* (pp.), *chapter* (chap.), and *section* (sec.).

    These theories have an interesting history (Lee,
    1966, chap. 2).

11. An Electronic Source

For an electronic source that does not show page numbers, use the paragraph number preceded by a ¶ symbol or the abbreviation para.

```
Conversation at the dinner table is an example of
a family ritual (Kulp, 2001, ¶ 3).
```

In the case of an electronic source that has neither page nor paragraph numbers, cite the heading in the source and the number of the paragraph following the heading in which the material is located.

```
Healthy eating is a never-ending series of free
choices (Shapiro, 2001, Introduction section,
para. 2).
```

If the source has no headings, you may not be able to specify an exact location.

12. Two or More Works within the Same Parenthetical Reference

List works by different authors in alphabetical order, separated by semicolons.

```
This theory is supported by several studies
(Barson & Roth, 1995; Rose, 2001; Tedesco, 2002).
```

List two or more works by the same author or authors in order of date of publication, with the earliest date first.

```
This theory is supported by several studies
(Rhodes & Dollek, 2000, 2002, 2003).
```

For two or more works by the same author published in the same year, designate the work whose title comes first alphabetically *a*, the one whose title comes next *b*, and so on; repeat the year in each citation.

```
This theory is supported by several studies
(Shapiro, 2003a, 2003b).
```

13. A Table

If you use a table from a source, give credit to the author in a note at the bottom of the table. Do not include this information in the reference list.

```
Note. From "Predictors of Employment and Earnings
Among JOBS Participants," by P. A. Neenan and D. K.
Orthner, 1996, Social Work Research, 20(4), p. 233.
```

(2) Reference List

The **reference list** gives the publication information for all the sources you cite. It should appear at the end of your paper on a new numbered page titled `References`. Entries on the reference list should be arranged alphabetically. Double-space within and between reference list entries, and indent the second and subsequent lines of each entry one-half inch (five spaces). (**See 34b** for full manuscript guidelines.)

SAMPLE APA REFERENCE LIST ENTRIES

 Print Sources

Entries for Books

Book citations include the author's name; the year of publication (in parentheses); the book title (italicized); and publication information. Capitalize only the first word of the title and subtitle and any proper nouns. Include any additional necessary information—edition, report number, or volume number, for example—in parentheses after the title.

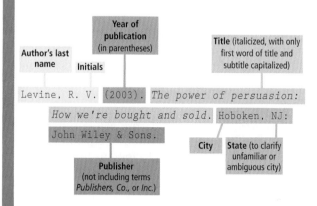

1. A Book with One Author

Use a short form of the publisher's name. Write out the names of associations, corporations, and university presses. Include the words `Book` and `Press`, but do not include terms such as `Publishers`, `Co.`, or `Inc.`

> Maslow, A. H. (1974). *Toward a psychology of being.* Princeton: Van Nostrand.

2. A Book with More Than One Author

List up to six authors—by last name and initials. For more than six authors, add et al. after the sixth name.

```
Wolfinger, D., Knable, P., Richards, H. L., &
    Silberger, R. (1990). The chronically
    unemployed. New York: Berman Press.
```

3. A Book with No Listed Author or Editor

```
Writing with a computer. (2000). Philadelphia:
    Drexel Press.
```

4. A Book with a Corporate Author

When the author and the publisher are the same, include the word Author at the end of the citation instead of repeating the publisher's name.

```
League of Women Voters of the United States.
    (2001). Local league handbook. Washington,
    DC: Author.
```

Editions, Multivolume Works, Forewords

5. An Edited Book

```
Lewin, K., Lippitt, R., & White, R. K. (Eds.).
    (1985). Social learning and imitation. New
    York: Basic Books.
```

6. A Work in Several Volumes

```
Jones, P. R., & Williams, T. C. (Eds.).
    (1990-1993). Handbook of therapy (Vols.
    1-2). Princeton: Princeton University Press.
```

7. The Foreword, Preface, or Afterword of a Book

```
Taylor, T. (1979). Preface. In B. B. Ferencz,
    Less than slaves (pp. ii-ix). Cambridge:
    Harvard University Press.
```

Parts of Books

8. A Selection from an Anthology

Give inclusive page numbers preceded by pp. (in parentheses) after the title of the anthology. The title of the selection is not enclosed in quotation marks.

Lorde, A. (1984). Age, race, and class. In P. S.
        Rothenberg (Ed.), *Racism and sexism: An*
        integrated study (pp. 352-360). New York:
        St. Martin's Press.

NOTE: If you cite two or more selections from the same anthology, give the full citation for the anthology in each entry.

9. An Article in a Reference Book

Edwards, P. (Ed.). (1987). Determinism. In *The*
        encyclopedia of philosophy (Vol. 2, pp.
        359-373). New York: Macmillan.

Government Reports

10. A Government Report

National Institute of Mental Health. (1987).
        Motion pictures and violence: A summary
        report of research (DHHS Publication No. ADM
        91-22187). Washington, DC: U.S. Government
        Printing Office.

Entries for Articles

Article citations include the author's name; the date of publication (in parentheses); the title of the article; the title of the periodical (italicized); the volume number (italicized); the issue number, if any (in parentheses); and the inclusive page numbers (including all digits). Capitalize only the first word of the article's title and subtitle. Do not underline or italicize the title of the article or enclose it in quotation marks. Give the periodical title in full, and capitalize all words except articles, prepositions, and conjunctions of fewer than four letters. Use p. or pp. when referring to page numbers in newspapers, but omit this abbreviation when referring to page numbers in journals and popular magazines.

Author's last name | Year of publication (in parentheses) | Title of article (only first word capitalized)

Wax, M. (1995). Knowledge, power, and ethics in
qualitative social research. *The American
Sociologist, 26*, 122-135.

Italicized volume number | Inclusive page numbers (include all digits) | Italicized title of periodical (capitalize all major words)

Scholarly Journals

11. An Article in a Scholarly Journal with Continuous Pagination through an Annual Volume

Miller, W. (1969). Violent crimes in city gangs.
Journal of Social Issues, 27, 581-593.

12. An Article in a Scholarly Journal with Separate Pagination in Each Issue

Williams, S., & Cohen, L. R. (1984). Child stress
in early learning situations. *American
Psychologist, 21*(10), 1-28.

Magazines and Newspapers

13. A Magazine Article

McCurdy, H. G. (1983, June). Brain mechanisms and
intelligence. *Psychology Today, 46*, 61-63.

14. A Newspaper Article

If an article appears on nonconsecutive pages, give all page numbers, separated by commas (for example, A1, A14). If the article appears on consecutive pages, indicate the full range of pages (for example, A7-A9).

James, W. R. (1993, November 16). The uninsured
and health care. *Wall Street Journal*, pp.
A1, A14.

15. A Letter to the Editor of a Newspaper

Williams, P. (2000, July 19). Self-fulfilling
stereotypes [Letter to the editor]. *Los
Angeles Times*, p. A22.

Entries for Miscellaneous Print Sources

Letters

16. A Personal Letter
References to unpublished personal letters, like references to all other personal communications, should be included only in the text of the paper, not in the reference list.

17. A Published Letter
Joyce, J. (1931). Letter to Louis Gillet. In
   Richard Ellmann, *James Joyce* (p. 631). New
   York: Oxford University Press.

Entries for Other Sources

Television Broadcasts, Films, CDs, Audiocassette Recordings, Computer Software

18. A Television Broadcast
Murphy J. (Executive Producer). (2002, March 4).
   The CBS evening news [Television broadcast].
   New York: Columbia Broadcasting Service.

19. A Television Series
Sorkin, A., Schlamme, T., & Wells, J. (Executive
   Producers). (2002). *The west wing*
   [Television series]. Los Angeles: Warner
   Bros. Television.

20. A Film
Spielberg, S. (Director). (1994). *Schindler's
   list* [Motion picture]. United States:
   Universal.

21. A CD Recording
Marley, B. (1977). Waiting in vain. On *Exodus*
   [CD]. New York: Island Records.

22. An Audiocassette Recording
Skinner, B. F. (Speaker). (1972). *Skinner on
   Skinnerism* [Cassette recording]. Hollywood,
   CA: Center for Cassette Studies.

23. Computer Software

```
Sharp, S. (1995). Career Selection Tests (Version
    5.0) [Computer software]. Chico, CA:
    Avocation Software.
```

Electronic Sources

APA guidelines for documenting electronic sources focus on Web sources, which often do not include all the bibliographic information that print sources do. For example, Web sources may not include page numbers or a place of publication. At a minimum, a Web citation should have a title, a date (the date of publication, update, or retrieval), and an electronic address (URL). If possible, also include the author(s) of a source. When you need to break the URL at the end of a line, break it after a slash or before a period (do not add a hyphen). Do not add a period at the end of the URL. (Current guidelines for electronic sources can be found on the APA Web site at <www.apa.org>.)

Entries from Internet Sites

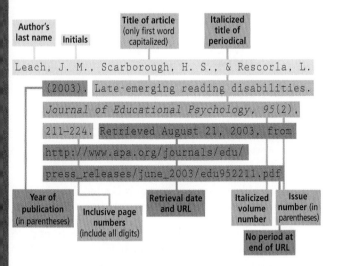

Author's last name **Initials** **Title of article** (only first word capitalized) **Italicized title of periodical**

Leach, J. M., Scarborough, H. S., & Rescorla, L. (2003). Late-emerging reading disabilities. *Journal of Educational Psychology, 95*(2), 211–224. Retrieved August 21, 2003, from http://www.apa.org/journals/edu/ press_releases/june_2003/edu952211.pdf

Year of publication (in parentheses) **Inclusive page numbers** (include all digits) **Retrieval date and URL** **Italicized volume number** **Issue number** (in parentheses)

No period at end of URL

Internet-Specific Sources

24. An Internet Article Based on a Print Source

If you have seen the article only in electronic format, include the phrase Electronic version in brackets after the title.

```
Winston, E. L. (2000). The role of art therapy in
     treating chronically depressed patients
     [Electronic version]. Journal of
     Bibliographic Research, 5, 54-72.
```

NOTE: If you have reason to believe the article you retrieved is different from the print version, add the date
you retrieved it and the URL.

25. An Article in an Internet-Only Journal

```
Hornaday, J., & Bunker, C. (2001). The nature of
     the entrepreneur. Personal Psychology, 23,
     Article 2353b. Retrieved November 21, 2001,
     from http://journals.apa.org/volume23/
     pre002353b.html
```

26. A Document from a University Web Site

```
Beck, E. (1997, July). The good, the bad & the
     ugly: Or, why it's a good idea to evaluate
     web sources. Retrieved January 7, 2002, from
     New Mexico State University Library Web
     site: http://lib.nmsu.edu/instruction/
     evalcrit.html
```

27. A Web Document (No Author Identified, No Date)

```
The stratocaster appreciation page. (n.d.).
     Retrieved July 27, 2002, from
     http://members.tripod.com/~AFH/
```

NOTE: The abbreviation n.d. stands for "no date."

28. An Email

As with all other personal communication, references to
personal email should be included only in the text of
your paper, not in the reference list.

29. A Message Posted to a Newsgroup

List the author's full name—or, if that is not available,
the screen name. In brackets after the title, provide information that will help readers access the message.

```
Shapiro, R. (2001, April 4). Chat rooms and
     interpersonal communication [Msg 7]. Message
     posted to news://sci.psychology
     .communication
```

30. A Searchable Database

```
Nowroozi, C. (1992). What you lose when you miss
     sleep. Nation's Business, 80(9), 73-77.
     Retrieved April 22, 2001, from Expanded
     Academic ASAP database.
```

Abstracts, Newspaper Articles

31. An Abstract

```
Guinot, A., & Peterson, B. R. (1995).
          Forgetfulness and partial cognition (Drexel
     University Cognitive Research Report No.
     21). Abstract retrieved December 4, 2001,
     from http://www.Drexel.edu/~guinot/
     deltarule-abstract.html
```

32. An Article in a Daily Newspaper

```
Farrell, P. D. (1997, March 23). New high-tech
     stresses hit traders and investors on the
     information superhighway. Wall Street
     Journal. Retrieved April 4, 1999, from
     http://wall-street.news.com/forecasts/
     stress/stress.html
```

(3) Content Footnotes

APA format permits content notes, indicated by super-scripts (raised numerals) in the text. The notes are listed on a separate numbered page, titled Footnotes, following the appendixes (or after the reference list if there are no appendixes). Double-space all notes, indenting the first line of each note one-half inch (or five to seven spaces) and beginning subsequent lines flush left. Number the notes with superscripts that correspond to the numbers in your text.

34b APA-Style Manuscript Guidelines

Social science papers have internal headings (internal sections may include an untitled introduction and the headings Method, Results, and Discussion). Each section of a social science paper is a complete unit with a beginning and an end so it can be read separately and still make sense out of context. The body of the paper may include charts, graphs, maps, photographs, flowcharts, or tables.

The following guidelines are based on the latest version of the *Publication Manual of the American Psychological Association*.

Checklist: Typing Your Paper

When typing your paper, use the student paper in **34c** as your model.

- ☐ Leave one-inch margins at the top and bottom and on both sides. Double-space your paper throughout.
- ☐ Indent the first line of every paragraph and the first line of every content footnote one-half inch (or five to seven spaces) from the left-hand margin.
- ☐ Set off a **long quotation** (more than forty words) in a block format by indenting the entire quotation five to seven spaces (or one-half inch) from the left-hand margin.
- ☐ Number all pages consecutively. Each page should include a **page header** (an abbreviated title) and a page number typed one-half inch from the top and one inch from the right-hand edge of the page. Leave five spaces (or one-half inch) between the page header and the page number.

See 38b

- ☐ Center and type major headings with uppercase and lowercase letters. Place minor headings flush left, typed with uppercase and lowercase letters and italicized.

See 38c

- ☐ Format items in a series as a numbered list.
- ☐ Arrange the pages of the paper in the following order:
  - Title page (page 1) with a page header, **running head,** title, and **byline** (your name)
  - Abstract (page 2)
  - Text of paper (beginning on page 3)
  - Reference list (new page)
  - Appendixes (start each on a new page)
  - Content footnotes (new page)

☐ If you use source material in your paper, citations should be consistent with **APA documentation style**.

See 34a

Checklist: Using Visuals

APA distinguishes between two types of visuals: **tables** and **figures** (charts, graphs, photographs, and diagrams). In manuscripts not intended for publication, tables and figures are included in the text. A short table or figure should appear on the page where it is discussed; a long table or figure should be placed on a separate page just after the page where it is discussed.

☐ Number all **tables** consecutively. Each table should have a *label* and a *title*.
- The **label** consists of the word Table (not in italics), along with an arabic numeral, typed flush left above the table.
- Double-space and type a brief explanatory **title** for each table (in italics) flush left below the label. Capitalize the first letters of principal words of the title.

Table 7

Frequency of Negative Responses of Dorm Students to Questions Concerning Alcohol Consumption

☐ Number all **figures** consecutively. Each figure should have a *label* and a *caption*.
- The **label** consists of the word *Figure* (typed flush left below the figure) followed by the figure number (both in italics).
- The **caption** explains the figure and serves as a title. Double-space the caption, but do not italicize it. Capitalize only the first word, and end the caption with a period. The caption follows the label (on the same line).

Figure 1. Duration of responses measured in seconds.

NOTE: If you use a table or figure from an outside source, include full source information in a note at the bottom of the table or figure. This information does not appear in your reference list.

Checklist: Preparing the APA Reference List

☐ Begin the reference list on a new page after the last page of text, numbered as the next page of the paper.

☐ Center the title `References` at the top of the page.

☐ List the items on the reference list alphabetically (with author's last name first).

☐ Type the first line of each entry at the left-hand margin. Indent subsequent lines one-half inch (or five to seven spaces).

☐ Separate the major divisions of each entry with a period and one space.

☐ Double-space the reference list within and between entries.

Checklist: Arranging Entries in the APA Reference List

☐ Single-author entries precede multiple-author entries that begin with the same name.

```
Field, S. (1987)
Field, S., & Levitt, M. P. (1984)
```

☐ Entries by the same author or authors are arranged according to date of publication, starting with the earliest date.

```
Ruthenberg, H., & Rubin, R. (1985)
Ruthenberg, H., & Rubin, R. (1987)
```

☐ Entries with the same author or authors and date of publication are arranged alphabetically according to title. Lowercase letters (*a*, *b*, *c*, and so on) that indicate the order of publication are placed within parentheses.

```
Wolk, E. M. (1996a). Analysis . . .
Wolk, E. M. (1996b). Hormonal . . .
```

34c Sample APA-Style Research Paper

The following student paper, "Sleep Deprivation in College Students," uses APA documentation style. It includes a title page, an abstract, a reference list, a table, and a bar graph.

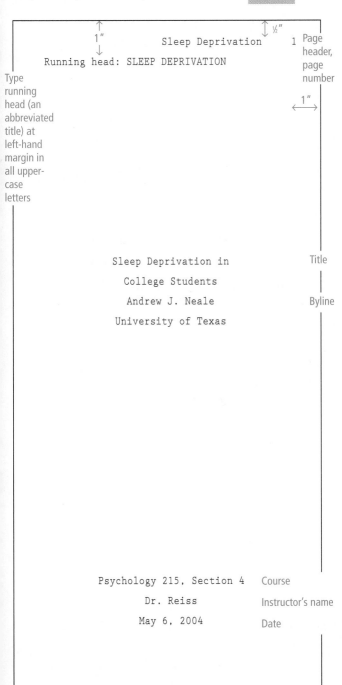

Sleep Deprivation   1   Page header, page number

Running head: SLEEP DEPRIVATION

Type running head (an abbreviated title) at left-hand margin in all upper-case letters

Sleep Deprivation in   Title
College Students
Andrew J. Neale   Byline
University of Texas

Psychology 215, Section 4   Course
Dr. Reiss   Instructor's name
May 6, 2004   Date

Center
heading

Abstract

A survey of 50 first-year college students
in an introductory biology class was
conducted. The survey consisted of 5
questions regarding the causes and results
of sleep deprivation and specifically
addressed the students' study methods and
the grades they received on the fall
midterm. The study's hypothesis was that
although students believe that forgoing
sleep to study will yield better grades,
sleep deprivation actually causes a
decrease in performance. In support of
this hypothesis, 43% of the students who
received either an A or a B on the fall
midterm deprived themselves of sleep in
order to cram for the test, whereas 90% of
those who received a C or a D were sleep
deprived.

Abstract
typed as a
single
paragraph
in block
format

Page
header
and
number
on every
page

Full title (centered)

1″

Sleep Deprivation   3

Sleep Deprivation in College Students

Indent ½″ (or five spaces) → For many college students, sleep is

Double-space

a luxury that they feel they cannot afford.

Bombarded with tests and assignments and

limited by a 24-hour day, students often

Introduction

attempt to make up time by doing without

sleep. Ironically, students may actually

impair their academic performance by

failing to get adequate sleep. According

Thesis statement

to several psychological and medical

studies, sleep deprivation can lead to

memory loss and health problems, both of

which are more likely to harm a student's

1″

academic performance than to help it.

1″

Sleep is often overlooked as an

essential component of a healthy

lifestyle. Millions of Americans wake up

daily to alarm clocks because their bodies

Literature review (¶s 2–7)

have not gotten enough sleep. This

indicates that for many people, sleep is

viewed as a luxury rather than a necessity.

As National Sleep Foundation Executive

Director Richard L. Gelula observes, "Some

of the problems we face as a society—

Quotation requires its own documentation and a page number. A ¶ number is included for Internet sources

from road rage to obesity—may be linked

to lack of sleep or poor sleep" (National

Sleep Foundation, 2002, ¶ 3). In fact,

according to the National Sleep

Foundation, "excessive sleepiness is

associated with reduced short-term memory

and learning ability, negative mood,

1″

Sleep Deprivation   4

inconsistent performance, poor
productivity and loss of some forms of
behavioral control" (2000, ¶ 2).

Focus
shifts to
student
sleep depri-
vation

Sleep deprivation is particularly
common among college students, many of
whom have busy lifestyles and are required
to memorize a great deal of material before
their exams. It is common for college
students to take a quick nap between
classes or fall asleep while studying in
the library because they are sleep
deprived. Approximately 44% of young
adults experience daytime sleepiness at
least a few days a month (National Sleep
Foundation, 2002). Many students face
daytime sleepiness on the day of an exam
because they stayed up all night studying.
These students believe that if they read
and review immediately before taking a
test—even though this usually means losing
sleep—they will remember more information
and thus get better grades. However, this
is not the case.

Student
uses past
tense
when dis-
cussing
other re-
searchers'
studies

A study conducted by professors Mary
Carskadon at Brown University in
Providence, Rhode Island, and Amy Wolfson
at the College of the Holy Cross in
Worcester, Massachusetts, showed that high
school students who got adequate sleep
were more likely to do well in their
classes (Carpenter, 2001). According to

their study of the correlation between
grades and sleep, students who went to bed
earlier on both weeknights and weekends
earned mainly A's and B's. The students who
received D's and F's averaged about 35
minutes less sleep per day than the high
achievers (cited in Carpenter).
Apparently, then, sleep is essential to
high academic achievement.

Cited in indicates an indirect source

Once students reach college and have
the freedom to set their own schedules,
however, many believe that sleep is a
luxury they can do without. For example,
students believe that if they use the time
they would normally sleep to study, they
will do better on exams. A recent survey of
144 undergraduate students in introductory
psychology classes contradicted this
assumption. According to this study, long
sleepers, or those individuals who slept 9
or more hours out of a 24-hour day, had
significantly higher grade point averages
(GPAs) than short sleepers, or individuals
who slept less than 7 hours out of a 24-
hour day. Therefore, contrary to the
belief of many college students, more
sleep is often required to achieve a high
GPA (Kelly, Kelly, & Clanton, 2001).

Many students believe that sleep
deprivation is not the cause of their poor
performance, but rather that a host of

other factors might be to blame. A study in the *Journal of American College Health* tested the effect that several factors have on a student's performance in school, as measured by students' GPAs. Some of the factors considered included exercise, sleep, nutritional habits, social support, time management techniques, stress management techniques, and spiritual health (Trockel, Barnes, & Egget, 2000). The most significant correlation discovered in the study was between GPA and the sleep habits of students. Sleep deprivation had a more negative impact on GPAs than any other factor did (Trockel et al.).

> First reference includes all three authors; *et al.* replaces second and third authors in subsequent reference in same paragraph

Despite these findings, many students continue to believe that they will be able to remember more material if they do not sleep at all before an exam. They fear that sleeping will interfere with their ability to retain information. Pilcher & Walters (1997), however, showed that sleep deprivation actually impaired learning skills. In this study, one group of students was sleep-deprived, while the other got 8 hours of sleep before the exam. Each group estimated how well they had performed on the exam. The students who were sleep-deprived believed their performance on the test was better than did those who were not sleep-deprived, but

Sleep Deprivation   7

actually the performance of the sleep-
deprived students was significantly worse
than that of those who got 8 hours of sleep
prior to the test (Pilcher & Walters, 1997,
cited in Bubolz, Brown, & Soper, 2001).
This study confirms that sleep deprivation
harms cognitive performance and reveals
that many students believe that the less
sleep they get, the better they will do.

A survey of students in an
introductory biology class at the
University of Texas demonstrated the
effects of sleep deprivation on academic
performance and supported the hypothesis
that despite students' beliefs, forgoing
sleep does not lead to better test scores.

Student
uses past
tense
when dis-
cussing
his own
research
study

Method

To determine the causes and results
of sleep deprivation, a study of the
relationship between sleep and test
performance was conducted. A survey of 50
first-year college students in an
introductory biology class was completed,
and their performance on the fall midterm
was analyzed.

Each student was asked to complete a
survey consisting of the following five
questions about their sleep patterns and
their performance on the fall midterm.

   1. Did you deprive yourself of sleep
      when studying for the fall midterm?

2. Do you regularly deprive yourself
   of sleep when studying for an exam?

3. What was your grade on the exam?

4. Do you feel your performance was
   helped or harmed by the amount of
   sleep you had?

5. Will you deprive yourself of sleep
   when you study for the final exam?

List is in-
dented ½″
(or five to
seven spaces)
and treated
as long block
quotation

To maintain confidentiality, the
students were not asked to put their names
on the survey. Also, to determine whether
the students answered question 3
truthfully, the group grade distribution
from the surveys was compared to the number
of A's, B's, C's, and D's shown in the
instructor's record of the test results.
The two frequency distributions were
identical.

Results

Analysis of the survey data indicated
a significant difference between the
grades of students who were sleep deprived
and the grades of those who were not. The

Table 1
introduced

results of the survey are presented in
Table 1.

The grades in the class were curved
so that out of 50 students, 10 received
A's, 20 received B's, 10 received C's, and
10 received D's. For the purposes of this
survey, an A or B on the exam indicates
that the student performed well. A grade of

Table 1

Results of Survey of Students in University of Texas Introduction to Biology Class Examining the Relationship between Sleep Deprivation and Academic Performance

Table placed on page where it is discussed

Grade Totals	Sleep-Deprived	Not Sleep-Deprived	Usually Sleep-Deprived	Improved	Harmed	Continue Sleep Deprivation?
A = 10	4	6	1	4	0	4
B = 20	9	11	8	8	1	8
C = 10	10	0	6	5	4	7
D = 10	8	2	2	1	3	2
Total	31	19	17	18	8	21

C or D on the exam is considered a poor grade.

Of the 50 students in the class, 31 (or 62%) said they deprived themselves of sleep when studying for the fall midterm. Of these students, 17 (or 34% of the class) answered yes to the second question, reporting they regularly deprive themselves of sleep before an exam.

Statistical findings in table reported

Of the 31 students who said they deprived themselves of sleep when studying for the fall midterm, only 4 earned A's, and the majority of the A's in the class were received by those students who were not sleep-deprived. Even more significant was the fact that of the 4 students who were sleep-deprived and got A's, only one

Sleep Deprivation   10

student claimed usually to be sleep-deprived on the day of an exam. Thus, assuming the students who earn A's in a class do well in general, it is possible that sleep deprivation did not help or harm these students' grades. Not surprisingly, of the 4 students who received A's and were sleep-deprived, all said they would continue to use sleep deprivation to enable them to study for longer hours.

The majority of those who used sleep deprivation in an effort to obtain a higher grade received B's and C's on the exam. A total of 20 students earned a grade of B on the exam. Of those students, only 9, or 18% of the class, said they were deprived of sleep when they took the test.

Students who said they were sleep-deprived when they took the exam received the majority of the poor grades. Ten students got C's on the midterm, and of these 10 students, 100% said they were sleep-deprived when they took their test. Of the 10 students (20% of the class) who got D's, 8 said they were sleep deprived.

Figure 1 introduced

Figure 1 shows the significant relation that was found between poor grades on the exam and sleep deprivation.

Discussion

For many students, sleep is viewed as a luxury rather than as a necessity.

Sleep Deprivation   11

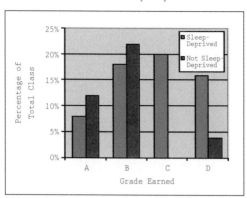

Figure placed on page where it is discussed

Figure 1. Results of survey of students in   Label
University of Texas introduction to biology   Caption
class examining the relationship between   (No
sleep deprivation and academic performance.   source
    informa-
    tion
    needed
Particularly during the exam period,   for stu-
students use the hours in which they would   dent's
    original
normally sleep to study. However, this   graph)
method does not seem to be effective. The
survey discussed here reveals a clear
correlation between sleep deprivation and
lower exam scores. In fact, the majority of
students who performed well on the exam,
earning either an A or a B, were not
deprived of sleep. Therefore, students who
choose studying over sleep should rethink
their approach and consider that sleep
deprivation may actually lead to impaired
academic performance.

1" Sleep Deprivation   12

References ←——————— Center

Bubolz, W., Brown, F., & Soper, B. (2001).

Indent ½" ——→ Sleep habits and patterns of college
(or five
spaces)   students: A preliminary study. *Journal*

of American College Health, 50, ←——
Double-space

131–135.   ←——

Carpenter, S. (2001). Sleep deprivation may

Entries   be undermining teen health. *Monitor on*
listed in
alphabetical   *Psychology, 32*(9). Retrieved March 9,
order
2004, from http://www.apa.org/monitor/

oct01/sleepteen.html

Kelly, W. E., Kelly, K. E., & Clanton, R.

C. (2001). The relationship between

sleep length and grade-point average

among college students. *College*

Student Journal, 35(1), 84–90.

National Sleep Foundation. (2000).

Adolescent sleep needs and patterns:

Research report and resource guide.

Retrieved March 16, 2004, from

http://www.sleepfoundation.org/

publications/sleep_and_teens_report1.pdf

National Sleep Foundation. (2002, April).

Epidemic of daytime sleepiness linked

to increased feelings of anger,

stress, and pessimism. Retrieved March

14, 2004, from http://www

.sleepfoundation.org/nsaw/

pk_pollresultsmood.html

Trockel, M., Barnes, M., & Egget, D.
     (2000). Health-related variables and
     academic performance among first-year
     college students: Implications for
     sleep and other behaviors. *Journal of
     American College Health, 49,* 125-131.

DIRECTORY OF CHICAGO-STYLE ENDNOTES AND BIBLIOGRAPHY ENTRIES

 Print Sources

Entries for Books

Authors

1. A book by one author (p. 263)
2. A book by two or three authors (p. 263)
3. A book by more than three authors (p. 264)
4. A book by a corporate author (p. 264)

Editions, Multivolume Works

5. An edited book (p. 265)
6. A subsequent edition of a book (p. 265)
7. A multivolume work (p. 265)

Parts of Books

8. A chapter in a book (p. 266)
9. An essay in an anthology (p. 266)

Religious Works

10. A religious work (p. 266)

Entries for Articles

Scholarly Journals

11. An article in a scholarly journal with continuous pagination through an annual volume (p. 267)
12. An article in a scholarly journal with separate pagination in each issue (p. 267)

Magazines and Newspapers

13. An article in a weekly magazine (signed/unsigned) (p. 268)
14. An article in a monthly magazine (signed/unsigned) (p. 268)
15. An article in a newspaper (signed/unsigned) (p. 269)

Entries for Miscellaneous Print and Nonprint Sources

Interviews

16. A personal interview (p. 269)
17. A published interview (p. 269)

Letters, Government Documents

18. A personal letter (p. 270)
19. A government document (p. 270)

Videotapes, DVDs, and Recordings

20. A videotape or DVD (p. 270)
21. A recording (p. 270)

search **Electronic Sources**

Entries from Internet Sites

Internet-Specific Sources

22. An article in an online journal (p. 271)
23. An article in an online magazine (p. 272)
24. An article in an online newspaper (p. 272)
25. A Web site or home page (p. 272)
26. An email message (p. 273)
27. A listserv message (p. 273)

Entries from Subscription Services

Documents from a Database

28. A scholarly journal article from a database (p. 273)

CHAPTER 35

Chicago Documentation Style

35a Using Chicago Style

The Chicago Manual of Style is used in history and in some social science and humanities disciplines. **Chicago style*** has two parts: *notes at the end of the paper* (**endnotes**) and *a list of bibliographic citations.* (Chicago style encourages the use of endnotes, but it allows the use of footnotes at the bottom of the page.)

---

*Chicago-style documentation follows the guidelines set in *The Chicago Manual of Style*, 15th ed. Chicago: University of Chicago Press, 2003. The manuscript guidelines and sample research paper at the end of this chapter follow guidelines set in Kate L. Turabian's *A Manual for Writers of Term Papers, Theses, and Dissertations*, 6th ed. Chicago: University of Chicago Press, 1993. Turabian style, which is based on Chicago style, addresses formatting concerns specific to college writers.

(1) Endnotes and Footnotes

The notes format calls for a **superscript** (raised numeral) in the text after source material you have either quoted or referred to. This numeral, placed after all punctuation marks except dashes, corresponds to the numeral that accompanies the note.

Endnote and Footnote Format: Chicago Style

In the Text

By November of 1942, the Allies had proof that the
Nazis were engaged in the systematic killing of Jews.[1]

In the Note

    1. David S. Wyman, *The Abandonment of the
Jews: America and the Holocaust 1941–1945* (New
York: Pantheon Books, 1984), 65.

Close-up: Subsequent References to the Same Work

In the first reference to a work, use the full citation; in subsequent references to the same work, list only the author's last name, followed by a comma, an abbreviated title, then a comma, and a page number.

First Note on Espinoza

    1. J. M. Espinoza, *The First Expedition of
Vargas in New Mexico, 1692* (Albuquerque:
University of New Mexico Press, 1949), 10–12.

Subsequent Note

    5. Espinoza, *First Expedition*, 29.

NOTE: *The Chicago Manual of Style* allows the use of the abbreviation *ibid.* ("in the same place") for subsequent references to the same work as long as there are no intervening references. *Ibid.* takes the place of the author's name and the work's title—but not the page number.

First Note on Espinoza

    1. J. M. Espinoza, *The First Expedition of
Vargas in New Mexico, 1692* (Albuquerque:
University of New Mexico Press, 1949), 10–12.

Subsequent Note

    2. Ibid., 23.

(2) Bibliography

In addition to the heading `Bibliography`, Chicago style allows `Selected Bibliography`, `Works Cited`, and `References`. Bibliography entries are arranged alphabetically. Double-space within and between entries.

SAMPLE CHICAGO-STYLE ENDNOTES AND BIBLIOGRAPHY ENTRIES

Print Sources

Entries for Books

Capitalize the first, last, and all major words of titles and subtitles. Chicago style recommends the use of italics for titles, but underlining to indicate italics is also acceptable.

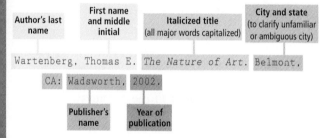

Author's last name	First name and middle initial	Italicized title (all major words capitalized)	City and state (to clarify unfamiliar or ambiguous city)

Wartenberg, Thomas E. *The Nature of Art.* Belmont, CA: Wadsworth, 2002.

Publisher's name | Year of publication

Authors

1. A Book by One Author
Endnote

    1. Robert Dallek, *An Unfinished Life: John F. Kennedy 1917–1963* (New York: Little Brown, 2003), 213.

Bibliography

Dallek, Robert. *An Unfinished Life: John F. Kennedy 1917–1963.* New York: Little Brown, 2003.

2. A Book by Two or Three Authors
Endnote
Two Authors

    2. Jack Watson and Grant McKerney, *A Cultural History of the Theater* (New York: Longman, 1993), 137.

Three Authors

> 2. Nathan Caplan, John K. Whitmore, and
> Marcella H. Choy, *The Boat People and Achievement
> in America: A Study of Economic and Educational
> Success* (Ann Arbor: University of Michigan Press,
> 1990), 51.

Bibliography
Two Authors

> Watson, Jack, and Grant McKerney. *A Cultural
>> History of the Theater*. New York: Longman,
>> 1993.

Three Authors

> Caplan, Nathan, John K. Whitmore, and Marcella H.
>> Choy. *The Boat People and Achievement in
>> America: A Study of Economic and Educational
>> Success*. Ann Arbor: University of Michigan
>> Press, 1990.

3. A Book by More Than Three Authors
Endnote
Chicago style favors and others rather than et al. in endnotes.

> 3. Robert E. Spiller and others, eds.,
> *Literary History of the United States* (New York:
> Macmillan, 1953), 24.

Bibliography
All authors' names are listed in the bibliography.

> Spiller, Robert E., Willard Thorp, Thomas H.
>> Johnson, and Henry Seidel Canby, eds.
>> *Literary History of the United States*. New
>> York: Macmillan, 1953.

4. A Book by a Corporate Author
If the title page of a publication issued by an organization does not identify a person as the author, the organization is listed as the author, even if its name is repeated in the title, in the series title, or as the publisher.

Endnote

4. National Geographic Society, *National Parks of the United States*, 3rd ed. (Washington, DC: National Geographic Society, 1997), 77.

Bibliography

National Geographic Society. *National Parks of the United States*. 3rd ed. Washington, DC: National Geographic Society, 1997.

Editions, Multivolume Works
5. An Edited Book
Endnote

5. William Bartram, *The Travels of William Bartram*, ed. Mark Van Doren (New York: Dover Press, 1955), 85.

Bibliography

Bartram, William. *The Travels of William Bartram*. Edited by Mark Van Doren. New York: Dover Press, 1955.

6. A Subsequent Edition of a Book
Endnote

6. Laurie G. Kirszner and Stephen R. Mandell, *The Wadsworth Handbook*, 7th ed. (Boston: Wadsworth, 2005), 52.

Bibliography

Kirszner, Laurie G., and Stephen R. Mandell. *The Wadsworth Handbook*. 7th ed. Boston: Wadsworth, 2005.

7. A Multivolume Work
Endnote

7. Kathleen Raine, *Blake and Tradition* (Princeton, NJ: Princeton University Press, 1968), 1:143.

Bibliography

Raine, Kathleen. *Blake and Tradition*. Vol. 1.
    Princeton, NJ: Princeton University Press,
    1968.

Parts of Books

8. A Chapter in a Book
Endnote

8. Roy Porter, "Health, Disease, and Cure,"
in *Quacks: Fakers and Charlatans in Medicine*
(Gloucestershire, UK: Tempus Publishing, 2003),
182–205.

Bibliography

Porter, Roy. "Health, Disease, and Cure," Chap. 5
    in *Quacks: Fakers and Charlatans in Medicine*
    Gloucestershire, UK: Tempus Publishing, 2003.

9. An Essay in an Anthology
Endnote

9. G. E. R. Lloyd, "Science and Mathematics,"
in *The Legacy of Greece*, ed. Moses Finley (New
York: Oxford University Press, 1981), 270.

Bibliography

Lloyd, G. E. R. "Science and Mathematics." In
    The Legacy of Greece, edited by Moses
    Finley, 256–300. New York: Oxford University
    Press, 1981.

Religious Works

10. A Religious Work
References to religious works (such as the Bible) are usually confined to the text or notes and not listed in the
bibliography. In citing the Bible, include the book (abbreviated), the chapter (followed by a colon), and the
verse numbers. Identify the version, but do not include a
page number.

Endnote

10. Phil. 1:9–11 (King James Version).

Entries for Articles

Scholarly Journals

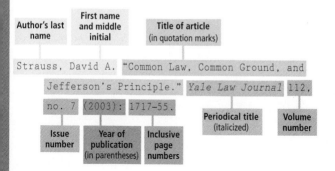

11. An Article in a Scholarly Journal with Continuous Pagination through an Annual Volume
Endnote

     11. John Huntington, "Science Fiction and the Future," *College English* 37 (Fall 1975): 341.

Bibliography

Huntington, John. "Science Fiction and the Future." *College English* 37 (Fall 1975): 340–58.

12. An Article in a Scholarly Journal with Separate Pagination in Each Issue
Endnote

     12. R. G. Sipes, "War, Sports, and Aggression: An Empirical Test of Two Rival Theories," *American Anthropologist* 4, no. 2 (1973): 80.

Bibliography

Sipes, R. G. "War, Sports, and Aggression: An Empirical Test of Two Rival Theories." *American Anthropologist* 4, no. 2 (1973): 65–84.

13. An Article in a Weekly Magazine (Signed/Unsigned)

Endnote

Signed

> 13. Pico Iyer, "A Mum for All Seasons,"
> *Time*, April 8, 2002, 51.

Unsigned

> 13. "Burst Bubble," *NewScientist*, July 27, 2002,
> 24.

NOTE: Although both endnotes above specify page numbers, the bibliography entries include page numbers only when the pages are consecutive.

Bibliography

Signed

> Iyer, Pico. "A Mum for All Seasons." *Time*, April
> 8, 2002.

Unsigned

> "Burst Bubble." *NewScientist*, July 27, 2002, 24–25.

14. An Article in a Monthly Magazine (Signed/Unsigned)

Endnote

Signed

> 14. Tad Suzuki, "Reflecting Light on Photo
> Realism," *American Artist*, March 2002, 47.

Unsigned

> 14. "Repowering the U.S. with Clean Energy
> Development." *BioCycle*, July 2002.

Bibliography

Signed

> Suzuki, Tad. "Reflecting Light on Photo Realism."
> *American Artist*, March 2002, 46–51.

Unsigned

> "Repowering the U.S. with Clean Energy
> Development." *BioCycle*, July 2002, 14.

15. An Article in a Newspaper (Signed/Unsigned)
Endnote

Because the pagination of newspapers can change from edition to edition, Chicago style recommends against giving page numbers for newspaper articles.

Signed

> 15. Francis X. Clines, "Civil War Relics Draw Visitors, and Con Artists," *New York Times*, August 4, 2002, national edition, sec. A.

Unsigned

> 15. "Feds Lead Way in Long-Term Care," *Atlanta Journal-Constitution*, July 21, 2002, sec. E.

Bibliography
Signed

> Clines, Francis X. "Civil War Relics Draw Visitors, and Con Artists." *New York Times*, August 4, 2002, national edition, sec. A.

Unsigned

> "Feds Lead Way in Long-Term Care." *Atlanta Journal-Constitution*, July 21, 2002, sec. E.

NOTE: Omit the article *the* from the newspaper's title. Include a city name in the title, even if it is not part of the actual title.

Entries for Miscellaneous Print and Nonprint Sources

Interviews
16. A Personal Interview
Endnote

> 16. Cornel West, interview by author, tape recording, June 8, 2003.

Bibliography

Personal interviews are not listed in the bibliography.

17. A Published Interview
Endnote

> 17. Gwendolyn Brooks, interview by George Stavros, *Contemporary Literature* 11, no. 1 (Winter 1970): 12.

Bibliography

Brooks, Gwendolyn. Interview by George Stavros. *Contemporary Literature* 11, no. 1 (Winter 1970): 1–20.

Letters, Government Documents

18. A Personal Letter
Endnote

18. Julia Alvarez, letter to the author, April 10, 2002.

Bibliography

Personal letters are not listed in the bibliography.

19. A Government Document
Endnote

19. U.S. Department of Transportation, *The Future of High-Speed Trains in the United States: Special Study, 2001* (Washington, DC: GPO, 2002), 203.

Bibliography

U.S. Department of Transportation. *The Future of High-Speed Trains in the United States: Special Study, 2001.* Washington, DC: GPO, 2002.

Videotapes, DVDs, and Recordings

20. A Videotape or DVD
Endnote

20. *Interview with Arthur Miller*, dir. William Schiff, 17 min., The Mosaic Group, 1987, videocassette.

Bibliography

Interview with Arthur Miller. Directed by William Schiff. 17 min. The Mosaic Group, 1987. Videocassette.

21. A Recording
Endnote

21. Bob Marley, "Crisis," *Bob Marley and the Wailers*, Kava Island Records 423 095-3, compact disc.

Bibliography

```
Marley, Bob. "Crisis." Bob Marley and the
     Wailers. Kava Island Records 423 095-3.
     Compact disc.
```

Electronic Sources

Internet citations for electronic sources include the author's name; the title of the document (enclosed in quotation marks); the title of the Internet site (italicized); the publication date (or, if no date is available, the abbreviation n.d.); the URL; and the date of access (in parentheses).

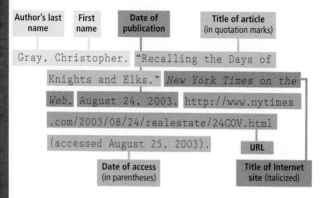

Entries from Internet Sites

Internet-Specific Sources

22. An Article in an Online Journal

Endnote

```
     22. Robert F. Brooks, "Communication as the
Foundation of Distance Education," Kairos: A
Journal of Rhetoric, Technology, and Pedagogy 7,
no. 2 (2002), http://english.ttu.edu/kairos/
index.html (accessed March 20, 2002).
```

Bibliography

```
Brooks, Robert F. "Communication as the
     Foundation of Distance Education." Kairos: A
     Journal of Rhetoric, Technology, and Pedagogy
     7, no. 2 (2002). http://english.ttu.edu/
     kairos/index.html (accessed March 20, 2002).
```

23. An Article in an Online Magazine
Endnote

    23. Steven Levy, "I Was a Wi-Fi Freeloader,"
Newsweek, October 9, 2002, http://www.msnbc
.com/news/816606.asp (accessed January 9, 2004).

Bibliography

Levy, Steven. "I Was a Wi-Fi Freeloader."
        Newsweek, October 9, 2002. http://www.msnbc
        .com/news/816606.asp (accessed January 9,
        2004).

24. An Article in an Online Newspaper
Endnote

    24. William J. Broad, "Piece by Piece, the
Civil War *Monitor* Is Pulled from the Atlantic's
Depths," *New York Times on the Web,* July 18,
2002, http://query.nytimes.com/search/advanced
(accessed June 15, 2004).

Bibliography

Broad, William J. "Piece by Piece, the Civil War
        Monitor Is Pulled from the Atlantic's
        Depths." *New York Times on the Web,* July 18,
        2002. http://query.nytimes.com/search/
        advanced (accessed June 15, 2004).

25. A Web Site or Home Page
Endnote

    25. David Perdue, "Dickens's Journalistic
Career," *David Perdue's Charles Dickens Page,*
September 24, 2002, http://www.fidnet.com/
~dap1955/dickens (accessed September 10, 2003).

Bibliography

Perdue, David. "Dickens's Journalistic Career."
        David Perdue's Charles Dickens Page.
        September 24, 2002. http://www.fidnet.com/
        ~dap1955/dickens (accessed September 10,
        2003).

26. An Email Message
Do not include the author's email address after his or her name.

Endnote
26. Meg Halverson, "Scuba Report," email message to author, April 2, 2004.

Bibliography
Email messages are not listed in the bibliography.

27. A Listserv Message
Include the name of the list and the date of the individual posting. Include the listserv address after the date of publication.

Endnote
27. Dave Shirlaw, email to Underwater Archeology discussion list, September 6, 2002, http://lists.asu.edu/archives/sub-arch.html (accessed May 12, 2002).

Bibliography
Listserv messages are not listed in the bibliography.

Entries from Subscription Services

Documents from a Database

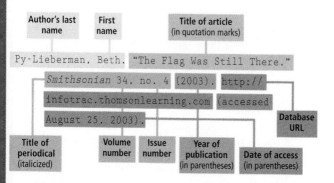

28. A Scholarly Journal Article from a Database
Include as much publication information as you can. Always give the URL of the service's main entrance; the date of access (in parentheses) is optional.

Endnote

    28. Richard J. Schaefer, "Editing Strategies
in Television Documentaries," *Journal of
Communication* 47, no. 4 (1997): 80, http://www
.galegroup.com/onefile (accessed October 2, 2003).

Bibliography

Schaefer, Richard J. "Editing Strategies in
        Television Documentaries." *Journal of
        Communication* 47, no. 4 (1997):80. http://
        www.galegroup.com/onefile (accessed October
        2, 2003).

35b Chicago-Style Manuscript Guidelines

Checklist: Typing Your Paper

When you type your paper, use the student paper in **35c** as your model.

- [ ] On the title page, include the full title of your paper as well as your name. Also include the course title, the instructor's name, and the date. Each element on the title page is considered a major heading and should appear entirely in capitals.
- [ ] Type your paper with a one-inch margin at the top, at the bottom, and on both sides.
- [ ] Double-space your paper throughout.
- [ ] Indent the first line of each paragraph one-half inch. Set off a long prose quotation (ten or more typed lines or more than one paragraph) from the text by indenting the entire quotation one-half inch from the left-hand margin. Do not use quotation marks. If the quotation is a full paragraph, include the paragraph indentation.
- [ ] Number all pages consecutively at the top of the page, with the number either centered or flush right. Page numbers should appear at a consistent distance (at least three-fourths of an inch) from the top edge. The title page is not numbered; the first full page of the paper is numbered page 1.
- [ ] Use superscript numbers to indicate in-text citations. Type superscript numbers at the end of cited material

(quotations, paraphrases, or summaries). Leave no space between the superscript number and the preceding letter or punctuation mark. The note number should be placed at the end of a sentence (or at the end of a clause). The number should come after any punctuation mark except for a dash, which it precedes.

☐ When you cite source material in your paper, use <u>Chicago documentation style</u>.

See 35a

Checklist: Using Visuals

According to *The Chicago Manual of Style*, there are two types of visuals: **tables** and **figures** (or **illustrations**), including charts, graphs, photographs, maps, and diagrams.

Tables

☐ Give each **table** a label and an arabic number (TABLE 1, TABLE 2, and so on).
☐ Give each table a descriptive title in the form of a sentence. Place the title after the table number.
☐ Place both the label and title above the table.
☐ Place source information below the table, introduced by the word *Source*. (If there is more than one source, begin with *Sources*.)

    Source: David E. Fisher and Marshall Jon Fisher,

    Tube: The Invention of Television (Washington,

    DC: Counterpoint Press, 1996), 185.

If the sources are listed in the bibliography, use a shortened form below the table.

    Source: Fisher and Fisher 1996.

Figures

☐ Give each **figure** a label, an arabic number, and a caption. The label Figure may be abbreviated Fig. (Figure 1, Fig. 1).
☐ Place both the label and caption below the figure, on the same line.
☐ Place source information in parentheses at the end of the title or caption.

    Fig. 1. Television and its influence on young

    children. (Photograph from ABC Photos.)

> ### Checklist: Preparing Chicago-Style Endnotes
>
> ☐ Begin the endnotes on a new page after the last page of the paper and preceding the bibliography.
> ☐ Type the title NOTES entirely in capitals and center it two inches from the top of the page.
> ☐ Number the page on which the endnotes appear as the next page of the paper.
> ☐ Type and number notes in the order in which they appear in the paper, beginning with number 1.
> ☐ Type the note number on (not above) the line, followed by a period and one space.
> ☐ Indent the first line of each note one-half inch (or five spaces); type subsequent lines flush with the left-hand margin.
> ☐ Double-space within and between entries.
> ☐ Break URLs after slashes, before punctuation marks, or before or after the symbols = and &.

> ### Checklist: Preparing a Chicago-Style Bibliography
>
> ☐ Type entries on a separate page after the endnotes.
> ☐ Type the title BIBLIOGRAPHY entirely in capitals, and center it two inches from the top of the page.
> ☐ List entries alphabetically according to the author's last name.
> ☐ Type the first line of each entry flush with the left-hand margin. Indent subsequent lines one-half inch (five spaces).
> ☐ Double-space within and between entries.

35c Sample Chicago-Style Research Paper (Excerpts)

The following student paper, "The Flu of 1918 and the Potential for Future Pandemics," was written for a history course. It uses Chicago-style documentation and includes a title page, a notes page, and a bibliography.

Title page is not numbered

THE FLU OF 1918 AND THE POTENTIAL FOR

FUTURE PANDEMICS

BY

RITA LIN

Title is centered and followed by name

AMERICAN HISTORY 301

DR. WALTER HIGH

MAY 3, 2004

Course title

Instructor's name

Date

Title
(centered)

Indent ½"
(or five
spaces)

Introduc-
tion

Superscript
numbers
refer to
endnotes

Double-space

The Flu of 1918 and the Potential for
Future Pandemics

     In November 2002, a mysterious new illness surfaced in China. By May 2003, what became known as SARS (Severe Acute Respiratory Syndrome) had been transported by air travelers to Europe, South America, South Africa, Australia, and North America, and the worldwide death toll had grown to 250.[1] By June 2003, there were more than 8,200 suspected cases of SARS in 30 countries and 750 deaths related to the outbreak, including 30 in Toronto. Just when SARS appeared to be waning in Asia, a second outbreak in Toronto, the hardest hit of all cities outside of Asia, reminded everyone that SARS remained a deadly threat.[2] As SARS continued to claim more victims and expand its reach, fears of a new pandemic spread throughout the world.

     The belief that a pandemic could occur in the future is not a far-fetched idea. During the twentieth century, there were three, and the most deadly one, in 1918, has several significant similarities to the SARS outbreak. As David Brown points out, in many ways, the 1918 influenza pandemic is a mirror reflecting the causes and symptoms, as well as the future potential, of SARS. Both are caused by a virus, result in respiratory illness, and

2

spread through casual contact and coughing. Outbreaks for both are often traced to one individual, quarantine is the major weapon against the spread of both, and both likely arose from mutated animal viruses. Moreover, as Brown observes, the greatest fear regarding SARS is that it will become so widespread that transmission chains will be undetectable, and health officials will be helpless to restrain outbreaks. Such was the case with the 1918 influenza, which also began mysteriously in China and was transported around the globe (at that time by World War I military ships). By the time the flu lost its power in the spring of 1919, in a year's time it had killed more than 50 million people worldwide,[3] more than twice as many as those who died during the four and a half years of World War I. Thus, if SARS is a reflection of the potential for a future flu pandemic—and experts believe it is—the international community needs to acknowledge the danger, accelerate its research, and develop an extensive virus-surveillance system.

Thesis statement

Clearly, the 1918 flu was different from anything previously known to Americans. Among the peculiarities of the pandemic was its origin and cause. In the spring of 1918, the virus, in relatively mild form,

History of 1918 pandemic

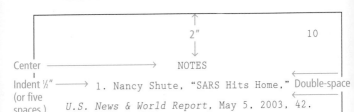

↑
2″   10
↓

Center ——————————→ NOTES

Indent ½″ ——————→ 1. Nancy Shute, "SARS Hits Home," ← Double-space
(or five
spaces) *U.S. News & World Report*, May 5, 2003, 42.

2. "Canada Waits for SARS News as

Endnotes Asia Under Control," *Sydney Morning Herald*
listed in
order in *on the Web*, June 2, 2003, http://www.smh
which
they ap- .com.au/text/articles/2003/06/01/
pear in
the paper 1054406076596.htm (accessed April 2, 2004).

3. David Brown, "A Grim Reminder in

SARS Fight: In 1918, Spanish Flu Swept the

Globe, Killing Millions," *MSNBC News*

Online, June 4, 2003, http://www.msnbc

.com/news/921901.asp (accessed April 2,

2004).

Subse- 4. Doug Rekenthaler, "The Flu
quent ref-
erences to Pandemic of 1918: Is a Repeat Performance
the same
source Likely?—Part 1 of 2," *Disaster Relief: New*
include
author's *Stories*, February 22, 1999, http://www
last name,
shortened .disasterrelief.org/Disasters/990219Flu/
title, and
page (accessed March 9, 2004).
number(s)
5. Lynette Iezzoni, *Influenza 1918:*

Ibid. is *The Worst Epidemic in American History*
used for a
subse- (New York: TV Books, 1999), 40.
quent ref-
erence to 6. "1918 Influenza Timeline,"
the same
source *Influenza 1918*, 1999, http://www.pbs.org/
when
there are wgbh/amex/influenza/timeline/index.html
no inter-
vening (accessed March 9, 2004).
references
7. Iezonni, *Influenza 1918*, 131-132.

8. Brown, "Grim Reminder."

9. Iezonni, *Influenza 1918*, 88-89.

10. Ibid, 204.

2″

13

BIBLIOGRAPHY ← Center

"1918 Influenza Timeline." *Influenza 1918*, 1999. http://www.pbs.org/wgbh/amex/influenza/timeline/index.html (accessed March 9, 2004).

Billings, Molly. "The Influenza Pandemic of 1918." *Human Virology at Stanford: Interesting Viral Web Pages*, June 1997. http://www.stanford.edu/group/virus/uda/index.html (accessed March 17, 2004).

Brown, David. "A Grim Reminder in SARS Fight: In 1918, Spanish Flu Swept the Globe, Killing Millions." *MSNBC News Online*, June 4, 2003. http://www.msnbc.com/news/921901.asp (accessed April 2, 2004).

"Canada Waits for SARS News as Asia Under Control." *Sydney Morning Herald on the Web*, June 2, 2003. http://www.smh.com.au/text/articles/2003/06/01/1054406076596.htm (accessed April 2, 2004).

Cooke, Robert. "Drugs vs. the Bug of 1918: Virus' Deadly Code Is Unlocked to Test Strategies to Fight It." *Newsday*, October 1, 2002.

Double-space

First line of each entry is flush with the left-hand margin; subsequent lines are indented 5 spaces

Entries are listed alphabetically according to the author's last name

DIRECTORY OF CSE REFERENCE LIST ENTRIES

Print Sources

Entries for Books

Authors

1. A book with one author (p. 285)
2. A book with more than one author (p. 285)

Editions

3. An edited book (p. 285)

Parts of Books

4. A chapter or other part of a book with a separate title but with the same author (p. 285)
5. A chapter or other part of a book with a different author (p. 286)

Religious Works, Classical Literature

6. A religious work (p. 286)
7. Classical literature (p. 286)

Entries for Articles

Scholarly Journals

8. An article in a journal paginated by issue (p. 286)
9. An article in a journal with continuous pagination (p. 287)

Magazines and Newspapers

10. A magazine article (signed/unsigned) (p. 287)
11. A newspaper article (signed/unsigned) (p. 287)

Entries for Miscellaneous Print and Nonprint Sources

Films, Videotapes, Recordings, Maps

12. An audiocassette (p. 288)
13. A film, videotape, or DVD (p. 288)
14. A map (p. 288)

Electronic Sources

Entries from Internet Sites

Internet-Specific Sources

15. An online book (p. 288)
16. An online journal (p. 289)

CHAPTER 36

CSE (Formerly CBE) and Other Documentation Styles

36a Using CSE Style

CSE style,* recommended by the Council of Science Editors (CSE), is used in biology, zoology, physiology, anatomy, and genetics. CSE style has two parts—*documentation in the text* and a *reference list.*

(1) Documentation in the Text

CSE style recommends two documentation formats: *citation-sequence format* and *name-year format.*

Citation-Sequence Format The **citation-sequence format** calls for either **superscripts** (raised numbers) in the text of the paper (the preferred form) or numbers inserted parenthetically in the text of the paper.

```
One study[1] has demonstrated the effect of low

dissolved oxygen.
```

These numbers correspond to a list of references at the end of the paper. When the writer refers to more than one source in a single note, the numbers are separated by a hyphen if they are in sequence and by a comma if they are not.

```
Some studies[2-3] dispute this claim.

Other studies[3,6] support these findings.
```

Name-Year Format The **name-year format** calls for the author's name and the year of publication to be inserted parenthetically in the text. If the author's name is used to introduce the source material, only the date of publication is needed in the parenthetical citation.

---

* CSE style follows the guidelines set in the style manual of the Council of Biology Editors: *Scientific Style and Format: The CBE Manual for Authors, Editors, and Publishers,* 6th ed. New York: Cambridge UP, 1994. The Council of Biology Editors has changed its name to the Council of Science Editors.

```
A great deal of heat is often generated during
this process (McGinness 1999).
```

```
According to McGinness (1999), a great deal of
heat is often generated during this process.
```

When two or more works are cited in the same parentheses, the sources are arranged chronologically (from earliest to latest) and separated by semicolons.

```
Epidemics can be avoided by taking tissue
cultures (Domb 1998) and by intervention with
antibiotics (Baldwin and Rigby 1984; Martin and
others 1992; Cording 1998).
```

NOTE: The citation `Baldwin and Rigby 1984` refers to a work by two authors; the citation `Martin and others 1992` refers to a work by three or more authors.

(2) Reference List

See
Ch. 34 The format of the reference list depends on the documentation format you use. If you use the name-year documentation format, your reference list will resemble the reference list for an **APA** paper. If you use the citation-sequence documentation style, your sources will be listed by number, in the order in which they appear in your paper, on a `References` page. Double-space within and between entries. Type the number flush left, followed by a period and one space. Align the second and subsequent lines with the first letter of the author's last name.

SAMPLE CSE CITATION-SEQUENCE REFERENCE LIST ENTRIES

 Print Sources

Entries for Books

List the author or authors by last name; after one space, list the initial or initials (unspaced) that represent the first and middle names (followed by a period); the title (not underlined, and with only the first word capitalized); the place of publication; the full name of the publisher (followed by a semicolon); the year (followed by a period); and the total number of pages (including back matter, such as the index).

Author's last name | Initials (unspaced) | Title (only first word capitalized)

1. Abbott EA. Flatland: a romance of many dimensions. Boston: Shambhala; 1999. 238 p.

Number of entry | City | Publisher | Year of publication | Total number of pages | Semicolon

Authors

1. A Book with One Author

> 1. Hawking SW. Brief history of time: from the big bang to black holes. New York: Bantam; 1995. 198 p.

NOTE: No comma follows the author's last name and no period separates the initials that represent the first and middle names.

2. Book with More Than One Author

> 2. Horner JR, Gorman J. Digging dinosaurs. New York: Workman; 1988. 210 p.

Editions

3. An Edited Book

> 3. Goldfarb TD, editor. Taking sides: clashing views on controversial environmental issues. 2nd ed. Guilford (CT): Dushkin; 1987. 323 p.

NOTE: The name of the publisher's state, province, or country can be added within parentheses to clarify the location. The two-letter postal service abbreviation can be used for the state or province.

Parts of Books

4. A Chapter or Other Part of a Book with a Separate Title but with the Same Author

> 4. Asimov I. Exploring the earth and cosmos: the growth and future of human knowledge. New York: Crown; 1984. Part III, The horizons of matter; p 245-94.

NOTE: No period follows the p when it precedes a page number.

5. A Chapter or Other Part of a Book with a Different Author

   5. Gingerich O. Hints for beginning observers.

      In: Mallas JH, Kreimer E, editors. The Messier

      album: an observer's handbook. Cambridge:

      Cambridge Univ Pr; 1978: p 194-5.

NOTE: When giving inclusive page numbers, give only the nonrepeated digits—for example, 197-8 (*not* 197-198).

Religious Works, Classical Literature

6. A Religious Work

   6. The New Jerusalem Bible. Garden City (NY):

      Doubleday; 1985. Luke 15:11-32. p 1715-6.

7. Classical Literature

   7. Homer. Odyssey; Book 17:319-32. In: Lombardo

      S, translator and editor. The essential Homer:

      selections from the Iliad and the Odyssey.

      Indianapolis: Hackett; 2000. p 391-2.

Entries for Articles

List the author or authors (last name first); the title of the article (not in quotation marks, and with only the first word capitalized); the abbreviated name of the journal (with all major words capitalized, but not italicized or underlined); the year (followed by a semicolon); the volume number (followed by a colon); and inclusive page numbers. No spaces separate the year, the volume, and the page numbers. Month names longer than three letters are abbreviated to their first three letters.

Scholarly Journals

8. An Article in a Journal Paginated by Issue

   8. Sarmiento JL, Gruber N. Sinks for

      anthropogenic carbon. Phy Today

      2002;55(8):30-6.

Author's last name   Initial   Title of article (only first word capitalized)

```
2. Davies P. How to build a time machine: it
   wouldn't be easy, but it might be possible.
   Sci Am 2002; 287(3):50-5.
```

Number of entry   Year of publication   Issue number (in parentheses)   Inclusive page numbers

Title of periodical (abbreviation)   Semicolon   Volume number

9. An Article in a Journal with Continuous Pagination

```
9. Brazil K, Krueger P. Patterns of family
   adaptation to childhood asthma. J Pediatr Nurs
   2002;17:167-73.
```

Omit the month (and day for weeklies) and issue number for journals with continuous pagination in volumes.

Magazines and Newspapers

10. A Magazine Article (Signed/Unsigned)
Signed

```
10. Nadis S. Using lasers to detect E.T.
    Astronomy 2002 Sep:44-9.
```

Unsigned

```
10. [Anonymous]. Brown dwarf glows with radio
    waves. Astronomy 2001 Jun:28.
```

11. A Newspaper Article (Signed/Unsigned)
Signed

```
11. Husted B. Don't wiggle out of untangling
    computer wires. Atlanta Journal-Constitution
    2002 Jul 21;Sect Q1(col 1).
```

Unsigned

```
11. [Anonymous]. Scientists find gene tied to
    cancer risk. New York Times 2002 Apr 22;Sect
    A:18(col 6).
```

Entries for Miscellaneous Print and Nonprint Sources

Films, Videotapes, Recordings, Maps

12. An Audiocassette

> 12. Ascent of man [audiocassette]. Bronowski J.
> New York: Jeffrey Norton Pub; 1974. 1
> audiocassette: 2-track, 55 min.

13. A Film, Videotape, or DVD

> 13. Women in science [videocassette]. Stoneberger
> B, Clark R, editor, American Society for
> Microbiology, producer. Madison (WI):
> Hawkhill; 1998. 1 videocassette: 42 min,
> sound, color, 1/2 in. Accompanied by: 1
> guide.

14. A Map
A Sheet Map

> 14. Amazonia: a world resource at risk
> [ecological map]. Washington: Nat Geographic
> Soc; 1992. 1 sheet.

A Map in an Atlas

> 14. Central Africa [political map]. In: Hammond
> citation world atlas. Maplewood (NJ):
> Hammond; 1996. p 114-5. Color, scale
> 1:13,800,000.

Electronic Sources

Entries from Internet Sites

Internet-Specific Sources

15. An Online Book

> 15. Bohm D. Causality and chance in modern
> physics [monograph online]. Philadelphia:
> Univ of Pennsylvania Pr; 1999. Available

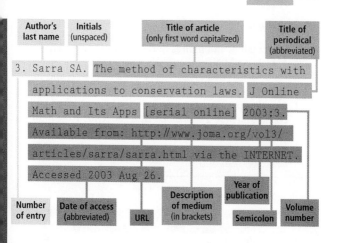

Author's last name | Initials (unspaced) | Title of article (only first word capitalized) | Title of periodical (abbreviated)

3. Sarra SA. The method of characteristics with
   applications to conservation laws. J Online
   Math and Its Apps [serial online] 2003:3.
   Available from: http://www.joma.org/vol3/
   articles/sarra/sarra.html via the INTERNET.
   Accessed 2003 Aug 26.

Number of entry | Date of access (abbreviated) | URL | Description of medium (in brackets) | Year of publication | Semicolon | Volume number

```
from: http://www.netlibrary.com/ebook_info
.asp?product_id517169 via the INTERNET.
Accessed 2002 Aug 17.
```

16. An Online Journal

```
16. Lasko P. The Drosophila melanogaster genome:
    translation factors and RNA binding proteins.
    J Cell Biol [serial online]
    2000;150(2):F51-6. Available from:
    http://www.jcb.org/search.dtl via the
    INTERNET. Accessed 2002 Aug 15.
```

36b CSE-Style Manuscript Guidelines

Checklist: Typing Your Paper

When you type your paper, use the student
paper in **36c** as your model.

☐ Type your name, the course, and the date flush left
  one inch from the top of the first page.
☐ If required, include an **abstract** (a 250-word summary of the paper) on a separate page following the
  title page.
☐ Double-space throughout.

(continued)

Typing your paper (continued)

☐ Insert tables and figures in the body of the paper. Number tables and figures in separate sequences (Table 1, Table 2; Figure 1, Figure 2; and so on).

☐ Number pages consecutively in the upper right-hand corner; include a shortened title above the page number.

See 36a
☐ When you cite source material in your paper, follow <u>CSE documentation style</u>.

Checklist: Preparing the CSE Reference List

☐ Begin the reference list on a new page after the last page of the paper, numbered as the next page.

☐ Center the title References, Literature Cited, or References Cited about one inch from the top of the page.

☐ List the entries in the order in which they first appear in the paper, *not alphabetically.*

☐ Number the entries consecutively; type the note numbers flush left on (not above) the line, followed by a period.

☐ Leave one space between the period and the first letter of the entry; align subsequent lines directly beneath the first letter of the author's last name.

☐ Double-space within and between entries.

36c Sample CSE-Style Research Paper (Excerpts)

The following student paper explores the dangers of global warming for humans and wildlife. The paper, which cites seven sources and includes a graph, illustrates the CSE citation-sequence format.

↑ 1"
↓

↕ ½"
Polar Ice Caps

Sara Castillo

Ecology 4223.01

April 10, 2004

Polar Ice Caps Could Melt by the ← Center title
End of This Century

Indent ½" (or five spaces) → The Arctic and Antarctica are
homes to the earth's polar ice caps, and Double-space
global warming appears to be melting them.
When polar temperatures increase, parts of Introduction
floating ice sheets and glaciers break off
1" and melt. This process could eventually ⟷ 1"
cause the ocean levels to rise and have
disastrous effects on plants, animals, and
human beings. There are ways to prevent
this disaster, but they will only be Thesis statement
effective if society has the will to
implement them immediately.

The polar ice caps are melting at a
rapid rate, and much of the scientific
community agrees that global warming is
one of the causes. The greenhouse effect,
the mechanism that causes global warming,
occurs when molecules of greenhouse gases
in the atmosphere reflect the rays of the
sun back to the earth. This mechanism
enables our planet to maintain a
temperature adequate for life. However, as Superscript numbers correspond
the concentration of greenhouse gases in to sources in the reference list
the atmosphere increases, more heat from
the sun is retained, and the temperature
of the earth rises.[1]

↑ 1" ↓

Polar Ice Caps

2

Greenhouse gases include carbon dioxide (CO_2), methane, and nitrous oxide.[2] Since the beginning of the industrial revolution in the late 1800s, people have been burning fossil fuels that create CO_2.[3] This CO_2 has led to an increase in the greenhouse effect and has contributed to the global warming that is melting the polar ice caps. As Figure 1 shows, the surface temperature of the earth has increased by about 1 degree Celsius (1.8 degrees Fahrenheit) since the 1850s.

Figure 1 introduced

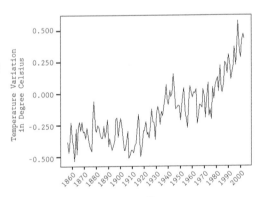

Figure placed close to where it is discussed

Figure 1   Global temperature variation from the average during the base period 1961-1990 (adapted from Climatic research unit: data: temperature 2003). Available from: http://www.cru.uea.ac.uk/cru/data/ temperature/ via the INTERNET. Accessed 2004 Mar 11.

Label, caption, and full source information

References

1. Edmonds A. A closer look at the
   greenhouse effect. Brookfield: Copper
   Beach Books; 1997. 32 p.

2. Smith RL, Smith TM. Elements of
   ecology. 5th ed. San Francisco:
   Benjamin Cummings; 2003. 534 p.

3. Pringle L. Global warming: the threat
   of earth's changing climate. New York:
   Sea and Star Books; 2001. 48 p.

4. Perkins S. Antarctic glacier thins and
   speeds up. Sci News 2001;159(5):70.

5. Pearce F. Arctic to lose all summer ice
   by 2100. New Scientist [serial online]
   2002;70(2):99-133. Available from:
   http://www.newscientist.com via the
   INTERNET. Accessed 2004 Mar 11.

6. [Anonymous]. The pacific decadal
   oscillation. BioSci 2000 Aug:32-39.

7. Woods M. Science on ice. Brookfield
   (CT): Millbrook Press; 1995. 96 p.

Double-space

Book with one author

Book with more than one author

Entries listed in order in which they first appear in the paper

Online journal

Print journal

36d Using Other Documentation Styles

The following style manuals describe documentation formats and manuscript guidelines used in various fields.

Chemistry

Dodd, Janet S. American Chemical Society. *The ACS Guide: A Manual for Authors and Editors.* 2nd ed. Washington: Amer. Chemical Soc., 1997.

Geology

United States Geological Survey. *Suggestions to Authors of the Reports of the United States Geological Survey.* 7th ed. Washington: GPO, 1991.

Government Documents

Garner, Diane L. *The Complete Guide to Citing Government Information Resources: A Manual for Writers and Librarians.* Rev. ed. Bethesda: Congressional Information Service, 1993.

United States Government Printing Office. *Style Manual.* Washington: GPO, 2000.

Journalism

Goldstein, Norm, ed. *Associated Press Stylebook and Briefing on Media Law.* 35th ed. New York: Associated P, 2000.

Law

The Bluebook: A Uniform System of Citation. Comp. Editors of *Columbia Law Review* et al. 16th ed. Cambridge: Harvard Law Rev. Assn., 1996.

Mathematics

American Mathematical Society. *AMS Author Handbook.* Providence: Amer. Mathematical Soc., 1998.

Medicine

Iverson, Cheryl. *Manual of Style: A Guide for Authors and Editors.* 9th ed. Chicago: Amer. Medical Assn., 1997.

Music

Holman, D. Kirn, ed. *Writing about Music: A Style Sheet from the Editors of 19th-Century Music.* Berkeley: U California P, 1988.

Physics

American Institute of Physics. *AIP Style Manual.* 5th ed. New York: Am. Inst. of Physics, 1995.

Scientific and Technical Writing

Rubens, Philip, ed. *Science and Technical Writing: A Manual of Style.* 2nd ed. New York: Routledge, 2001.

Developing Strategies for Academic Success

37 Ten Habits of Successful Students 298
37a Learn to Manage Your Time Effectively 298
37b Put Studying First 299
37c Be Sure You Understand School and Course Requirements 300
37d Be an Active Learner in the Classroom 300
37e Be an Active Learner Outside the Classroom 301
37f Take Advantage of College Services 302
37g Use the Library 303
37h Use Technology 303
37i Make Contacts—and Use Them 304
37j Be a Lifelong Learner 304

38 Designing Effective Documents 305
38a Creating an Effective Visual Format 305
38b Using Headings 306
38c Constructing Lists 307
38d Using Visuals 308

39 Creating a Web Site 312
39a Planning Your Web Site 313
39b Designing Your Web Site 313
39c Providing Links 314
39d Editing and Proofreading Your Web Site 314
39e Posting Your Web Site 315

40 Writing for the Workplace 315
40a Writing Letters of Application 316
40b Designing Résumés 318
40c Writing Memos 321
40d Writing Emails 323

41 Making Oral Presentations 324
41a Getting Started 324
41b Planning Your Speech 325
41c Preparing Your Notes 325
41d Using Visual Aids 326
41e Rehearsing Your Speech 329
41f Delivering Your Speech 329

CHAPTER 37

Ten Habits of Successful Students

Successful students have *learned* to be successful: they have developed specific strategies for success, and they apply those strategies to their education. If you take the time, you can learn the habits of successful students and apply them to your own college education—and, later on, to your career.

37a Learn to Manage Your Time Effectively

College makes many demands on your time. It is hard, especially at first, to balance studying, coursework, family life, friendships, and a job. But if you don't take control of your schedule, it will take control of you; if you don't learn to manage your time, you will always be behind, struggling to catch up.

Fortunately, there are two tools that can help you manage your time: a **personal organizer** and a **monthly calendar.** Carry your organizer with you at all times, and post your calendar in a prominent place (perhaps above your desk or next to your phone). Remember to record *in both places* school-related deadlines, appointments, and reminders (every due date, study group meeting, conference appointment, and exam) as well as outside responsibilities, such as work hours and medical appointments. (Be sure to record tasks and dates as soon as you learn of them.)

You can also use your organizer to help you plan a study schedule: block out times to study or to complete assignment-related tasks—such as a library database search for a research paper—in addition to appointments and deadlines. Make these entries in pencil so you can adjust your schedule as new responsibilities arise.

Remember: your college years can be a very stressful time, but although some degree of stress is inevitable, it can be kept in check. If you are organized, you will be better able to handle the pressures of a college workload.

37b Put Studying First

To be a successful student, you need to understand that studying is something you do *regularly*, not right before an exam. You also need to know that studying does not mean just memorizing facts; it also means reading, rereading, and discussing ideas until you understand them.

To make studying a regular part of your day, set up a study space that includes everything you need (supplies, good light, a comfortable chair) and does not include anything you do not need (clutter, distractions). Then, set up a tentative study schedule that reflects your priorities. Try to designate at least two hours each day to complete assignments due right away, to work on those due later on, and to reread class notes. When you have exams and papers, you can adjust your schedule accordingly.

Successful students often form **study groups,** and you should use this strategy whenever you can—particularly in a course you find challenging. A study group of four or five students who meet regularly (not just the night before an exam) can make studying more focused and effective as well as less stressful. By discussing concepts with your classmates, you can try out your ideas and get feedback, clarify complex concepts, and formulate questions for your instructor.

Checklist: Working in a Study Group

Working collaboratively in a **study group** requires some degree of organization. To get the most out of your study group, you need to set some ground rules.

- ☐ Meet regularly.
- ☐ Decide in advance who will be responsible for particular tasks.
- ☐ Set deadlines.
- ☐ Listen when someone else is speaking.
- ☐ Don't reject other people's ideas and suggestions without considering them very carefully.
- ☐ Take stock of problems and progress at regular intervals.
- ☐ Be mindful of other students' learning styles and special needs.

37c Be Sure You Understand School and Course Requirements

To succeed in school, you need to know what is expected of you—and, if you are not sure, you need to ask.

When you first arrived at school, you probably received a variety of orientation materials—a student handbook, library handouts, and so on—that set forth the rules and policies of your school. Read these documents carefully (if you have not already done so). If you do not understand something, ask your peer counselor or your adviser for clarification.

You also need to know the specific requirements of each course you take. Each course syllabus explains the instructor's policies about attendance and lateness, assignments and deadlines, plagiarism, and classroom etiquette. In addition, a syllabus may explain penalties for late assignments or missed quizzes, explain how assignments are graded, tell how much each assignment is worth, or note additional requirements, such as field work or group projects. Requirements vary significantly from course to course, so read each syllabus (as well as any supplementary handouts) carefully.

ESL Tip

If you did not attend high school in the United States, some of your instructors' class policies and procedures may seem strange to you. To learn more about the way US college classes are run, read the syllabus for each of your courses, and talk to your instructors about your concerns. You may also find it helpful to talk to older students with cultural backgrounds similar to your own. For specific information on adjusting to the US college classroom, **see Chapter 42.**

37d Be an Active Learner in the Classroom

Education is not about sitting passively in class and waiting for information and ideas to be given to you. It is up to you to be an active participant in your own education.

First, take as many small classes as you can. Small classes enable you to interact with other students and with your instructor. If a large course has recitation sections, be sure to attend these regularly even if they are not required. Also, be sure to take classes that require writing. Good writing skills are essential to your success as a student (and as a college graduate entering the workforce), and you will need all the practice you can get.

Attend class regularly, and arrive on time. Listen attentively, and take careful, complete notes. (Try to review these notes later with other students to make sure you have not missed anything important.) Do your homework on time, and keep up with the reading. When you read an assignment, interact with the text (for example, underlining the text and making marginal annotations) instead of just looking at what is on the page. If you have time, read beyond the assignment, looking on the Internet and in books, magazines, and newspapers for related information.

Finally, participate in class discussions: ask and answer questions, volunteer opinions, and give helpful feedback to other students. By participating in this way, you learn to consider other points of view, to test your ideas, and to respect the ideas of others.

ESL Tip

Especially in small classes, US instructors usually expect students to participate in class discussion. If you feel nervous about speaking up in class, you might start by expressing your support of a classmate's opinion.

37e Be an Active Learner Outside the Classroom

Taking an active role in your education is also important outside the classroom. Do not be afraid to approach your instructors; visit them during their office hours, and keep in touch with them by email. Get to know your major adviser well, and be sure he or she knows who you are and where your academic interests lie. Make appointments, ask questions, and explore possible solutions to problems: this is how you learn.

In addition, become part of your school community. Read your school newspaper, check the Web site regularly, join clubs, and apply for internships. This participation can help you develop new interests and friendships as well as enhance your education.

Finally, participate in the life of your community outside your school. Try to arrange an **internship,** a job that enables you to gain practical experience. (Many businesses, nonprofit organizations, and government agencies offer internships—paid or unpaid—to qualified students.) Take service learning courses, if they are offered at your school, or volunteer at a local school or social agency. As successful students know, education is more than just attending classes.

37f   Take Advantage of College Services

Colleges and universities offer students a wide variety of support services. For example, if you are struggling with a particular course, you can go to the tutoring service offered by your school's academic support center or by an individual department. If you need help with writing or revising a paper, you can make an appointment with the writing lab, where tutors will give you advice. If you are having trouble deciding on what courses to take or what to major in, you can see your academic adviser. If you are having trouble adjusting to college life, your peer counselor or (if you live in a dorm) your resident adviser may be able to help you. Finally, if you have a personal or family problem you would rather not discuss with another student, you can make an appointment at your school's counseling center, where you can get advice from professionals who understand student problems.

ESL Tip

Many ESL students find using the writing lab (sometimes called a writing center) very helpful. In fact, many writing labs have tutors who specialize in working with ESL students. Most writing labs provide assistance with assignments for any course, and they often assist with writing job application letters and résumés.

Of course, other services are available—for example, at your school's computer center, job placement service, and financial aid office. Your academic adviser or instructors can tell you where to find the help you need, but it is up to you to make the appointment.

37g Use the Library

Because so much material is available on the Internet, you may think your college library is outdated or even obsolete. But learning to use the library is an important part of your education. See Ch. 29

First, the library can provide a quiet place to study—something you may need if you have a large family or noisy roommates. The library also contains materials that cannot be found online—rare books, special collections, audiovisual materials—as well as electronic databases that contain material you will not find on the free Internet.

Finally, the library is the place where you have access to the expert advice of your school's reference librarians. These professionals can answer questions, guide your research, and point you to sources that you might never have found on your own.

37h Use Technology

Technological competence is essential to success in college. For this reason, it makes sense to develop good word-processing skills and to be comfortable with the Internet. You should also know how to send and receive email from your university account as well as how to attach files to your email. Beyond the basics, you should learn how to manage the files you download, how to evaluate Web sites, and how to use the electronic resources of your library. You might also find it helpful to know how to scan documents (containing images as well as text) and how to paste these files into your documents. See Ch. 30

If you do not have these skills, you need to locate campus services that will help you get them. Workshops and online tutorials may be available through your school library, and individual assistance with software and hardware is available in computer labs.

Part of being technologically savvy in college involves being aware of the online services your campus has to offer. For example, many campuses rely on customizable information-management systems called **portals.** Not unlike commercial services, such as Yahoo! or America Online, a portal requires you to log in with a user ID and password to access services, such as locating and contacting your academic adviser and viewing your class schedule and grades.

Finally, you need to know not only how to use technology to enhance a project—for example, how to use *Power-Point* for an oral presentation or *Excel* to make a table— but also when to use technology (and when *not* to).

See
38d1

37i   Make Contacts—and Use Them

One of the most important things you can do for yourself is to make academic and professional contacts that you can use during college and after you graduate.

Your first contacts are your classmates. Be sure you have the names, phone numbers, and email addresses of at least two students in each of your classes. These contacts will be useful to you if you miss class, if you need help understanding your notes, or if you want to start a study group.

You should also build relationships with students with whom you participate in college activities, such as the college newspaper or the tutoring center. These people are likely to share your goals and interests, so you may want to get feedback from them as you choose a major, consider further education, and make career choices.

Finally, develop relationships with your instructors, particularly those in your major area of study. One of the things cited most often in studies of successful students is the importance of **mentors,** experienced individuals whose advice they trust. Long after you leave college, you will find these contacts useful.

37j   Be a Lifelong Learner

Your education should not stop when you graduate from college. To be a successful student, you need to be a lifelong learner.

Get in the habit of reading newspapers; know what is happening in the world outside school. Talk to people outside the college community so that you don't forget there are issues that have nothing to do with courses and grades. Never miss an opportunity to learn: try to get in the habit of attending plays and concerts sponsored by your school or community and lectures offered at your local library or bookstore.

And think about the life you will lead after college. Think about who you want to be and what you have to do to get there. This is what successful students do.

CHAPTER 38

Designing Effective Documents

Document design refers to the conventions that determine the way a document—a research paper, memo, report, business letter, or résumé, for example—looks on a page. A well-designed document is not only pleasing to look at, it is also easy to read. In general, well-designed documents have the following characteristics:

- An effective format
- Clear headings
- Useful lists
- Attractive visuals

38a Creating an Effective Visual Format

Margins Margins frame a page and keep it from looking overcrowded. In general, a document should have at least a one-inch margin on all sides. Keep in mind, however, that specific assignments often have specific requirements for margins. Before you prepare an academic document, consult the appropriate style sheet.

Except in documents such as flyers and brochures, in which you might want to isolate some blocks of text for emphasis, you should **justify** (uniformly align, except for paragraph indentations) the left-hand margin. You can either leave a ragged edge on the right or justify your text so all the words are aligned evenly along the right margin.

Line Spacing Line spacing refers to the amount of space between the lines of a document. The conventions of the type of writing you do determine line spacing. For example, the paragraphs of reports and business letters are usually single-spaced and separated by a double space (and not indented); the paragraphs of academic papers are usually double-spaced and indented.

White Space White space is the area of a page that is intentionally left blank. Used effectively, white space focuses readers' attention on the material you are isolating. You can use white space around a block of text—a paragraph or a section, for example—or around visuals, such as charts, graphs, and photographs.

Color Color can emphasize and clarify information—such as the headings in a report or the bars in a bar graph—while at the same time making it visually appealing. Keep in mind, however, that too many colors can distract readers and obscure your visual emphasis.

Typeface and Type Size Typefaces are distinctively designed sets of numbers and letters. In your academic writing, you should select a typeface that is simple and direct—Courier, Times New Roman, or Arial, for example—and avoid fancy typefaces that call attention to themselves—*Calligraphy* or *Script*, for example. For most of your academic papers, use 10- or 12-point type (although headings may sometimes be larger).

http://kirsznermandell.wadsworth.com

Computer Tip: Formatting Features

Most word-processing programs enable you to create borders, horizontal rules, boxes, and shaded areas of text. Border and shading options are usually found under the Format menu of your word-processing program. With these features, you can select line style, thickness, and color and adjust white space, boxed text, and the degree of shading.

38b Using Headings

Headings perform some useful functions in a text:

- **Headings tell readers that a new idea is being introduced.** In this way, headings tell readers what to expect in a section before they actually read it.
- **Headings emphasize key ideas.** By summarizing an idea and isolating it from the text around it, headings help readers identify important information.
- **Headings indicate how information is organized in a text.** Headings use various typefaces and type sizes (as well as indentation) to indicate the relative importance of ideas.

Number of Headings The number of headings depends on the document. A long, complicated document will need more headings than a shorter, less complex one. Keep in mind that too few headings may not be of much use, but too many headings will make your document look like an outline.

Phrasing Headings can be single words—*Summary* or *Introduction*, for example. They can also be phrases (always stated in <u>parallel</u> terms): *Choosing a dog, Caring for your dog, Housebreaking your dog.* Sometimes, they can even be questions (*How do you choose a dog?*) or statements (*Choose the right dog.*). Whether they are single words, phrases, or questions, headings should be brief, descriptive, and to the point.

See Ch. 13

Indentation In general, the more important a heading is, the closer it is to the left-hand margin: first-level headings are justified left, second-level headings are indented five spaces, and third-level headings are indented another two or three spaces. (Alternatively, headings may be *centered*, with different levels of subheadings placed *flush left* and *run into the text.*)

Consistency Headings at the same level should be in the same format. For example, if one first-level heading is boldfaced and centered, all other first-level headings must be boldfaced and centered. Using consistent headings reinforces the hierarchy of ideas and makes a document easier to understand.

Typefaces You can emphasize headings by using **bold-face,** *italics,* or ALL CAPITAL LETTERS. Used in moderation, these distinctive typefaces make a text more readable. Used excessively, however, they slow readers down.

38c Constructing Lists

A list makes material easier to understand by breaking complicated statements into a series of key ideas. Lists are easiest to read when all the elements are parallel and about the same length. When rank is important, number the items on the list; when it isn't, use **bullets** (as in the list below). Make sure you introduce the list with a complete sentence followed by a colon.

We must take several steps to reduce spending:
- We must cut our workforce by 10 percent.
- We must use less expensive vendors.
- We must decrease overtime payments.

Because the items on the list above are complete sentences, each ends with a period. Do not use periods if the items are not sentences.

Remember, use lists in moderation. Too many lists are visually distracting and make a document choppy and hard to follow.

Figure 38.1 shows a page from a student's report that incorporates some of the effective design elements discussed on the preceding pages.

Figure 38.1 A well-designed page from a student's report.

38d Using Visuals

Visuals, such as tables, graphs, diagrams, and photographs, can enhance your documents. You can create your own tables and graphs by using a computer program such as *Excel, Lotus,* or *Microsoft Word*. You can also get diagrams and photographs by photocopying or scanning them from a print source, or by downloading them from the Internet or from CD-ROMs or DVDs. Introduce each visual in the text of your paper to provide context, and label it according to the appropriate style sheet. If you use a visual from a source, you must supply appropriate <u>documentation</u>.

See
Pt.7

(1) Tables

Tables present data in a condensed, visual format—arranged in rows and columns. Tables may contain numerical data, text, or a combination of the two. Keep in mind that tables may distract readers, so include only those necessary to support your discussion. (The table in Figure 38.2 reports the student writer's original research and therefore needs no documentation.)

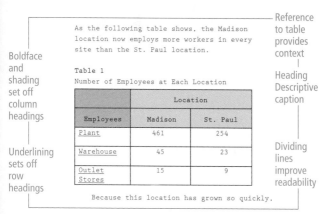

Figure 38.2 Sample table from a student paper.

(2) Graphs

Whereas tables present specific numerical data, graphs show the general pattern or trend that the data suggest. Because graphs tend to be more general (and therefore less accurate) than tables, they are frequently accompanied by tables. Figure 38.3 is an example of a bar graph showing data from a source.

(3) Diagrams

A diagram calls readers' attention to specific details of a structure, object, or device. Diagrams are often used in scientific and technical writing to clarify concepts that are difficult to explain in words. Figure 38.4, which

illustrates the sections of an orchestra, serves a similar
purpose in a music education paper.

the demographics of college students is changing.
According to a 2002 US Department of Education report
entitled <u>Nontraditional Undergraduates</u>, the percentage
of students who could be classified as "nontraditional"

**Reference
to graph
provides
context**

has increased over the last decade (see fig 1).

Data

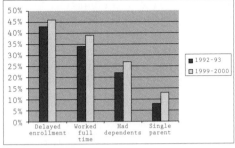

**Label and
citation**

Fig. 1. United States. Dept. of Educ., Office of Educ.
Research and Improvement, Natl. Center for Educ.
Statistics, <u>Nontraditional Undergraduates</u>, NCES 2002-
012 (Washington: US Dept. of Educ., 2002) 4, 27 Feb.
2003 <http://nces.ed.gov/pubs2002/2002012.pdf>.

Figure 38.3 Sample graph from a student paper.

**Reference
to diagram
provides
context**

The sections of an orchestra are arranged precisely to
allow for a powerful and cohesive performance. Fig. 1
illustrates the placement of individual sections of
an orchestra.

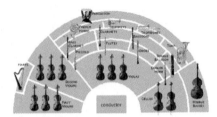

**Label,
descriptive
caption,
and
citation**

Fig. 1. The sections of an orchestra, <u>The Lyric Opera
of Waco: Education Outreach</u>, 23 Aug. 2002, 11 Nov.
2003 <http://www.lyricoperaofwaco.org/education/
orchestra/>.

Figure 38.4 Sample diagram from a student paper.

(4) Photographs

Photographs enable you to show exactly what something or someone looks like. Although computer technology that enables you to paste photographs directly into a text is widely available, you should use it with restraint. Not every photograph will support or enhance your written text; in fact, an irrelevant photograph will distract readers. The photograph of a wooded trail in Figure 38.5 illustrates the student writer's description.

Photo placed appropriately within text with consistent white space above and below

```
travelers are well advised to be prepared,
to always carry water and dress for the
conditions. Loose fitting, lightweight
wicking material covering all exposed skin
is necessary in summer, and layers of warm
clothing are needed for cold weather
outings. Hats and sunscreen are always a
good idea no matter what the temperature,
although most of the trails are quite
shady with huge oak trees. Figure 1 shows
a shady portion of the trail.
```

Reference to photo provides context

Figure 1 Greenbelt Trail in springtime (author photo)

Label and descriptive caption

Figure 38.5 Sample photograph from a student paper.

Checklist: Using Visuals

☐ Use a visual only when it contributes something important to your discussion, not for embellishment.
☐ Place the visual in the text only if you plan to refer to it in your paper (if not, place the visual in an appendix).
☐ Introduce each visual with a complete sentence that provides context.
☐ Follow each visual with a discussion that explains its significance.
☐ Leave wide margins around each visual.

(continued)

Using visuals (continued)

☐ Place the visual as close as possible to the section of your paper in which it is discussed.
☐ Label each visual appropriately.
☐ Document each visual borrowed from a source.

CHAPTER 39

Creating a Web Site

At some point in your college career, you may be asked to create a personal home page or even a full Web site—for example, to fulfill a course assignment or to market your job skills. Like other documents, Web pages follow specific conventions of document design. The easiest way to create a Web page is to use one of the many Web creation software packages that are commercially available. These programs automatically convert text and graphics into HTML (the programming language by which standard documents are converted into World Wide Web hypertext documents) so that they can be posted on the Web.

A personal **home page** usually contains information about how to contact the author, a brief biography, and links to other Web sites. A home page can be the first page of a **Web site,** a group of related Web pages. Basic Web pages contain only text, but more advanced Web pages include photographs, animation, and even film clips. You can get ideas for your Web site by examining other sites and determining what appeals to you. Keep in mind, however, that although you may borrow formatting ideas from a Web site, it is never acceptable to replicate the exact appearance of another site or to appropriate a site's content.

Close-up: Web Sites and Copyright

As a rule, you should assume that any material on the Web is copyrighted unless the author makes an explicit statement to the contrary. This means that you must receive written permission if you are going to reproduce this material on your Web site. The only exception to this rule is the **fair use doctrine,** which allows the use of copyrighted material for the purpose of commentary, parody, or research and education. How much of the work you use is also of consideration, and so is the purpose of your use—whether or not you are using it commercially. As of now, you do not usually have to get permission to provide a link to material on another Web site. (Material you quote in a research paper for one of your classes falls under the fair use doctrine and does not require permission.)

39a Planning Your Web Site

Begin by sketching a basic plan of your Web site's content. Then, consider how your Web pages will be connected and what links you will provide to other Web sites. Your home page should provide an overview of your site and give readers a clear sense of what material the site will contain. Beginning with the home page, users will navigate from one piece of information to another.

As you plan your Web site, consider how your pages will be organized. If your site is relatively uncomplicated, you can arrange pages so that one page leads sequentially to the next. If your site is relatively complicated, however, you will have to group pages under headings or categories in order of their importance. A home page of a student's Web site, shown in Figure 39.1, indicates that information is grouped under various headings—*About me, Résumé, Portfolio, Services,* and *Contact.*

39b Designing Your Web Site

When you design your Web site, lay out text and graphics so that they present your ideas clearly and logically. Because your home page is the first thing readers will encounter, it should be clear and easy to follow. Place related items next to each other, and use text sparingly. Make sure you identify text on the same topic by highlighting it in the same color or by using the same font or graphic. Remember, however, that using too many graphics or elaborate type will distract and confuse readers.

Figure 39.1 Home page of student's Web site.

39c Providing Links

Your home page will include buttons and links. **Buttons**—graphic icons, such as arrows or pictures—enable readers to move from one page of a Web site to another. **Links**—short for **hyperlinks**, words or URLs (electronic addresses) highlighted and underlined in blue—enable readers to navigate from one site to another. When you provide a link, you are directing people to a specific Web site, so be sure that the site is up and running and that the information that appears there is reliable.

39d Editing and Proofreading Your Web Site

Before you post your site, edit and proofread it just as you would any other document. In addition, if you have included links on your Web site, be sure you have entered the full Web address (beginning with http://). If you have used a colored background or text, be sure you have avoided color combinations that make your pages difficult to read (purple on black, for example). Finally, make certain that you have received permission to use all material—graphics as well as text—that you have borrowed from a source and that you have documented this material.

39e Posting Your Web Site

Once you have designed a Web site, you will need to upload (post) it so you can view it on the Web. Most commonly, Web pages are posted with **FTP** (File Transfer Protocol) software. See 30b4

To get your site up on the Web, you transfer your files to an **Internet server,** a computer that is connected at all times to the Internet. Your Internet service provider will instruct you on how to use FTP to transfer your files. Once your site is up and running, any mistakes you have made will be apparent as soon as you view your pages on the Web.

Checklist: Designing a Web Site

- ☐ Plan the content of your site.
- ☐ Consider how you want your site to be organized.
- ☐ Draw a basic plan of your site.
- ☐ Lay out text and graphics so that they present your ideas clearly and logically.
- ☐ Keep both text and graphics simple.
- ☐ Provide clear and informative links.
- ☐ Proofread your text.
- ☐ Make sure your site looks the way you want it to.
- ☐ Make sure all your links are active.
- ☐ Make sure you have acknowledged all material that you have borrowed from a source.
- ☐ Post your site to an Internet server.

CHAPTER 40

Writing for the Workplace

Whether you are writing letters of application, résumés, memos, or email, you should always be concise, avoid digressions, and try to sound as natural as possible.

40a Writing Letters of Application

A letter of application summarizes your qualifications for a particular job. Begin by identifying the job you are applying for and telling where you heard about it. In the body of your letter, provide the specific information that will convince readers you are qualified for the position. Conclude by reinforcing your desire for the job and by stating that you have enclosed your résumé and that you will be available for an interview. (Be sure to include your phone number and email address.) Finally, proofread carefully to make sure there are no errors in spelling or punctuation.

Figure 40.1 An effective letter of application will improve your chances of getting an interview.

Sample Letter of Application

246 Hillside Drive
Urbana, IL 61801
kr237@metropolis.105.com
October 20, 2004   *Heading*

Mr. Maurice Snyder, Personnel Director   *Inside address*
Guilford, Fox, and Morris
22 Hamilton Street
Urbana, IL 61822

Dear Mr. Snyder: *Salutation*

My college advisor, Dr. Raymond Walsh, has told me that you are interested in hiring a part-time accounting assistant. I believe that my academic background and my work experience qualify me for this position.

    Body

I am presently a junior accounting major at the University of Illinois. During the past year, I have taken courses in taxation, trusts, and business law. I am also proficient in *Lotus* and *ClarisWorks*. Last spring, I gained practical accounting experience by working in our department's tax clinic.

    ←—— *Double-space*

After I graduate, I hope to get a master's degree in taxation and then return to the Urbana area. I believe that my experience in taxation as well as my ←—— *Single-space* familiarity with the local business community will enable me to make a contribution to your firm.

I have enclosed a résumé for your examination. I will be available for an interview any time after midterm examinations, which end October 25. I look forward to hearing from you.

Sincerely yours,   *Complimentary close*

Sandra Kraft   *Written signature*

Sandra Kraft   *Typed signature*
Enc.: Résumé   *Additional data*

NOTE: After you have been interviewed, you should send a **follow-up letter** to the person (or persons) who interviewed you. First, thank your interviewer for taking the time to see you. Then, briefly summarize your qualifications and your interest in the position. Because so few applicants write follow-up letters, such letters can have a very positive effect on the recipient.

40b Designing Résumés

A résumé lists relevant information about your education, job experience, goals, and personal interests. The most common way to arrange the information in your résumé is in chronological order, listing your education and work experience in sequence, moving from earliest to latest. Your résumé should be brief (one page, if possible), clear, and logically organized. Emphasize important information with italics, bullets, boldface, or different fonts. Print your résumé on high-quality paper, and proofread carefully for errors.

Close-up: Scannable Résumés

Although the majority of résumés are submitted on paper, an increasing number of résumés are designed to be **scannable;** that is, to be scanned and entered into an electronic database. If you submit such a résumé, format it accordingly. Because scanners will not pick up columns, bullets, or italics, you should not use them in a scannable résumé. Whereas in print résumés you use strong action verbs to describe your accomplishments (*performed computer troubleshooting*, for example), in a scannable résumé you use key nouns or adjectives (*computer troubleshooter*, for example) to attract employers who carry out a keyword search for applicants with certain skills. (To facilitate such a search, you should include a Keyword section on your scannable résumé.)

Sample Résumé

KAREN L. OLSON

SCHOOL
3812 Hamilton St. Apt. 18
Philadelphia, PA 19104
215-382-0831
olsont@dunm.ocs.drexel.edu

HOME
110 Ascot Ct.
Harmony, PA 16037
412-452-2944

EDUCATION

Drexel University, Philadelphia, PA 19104
Bachelor of Science in Graphic Design
Anticipated Graduation: June 2004
Cumulative Grade Point Average: 3.2 on a 4.0 scale

COMPUTER SKILLS

Hardware: Familiar with both Macintosh and PC systems
Software: *Adobe Illustrator, Photoshop,* and *Type Align;*
QuarkXPress; CorelDRAW; Micrografx Designer

EMPLOYMENT EXPERIENCE

The Triangle, Drexel University, Philadelphia, PA 19104
January 2001–present
Graphics Editor. Design all display advertisements submitted to
Drexel's student newspaper.

Unisys Corporation, Blue Bell, PA 19124
June–September 2001, Cooperative Education
Graphic Designer. Designed interior pages as well as covers for target marketing brochures. Created various logos and spot art designed for use on interoffice memos and departmental publications.

Charming Shoppes, Inc., Bensalem, PA 19020
June–December 2000, Cooperative Education
Graphic Designer/Fashion Illustrator. Created graphics for future
placement on garments. Did some textile designing. Drew flat illustrations of garments to scale in computer. Prepared presentation boards.

Design And Imaging Studio, Drexel University, Philadelphia, PA
19104
October 2000–June 2001
Monitor. Supervised computer activity in studio. Answered telephone. Assisted other graphic design students in using computer
programs.

ACTIVITIES AND AWARDS

Kappa Omicron Nu Honor Society, vice president: 2002–present;
Dean's List: 2000–2001; Graphics Group, vice president:
2001–present

REFERENCES AND PORTFOLIO

Available upon request.

Sample Résumé: Scannable

CONSTANTINE G. DOUKAKIS

2000 Clover Lane   Phone: (817) 735-9120
Fort Worth, TX 76107   E-Mail: Douk@aol.com

Employment Objective: Entry-level position in an organization that will enable me to use my academic knowledge and the skills that I learned in my work experience.

EDUCATION:

University of Texas at Arlington, Bachelor of Science in Civil Engineering, June 2004. Major: Structural Engineering. Graduated Magna Cum Laude. Overall GPA: 3.75 on a 4.0 base.

SCHOLASTIC HONORS AND AWARDS:

Member of Phi Eta Sigma First-Year Academic Honor Society, Chi Epsilon Civil Engineering Academic Society, Tau Beta Pi Engineering Academic Society, Golden Key National Honor Society.

Jack Woolf Memorial Scholarship for Outstanding Academic Performance.

COOPERATIVE EMPLOYMENT EXPERIENCE:

Johnson County Electric Cooperative, Cleburne, TX, Jan. to June 2003. Junior Engineer in Plant Dept. of Maintenance and Construction Division. Inspected and supervised in-plant construction. Devised solutions to construction problems. Estimated costs of materials for small construction projects. Presented historical data relating to the function of the department.

Dallas-Fort Worth International Airport, Tarrant County, TX, Dec. 2001 to June 2002. Assistant Engineer. Supervised and inspected airfield paving, drainage, and utility projects as well as terminal building renovations. Performed on-site and laboratory soil tests. Prepared concrete samples for load testing.

Dallas-Fort Worth International Airport, Tarrant County, TX, Jan.–June 2001. Draftsman in Design Office. Prepared contract drawings and updated base plans as well as designed and estimated costs for small construction projects.

KEY WORDS:

Organizational and leadership skills. Written and oral communication skills, C++, IBM, Macintosh, DOS, Windows 2000, and Mac OS. Word, Excel, FileMakerPro, PowerPoint, WordPerfect, Internet client software. Computer model development. Technical editor.

40c Writing Memos

Memos communicate information within an organization. A memo can be short or long, depending on its purpose.

Begin your memo with a purpose statement that presents your reason for writing it. Follow this statement with a summary section that tells readers what to expect in the rest of the memo. Then, in the body of your memo, present your support: the detailed information that supports the main point of your memo. If your document is short, use numbered or bulleted lists to emphasize information. If it is long, use headings to designate the various parts of the memo (*Summary, Background, Benefits*, and so on). End your memo with a statement of your conclusions and recommendations.

Figure 40.2 Memos are frequently emailed within an organization to facilitate their distribution.

Sample Memo

TO: Ina Ellen, Senior Counselor
FROM: Kim Williams, Student Tutor Supervisor   Opening compone
SUBJECT: Construction of a Tutoring Center
DATE: November 10, 2004

This memo proposes the establishment of a tutoring center in the Office of Student Affairs.   Purpose statemen

BACKGROUND
Under the present system, tutors must work with students at a number of facilities scattered across the university campus. As a result, tutors waste a lot of time running from one facility to another and are often late for appointments.

NEW FACILITY
I propose that we establish a tutoring facility adjacent to the Office of Student Affairs. The two empty classrooms next to the office, presently used for storage of office furniture, would be ideal for this use. We could furnish these offices with the desks and file cabinets already stored in these rooms.   Body

BENEFITS
The benefits of this facility would be the centralizing of the tutoring services and the proximity of the facility to the Office of Student Affairs. The tutoring facility could also use the secretarial services of the Office of Student Affairs.

Conclusion

RECOMMENDATIONS
To implement this project, we would need to do the following:

1. Clean up and paint rooms 331 and 333
2. Use folding partitions to divide each room into five single-desk offices
3. Use stored office equipment to furnish the center

I am certain these changes would do much to improve the tutoring service. I look forward to discussing this matter with you in more detail.

40d Writing Emails

In many workplaces, virtually all internal (and some external) communications are transmitted as email. Although personal email tends to be quite informal, business email observes the conventions of standard written communication.

Close-up: Writing Emails

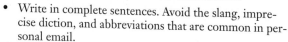

The following rules can help you communicate effectively in an electronic business environment:

- Write in complete sentences. Avoid the slang, imprecise diction, and abbreviations that are common in personal email.
- Use an appropriate tone. Address readers with respect, just as you would in a standard business letter.
- Include a subject line that clearly identifies your content. If your subject line is vague, your email may be deleted without being read.
- Make your message as short as possible. Because most emails are read on the screen, long discussions are difficult to follow.
- Use short paragraphs, leaving an extra space between paragraphs.
- Use lists and internal headings to focus your discussion and to break it into manageable parts. This strategy will make your message easier to understand.
- Take the time to edit your email after you have written it. Delete excess words and phrases.
- Proofread carefully before sending your email. Look for errors in grammar, spelling, and punctuation.
- Make sure that your list of recipients is accurate and that you do not send your email to unintended recipients.
- Do not send your email until you are absolutely certain that your message says exactly what you want it to say.
- Do not forward an email unless you have the permission of the sender.
- Watch what you write. Keep in mind that email written at work is the property of the employer, who has the legal right to access it—even without your permission.

CHAPTER 41

Making Oral Presentations

At school and on the job, you may sometimes be called upon to make oral presentations. Although many people are uncomfortable about making oral presentations, the guidelines that follow can make the experience easier and less stressful.

41a Getting Started

Just as with writing an essay, the preparation phase of an oral presentation is as important as the speech itself. The time you spend here will make your job easier later on.

Identify Your Topic The first thing you should do is identify the topic of your speech. Once you have a topic, you should decide how much information, as well as what kind of information, you will need.

Consider Your Audience The easiest way to determine what kind of information you will need is to consider the nature of your <u>audience</u>. Is your audience made up of experts or of people who know very little about your topic? How much background information will you have to provide? Can you use technical terms, or should you avoid them? Do you think your audience will be interested in your topic, or will you have to create interest? What opinions or ideas about your topic will the members of your audience bring with them?

See 1b

Consider Your Purpose Your speech should have a specific <u>purpose</u> that you can sum up concisely—for example, *to suggest ways to make registration easier for students.* To help you zero in on your purpose, ask yourself what you are trying to accomplish with your presentation.

See 1a

Consider Your Constraints How much time do you have for your presentation? (Obviously a ten-minute presentation requires more information and preparation than a three-minute presentation.) Do you already know enough about your topic, or will you have to do research?

41b Planning Your Speech

In the planning phase, you focus your ideas about your topic and develop a thesis; then, you decide what specific points you will discuss and divide your speech into a few manageable sections.

Develop a Thesis Statement Before you can actually begin to plan your speech, you should develop a thesis statement that clearly and concisely presents your main idea—the key idea you want to present to your audience. If you know a lot about your topic, you can develop a thesis on your own. If you do not, you will have to gather information and review it before you can decide on a thesis. As you plan your speech, remember to refer to your thesis to keep yourself on track.

Decide on Your Points Once you have developed a thesis, you can decide what points you will discuss. Unlike readers, who can reread a passage until they understand it, listeners must understand information the first time they hear it. For this reason, speeches usually focus on points that are clear and easy to follow. Usually, your thesis statement states or strongly implies these points.

Outline the Individual Parts of Your Speech Every speech has a beginning, a middle, and an end. Your **introduction** should introduce your subject, engage your audience's interest, and state your thesis—but it should not present an in-depth discussion or a summary of your topic. The **body,** or middle section, of your speech should present the points that support your thesis. It should also include the facts, examples, and other information that will clarify your points and help convince listeners that your thesis is reasonable. Your **conclusion** should bring your speech to a definite end and reinforce your thesis.

41c Preparing Your Notes

Most people use notes of some form when they give a speech. Each system of notes has advantages and disadvantages.

Full Text Some people like to write out the full text of their speech and refer to it during their presentation. If the type is large enough, and if you triple-space, this strategy can be useful. One disadvantage of using the full text of your speech is that it is easy to lose your place and become disoriented; another is that you may find yourself simply reading the speech.

3 x 5 Cards Some people write parts of their speech—for example, a list of key points or definitions—on 3 × 5 notecards, which can be flipped through easily. They are also small, so they can be placed inconspicuously on a podium or a table. With some practice, you can use notecards effectively. You have to be careful, however, not to become so dependent on the cards that you lose eye contact with your audience or begin fidgeting with the cards as you give your speech.

Outlines Some people like to refer to an outline when they give a speech. As they speak, they can glance down at the outline to get their bearings or to remind themselves of a point they may have forgotten. Because an outline does not contain the full text of a speech, the temptation to read is eliminated. However, if for some reason you draw a blank, an outline gives you very little to fall back on.

41d Using Visual Aids

Visual aids—such as overhead transparencies or posters, can reinforce important information and make your speech easier to understand. For a simple speech, a visual aid may be no more than a definition or a few key terms, names, or dates written on the board. For a more complicated presentation, you might need charts, graphs, diagrams, or photographs—or even objects. The major consideration for including a visual aid is whether it actually adds something to your speech.

If you are using equipment such as a slide projector or a laptop to display a visual, make sure you know how to operate it—and have a contingency plan in case the equipment doesn't work the way it should. In addition, make sure that whatever visual you use is large enough for everyone in your audience to see. Printing or typing should be neat and free of errors. Graphics should be clearly labeled and easy to see.

Microsoft PowerPoint, the most commonly used **presentation software** package, enables you to organize an oral presentation and prepare attractive, professional slides (see Figure 41.1). This program contains many options for backgrounds, color schemes, and special effects, and also enables you to enhance your slides with sound and video.

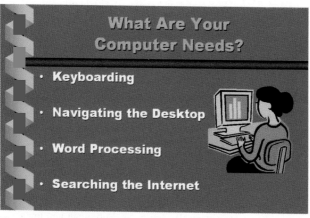

Figure 41.1 Sample *PowerPoint* slide.

http://kirsznermandell.wadsworth.com

Computer Tip: Using *PowerPoint*

If possible, use the same computer that you used to prepare your *PowerPoint* slides when you deliver your speech. That way, you will be sure that you will be able to open your files and that all the multimedia effects you included with your slides will work.

Using Visual Aids in Your Presentations

Visual Aid	Advantages	Disadvantages
Computer presentations	Clear Easy to read Professional Graphics, video, sound, and animated effects Portable (disk or CD-ROM)	Special equipment needed Expertise needed Special software needed Software might not be compatible with all computer systems

(continued)

Using Visual Aids in Your Presentations (*continued*)

Visual Aid	Advantages	Disadvantages
Overhead projectors	Transparencies are inexpensive Transparencies are easily prepared with computer or copier Transparencies are portable Transparencies can be written on during presentation Projector is easy to operate	Transparencies can stick together Transparencies can be placed upside down Transparencies must be placed on projector by hand Some projectors are noisy Speaker must avoid projector's power cord during presentation
Slide projector	Colorful Professional Projector is easy to use Order of slides can be reversed during presentation Portable (slide carousel)	Slides are expensive to produce Special equipment needed for lettering and graphics Dark room needed for presentation Slides can jam in projector
Posters or flip charts	Low-tech and personal Good for small-group presentations Portable	May not be large enough to be seen in some rooms Artistic ability needed May be expensive if prepared professionally Must be secured to an easel
Chalkboards or whiteboards	Available in most rooms Easy to use Easy to erase or change information during presentation	Difficult to draw complicated graphics Handwriting must be legible Must catch errors as you write Cannot face audience when writing or drawing Very informal

> ### Checklist: Designing Visuals
>
> ☐ Do not put more than three or four points on a single visual.
> ☐ Use single words or short phrases, not sentences or paragraphs.
> ☐ Limit the number of visuals. For a three- to five-minute presentation, five or six visuals are enough.
> ☐ Use the same size font and the same color consistently on each visual.
> ☐ Use type that is large enough for your audience to see (50-point type for major headings and 30–34 point type for text).
> ☐ Do not use elaborate graphics or special effects just because your computer software enables you to do so (this is especially relevant for users of *Microsoft Power-Point*).
> ☐ Check your visuals for correctness. Make sure your graphics do not contain typos, mislabelings, or other errors.

41e Rehearsing Your Speech

You should practice your speech often—at least five times. Do not try to memorize your entire speech, but be sure you know it well enough so that you can move from point to point without constantly looking at your notes. If possible, rehearse your speech in the actual room you will be using, and try standing in the back of the room to make sure that your visuals can be seen clearly. Finally, time yourself. Make certain that your three-minute speech actually takes three minutes to deliver.

41f Delivering Your Speech

The most important part of your speech is your delivery. Keep in mind that a certain amount of nervousness is normal, so try not to focus on your nervousness too much. While you are waiting to begin, take some deep breaths and calm down. Once you get to the front of the room, do not start right away. Take the time to make sure that everything you will need is there and that all your equipment is positioned properly.

Before you speak, make sure that both feet are flat on the floor and that you are facing the audience. When you begin speaking, pace yourself. Speak slowly and clearly, and look at the entire audience, one person at a time. Make sure that you speak *to* your audience, not *at* them. Even though your speech is planned, it should sound natural and conversational. Speak loudly enough for everyone in the room to hear you, and remember to vary your pitch and your volume so that you do not speak in a monotone. Try using pauses to emphasize important points and to give listeners time to consider what you have said. Finally, sound enthusiastic about your subject. If you appear to be bored or distracted, your audience will be too.

Your movements should be purposeful and natural. Do not pace or lean against something. Move around only when the need arises—for example, to change a visual, to point to a chart, or to distribute something. Never turn your back to your audience; if you have to write on the board, make sure that you are angled toward the audience. Try to use hand movements to emphasize points, but do not play with pens or notecards as you speak, and do not put your hands in your pockets.

Finally, dress appropriately for the occasion. How you look will be the first thing that listeners notice about you. (Although shorts and a T-shirt may be appropriate for an afternoon in the park, they are not suitable for a classroom presentation.) Dressing appropriately not only demonstrates your respect for your audience but also shows that you deserve to be taken seriously.

ESL Tip

Some ESL students are nervous about delivering a speech, especially if they have noticeable accents. However, even students who have difficulties with English can deliver effective speeches by following the tips in this section on body language, eye contact, and pacing.

Resources for Bilingual and ESL Writers

42 Adjusting to the US Classroom   332
42a Understanding the Writing Process   332
42b Understanding English Language Basics   334
42c Learning to Edit Your Work   334

43 Understanding Grammar and Usage   336
43a Solving Verb-Related Problems   336
43b Solving Noun-Related Problems   341
43c Using Pronouns   343
43d Using Adjectives and Adverbs   345
43e Using Prepositions   346
43f Understanding Word Order   348

CHAPTER 42

Adjusting to the US Classroom

If you went to school outside of the United States, you may not be familiar with the way writing is taught in US composition classes.

Close-up: Adjusting to the US Classroom

Here are some aspects of US classrooms that may be unfamiliar to you:

- **Punctuality** Students are expected to be in their seats and ready to begin class at the scheduled time. If you are late repeatedly, your grade may be lowered.
- **Student–Instructor Relationships** The relationship between students and instructors may be more casual or friendly than you are used to. However, instructors still expect students to abide by the rules they set.
- **Class Discussion** Instructors typically expect students to volunteer ideas in class and may even enjoy it when students disagree with their opinions (as long as the students can make good arguments for their positions). Rather than being a sign of disrespect, this is usually considered to be evidence of interest and involvement in the topic under discussion.

42a Understanding the Writing Process

See Ch. 2

Typically, US composition instructors teach writing as a process. This process usually includes the following components:

- **Planning and shaping your writing** Your instructor will probably help you get ideas for your writing by assigning relevant readings, conducting class discussions, and asking you to keep a journal or engage in freewriting and brainstorming.

See 2a2

- **Writing multiple drafts** After you write your paper for the first time, you will probably get feedback from your instructor or your classmates so that you can **revise** (improve) your paper before receiving a grade on it. Instructors expect students to use the suggestions they receive to make significant improvements to their papers. (For more information on the drafting process, see 2c.)

- **Looking at sample papers** Your instructor may provide the class with sample papers of the type that he or she has assigned. Such samples can help you understand how to complete the assigned paper. Sometimes the samples are strong papers that can serve as good examples of what to do. However, most samples will have both strengths and weaknesses, so be sure you understand your instructor's opinion of the samples he or she provides.
- **Engaging in** <u>peer review</u> (sometimes called peer editing) Your instructor may ask the class to work in small groups or in pairs to exchange ideas about an assigned paper. You will be expected to provide other students with feedback on the strengths and weaknesses of their papers. Afterward, you should think carefully about your classmates' comments and make changes to improve your paper. See 28h3
- **Attending conferences** Your instructor may schedule one or more appointments with you to discuss your writing and may ask you to bring a draft of the paper you are working on. Your instructor may also be available to help you with your paper without an appointment during his or her office hours. In addition, many educational institutions have **writing centers**, where tutors help students get started on their papers or improve their drafts. When you meet with your instructor or writing center tutor, bring a list of specific questions about your paper, and be sure to make careful notes about what you discuss. You can refer to these notes when you revise your paper.

Close-up: Using Your Native Language

Depending on your language background and skills, you may find it helpful to use your native language in some stages of your writing. When you are making notes about the content of your paper, you may be able to generate more ideas and record them more quickly if you do some of the work in your native language. Additionally, when you are drafting your paper and cannot think of a particular word in English, it may be better simply to write the word in your native language (and come back to it later) so you do not lose your train of thought. However, if you use another language a great deal as you draft your writing and then try to translate your work into English, the English may sound awkward or be hard for readers to understand. The best strategy when you draft your papers is to write in English as much as you can, using the vocabulary and structures that you already know.

42b Understanding English Language Basics

Getting used to writing and editing your work in English will be easier if you understand a few basic principles:

ESL 43a

- **In English, words may change their form according to their function.** For example, <u>verbs</u> change form to communicate whether an action is taking place in the past, present, or future.

- **In English, context is extremely important to understanding function.** In the following sentences, for instance, the very same words can perform different functions according to their relationships to other words.

  > Juan and I are taking a <u>walk</u>. (*Walk* is a noun, a direct object of the verb *taking*, with an article, *a*, attached to it.)

  > If you <u>walk</u> instead of driving, you will help conserve the Earth's resources. (*Walk* is a verb, the predicate of the subject *you*.)

See Ch. 22

- **Spelling in English is not always phonetic and sometimes may seem illogical.** <u>Spelling</u> in English may be related more to the history of the word and to its origins in other languages than to the way the word is pronounced. Therefore, learning to spell correctly is often a matter of memorization, not sounding out the word phonetically. For example, "ough" is pronounced differently in *tough*, *though*, and *thought*.

ESL 43f

- <u>Word order</u> **is extremely important in English sentences.** In English sentences, word order may indicate which word is the subject of the sentence and which is the object, whether the sentence is a question or a statement, and so on.

42c Learning to Edit Your Work

See 2d

<u>Editing</u> your paper involves focusing on grammar, spelling, punctuation, and mechanics. The approach you take to editing for grammar errors should depend on your strengths and weaknesses in English.

If you learned English mostly by speaking it, if you have strong oral skills, and if you usually make correct judgments about English by instinct, the best approach for you may be reading your paper aloud and listening for mistakes, correcting them by deciding what sounds right. You may even find that as you read aloud, you automatically correct your written mistakes as you speak. (Be sure to transfer those corrections to your paper.) In addition to proofreading your paper from beginning to end, you might find it helpful to start from the end of the paper, reading and proofreading sentence by sentence. This strategy can keep you from being distracted by your ideas, allowing you to focus on grammar alone.

If you learned English mostly by reading, studying grammar rules, and/or translating between your native language and English, you may not feel that you have good instincts about what sounds right in English. If this is the case, you should take a different approach to editing your papers. First, identify the errors you make most frequently by looking at earlier papers your instructor has marked or by asking your instructor for help. Once you have identified your most common errors, read through your paper, checking each sentence for these errors. Try to apply the grammar and mechanics rules you already know, or check the relevant grammar explanations in **Chapter 43** for help.

After you check your paper for grammar errors, you should check again to make sure that you have used proper punctuation, capitalization, and spelling. If you have difficulty with spelling, you can use a spell checker to help you, but remember that spell checkers cannot catch every error. After you have made grammar and mechanics corrections on your own, you can seek outside help in identifying errors you might have missed. You should also keep a notebook with a list of your most frequent grammatical errors and review these errors frequently.

CHAPTER 43

Understanding Grammar and Usage

For ESL writers (as for many native English writers), grammar can be a persistent problem. Grammatical knowledge in a second language usually develops slowly, with time and practice, and much about English is idiomatic (not subject to easy-to-learn rules). This chapter is designed to provide you with the tools you will need to address some of the most common grammatical errors made by ESL writers.

43a Solving Verb-Related Problems

(1) Subject-Verb Agreement

^{See} ^{A1.3} English <u>verbs</u> change their form according to person, number, and tense. The verb in a sentence must agree with the subject in person and number. <u>Person</u> refers to ^{See} ^{12a4} *who* or *what* is performing the action of the verb (for example, *myself*, *you*, or someone else), and <u>number</u> refers to *how many* people or things are performing the action (one or more than one). In English, the rules for <u>subject-</u> ^{See} ^{6a} <u>verb agreement</u> are very important. Unless you use the correct person and number in the verbs in your sentences, you will confuse your English-speaking audience by communicating meanings you do not intend.

(2) Tense

^{See} ^{7b} <u>Tense</u> refers to *when* the action of the verb takes place. One problem that many nonnative speakers of English have with English verb tenses results from the large ^{See} ^{7a} number of <u>irregular verbs</u> in English. For example, the first-person singular present tense of *be* is not "I be" but "I am," and the past tense is not "I beed" but "I was."

Close-up: Choosing the Simplest Verb Forms

Some nonnative English speakers use verb forms that are more complicated than they need to be. They may do this because their native language uses more complicated verb forms than English does or because they "overcorrect" their verbs into complicated forms. Specifically, nonnative speakers tend to use progressive and perfect verb forms instead of simple verb forms. To communicate your ideas clearly to an English-speaking audience, choose the simplest possible verb form.

(3) Auxiliary Verbs

The **auxiliary verbs** (also known as **helping verbs**) *be*, *have*, and *do* are used to create some present, past, and future forms of verbs in English: "<u>Julio *is taking*</u> a vacation"; "<u>I *have been*</u> tired lately"; "<u>He *does*</u> not *need* a license." The auxiliary verbs *be*, *have*, and *do* change form to reflect the time frame of the action or situation and to agree with the subject; however, the main verb remains in simple present or simple past form.

Close-up: Auxiliary Verbs

Only auxiliary verbs, not the verbs they "help," change form to indicate person, number, and tense.

Present: We <u>have</u> to eat.

Past: We <u>had</u> to eat. (*not* "we had to ate.")

<u>Modal auxiliaries</u> (such as *can* and *should*) do not change form to indicate tense, person, or number.

See A1.3

---

(4) Negative Verbs

The meaning of a verb may be made negative in English in a variety of ways, chiefly by adding the words *not* or *does not* to the verb (is, *is not*; can ski, *can't* ski; drives a car, *does not* drive a car).

Close-up: Correcting Double Negatives

A **double negative** occurs when the meaning of a verb is negated not just once but twice in a single sentence.

Henry doesn't have ~~no~~ ^{any} friends. (*or* Henry ~~doesn't have~~ ^{has} no friends.)

I looked for articles in the library, but there ~~weren't~~ none. (*or* I looked for articles in the library, but there weren't ^{any} ~~none~~.)

---

(5) Phrasal Verbs

Many verbs in English are composed of two or more words—for example, *check up on, run for, turn into,* and *wait on.* These verbs are called **phrasal verbs.** It is important to become familiar with phrasal verbs and their definitions so you will recognize these verbs as phrasal verbs (instead of as verbs that are followed by prepositions). However, knowing the definitions of the individual words that make up these verbs is not always enough to enable you to define the phrasal verbs accurately. Even after consulting a dictionary, you will need to pay close attention to the use of these verbs in speech and writing.

Sometimes the words that make up a phrasal verb can be separated from each other by a direct object. In these **separable phrasal verbs,** the object can come either before or after the preposition. For example, "<u>Ellen *turned down*</u> the job offer" and "<u>Ellen *turned*</u> the job offer <u>*down*</u>" are both correct. However, when the object is a pronoun, the pronoun must come before the preposition. Therefore, "<u>Ellen turned</u> *it* <u>down</u>" is correct, but "<u>Ellen turned down</u> *it*" is incorrect.

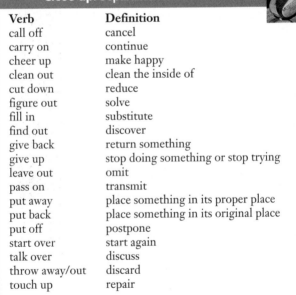

Close-up: Separable Phrasal Verbs	
Verb	**Definition**
call off	cancel
carry on	continue
cheer up	make happy
clean out	clean the inside of
cut down	reduce
figure out	solve
fill in	substitute
find out	discover
give back	return something
give up	stop doing something or stop trying
leave out	omit
pass on	transmit
put away	place something in its proper place
put back	place something in its original place
put off	postpone
start over	start again
talk over	discuss
throw away/out	discard
touch up	repair

However, some phrasal verbs—such as *look into, make up for,* and *break into*—consist of words that can never be separated. With these **inseparable phrasal verbs,** you do not have a choice about where to place the object; the object must always follow the preposition. For example, "<u>Anna</u> *cared for* her niece" is correct, but "<u>Anna</u> *cared* her niece *for*" is incorrect.

Close-up: Inseparable Phrasal Verbs	
Verb	**Definition**
come down with	develop an illness
come up with	produce
do away with	abolish
fall behind in	lag
get along with	be congenial with
get away with	avoid punishment
keep up with	maintain the same achievement or speed
look up to	admire
make up for	compensate
put up with	tolerate
run into	meet by chance
see to	arrange
show up	arrive
stand by	wait or remain loyal to
stand up for	support
watch out for	beware of or protect

(6) Voice

Verbs may be in either active or passive <u>voice</u>. When the subject of a sentence performs the action of the verb, the verb is in **active voice.** When the action of the verb is performed on the subject, the verb is in **passive voice.**

See 7d

> <u>Karla and Miguel</u> <u>purchased</u> the plane tickets. (active voice)

> <u>The plane tickets</u> <u>were purchased</u> by Karla and Miguel. (passive voice)

Because your writing will usually be clearer and more concise if you use the active voice, you should use the passive voice only when you have a good reason to do so. For example, in scientific writing, it is common for writers to use the passive voice in order to convey the idea of scientific objectivity (lack of bias).

(7) Transitive and Intransitive Verbs

Many nonnative English speakers find it difficult to decide whether or not a verb needs an object and in what order direct and indirect objects should appear in a sentence. Learning the difference between transitive verbs and intransitive verbs can help you with such problems.

A **transitive verb** is a verb that has a direct object: "My father asked a question" (subject + verb + direct object). In this example, *asked* is a transitive verb; it needs an object to complete its meaning.

An **intransitive verb** is a verb that does not take an object: "The doctor smiled" (subject + verb). In this example, *smiled* is an intransitive verb; it does not need an object to complete its meaning.

A transitive verb may be followed by a direct object or by both an indirect object and a direct object. (An indirect object answers the question "To whom?" or "For whom?") The indirect object may come before or after the direct object. If the indirect object follows the direct object, the preposition *to* or *for* must precede the indirect object.

  s   v   do
Keith wrote a letter. (subject + verb + direct object)

  s   v   io   do
Keith wrote his friend a letter. (subject + verb + indirect object + direct object)

  s   v   do   io
Keith wrote a letter *to* his friend. (subject + verb + direct object + *to/for* + indirect object)

Some verbs in English look similar and have similar meanings, except that one is transitive and the other is intransitive. For example, *lie* is intransitive, *lay* is transitive; *sit* is intransitive, *set* is transitive; *rise* is intransitive, *raise* is transitive. Knowing whether a verb is transitive or intransitive will help you with troublesome verb pairs like these and help you place the words in the correct order.

NOTE: It is also important to know whether a verb is transitive or intransitive because only transitive verbs can See 7d be used in the passive voice. To determine whether a verb is transitive or intransitive—that is, to determine whether or not it needs an object—consult the example phrases in a dictionary.

43b Solving Noun-Related Problems

A <u>noun</u> names things: people, animals, objects, places, feelings, ideas. If a noun names one thing, it is <u>singular</u>; if a noun names more than one thing, it is <u>plural</u>.

See 22b7

See A1.1

(1) Recognizing Noncount Nouns

Some English nouns do not have a plural form. These are called **noncount nouns** because what they name cannot be counted.

Close-up: Noncount Nouns

The following commonly used nouns are non-count nouns. These words have no plural forms. Therefore, you should never add -*s* to them.

advice	homework
clothing	information
education	knowledge
equipment	luggage
evidence	merchandise
furniture	revenge

---

(2) Using Articles with Nouns

English has two **articles,** indefinite and definite.

Use an **indefinite article** (*a* or *an*) with a noun when readers are not familiar with the noun you are naming—when you are introducing the noun for the first time, for example. To say, "Jatin entered *a* building," signals to the audience that you are introducing the idea of the building for the first time. The building is indefinite, or not specific, until it has been identified.

The indefinite article *a* is used when the word following it (which may be a noun or an adjective) begins with a consonant or with a consonant sound: *a tree, a onetime offer.* The indefinite article *an* is used if the word following it begins with a vowel (*a, e, i, o,* or *u*) or with a vowel sound: *an apple, an honor.*

Use the **definite article** (*the*) when the noun you are naming has already been introduced, when the noun is already familiar to readers, or when the noun to which you refer is specific. To say, "Jatin entered *the* building," signals to readers that you are referring to the same building you mentioned earlier. The building has now become specific and may be referred to by the definite article.

Close-up: Using Articles with Nouns

There are two exceptions to the rules governing the use of articles with nouns:

1. **Plural** nouns do not require **indefinite articles:** "I love horses," not "I love <u>a</u> horses." (Plural nouns do, however, require definite articles: "I love <u>the</u> horses in the national park near my house.")
2. **Noncount nouns** may not require articles: "Love conquers all," not "<u>A</u> love conquers all" or " <u>The</u> love conquers all."

---

(3) Using Other Determiners with Nouns

^{ESL}
_{43d} **Determiners** are words that function as <u>adjectives</u> to limit or qualify the meaning of nouns. In addition to articles, **demonstrative pronouns, possessive nouns and pronouns, numbers** (both **cardinal** and **ordinal**), and other words indicating *number* and *order* can function in this way.

Close-up: Using Other Determiners with Nouns

- **Demonstrative pronouns** (*this, that, these, those*) communicate
  1. the relative nearness or farness of the noun from the speaker's position (*this* and *these* for things that are *near, that* and *those* for things that are *far*): *this* book on my desk, *that* book on your desk; *these* shoes on my feet, *those* shoes in my closet.
  2. the *number* of things indicated (*this* and *that* for *singular* nouns, *these* and *those* for *plural* nouns): *this* (or *that*) flower in the vase, *these* (or *those*) flowers in the garden.
- **Possessive nouns** and **possessive pronouns** (*Ashraf's, his, their*) show who or what the noun belongs to: *Maria's* courage, *everybody's* fears, the *country's* natural resources, *my* personality, *our* groceries.

- **Cardinal** numbers (*three, fifty, a thousand*) indicate how many of the noun you mean: *seven* continents. **Ordinal** numbers (*first, tenth, thirtieth*) indicate in what order the noun appears among other items: *third* planet.
- Words other than numbers may indicate **amount** (*many, few*) and **order** (*next, last*) and function in the same ways as cardinal and ordinal numbers: *few* opportunities, *last* chance.

43c   Using Pronouns

Any English noun may be replaced by a <u>pronoun</u>. Pronouns enable you to avoid repeating a noun over and over. For example, *doctor* may be replaced by *he* or *she*, *books* by *them*, and *computer* by *it*.

See A1.2

(1) Pronoun Reference

<u>Pronoun reference</u> is very important in English sentences, where the noun the pronoun replaces (the **antecedent**) must be easily identified. In general, you should place the pronoun as close as possible to the noun it replaces so the noun to which the pronoun refers is clear. If this is impossible, use the noun itself instead of replacing it with a pronoun.

See 8c

Unclear: When Tara met Emily, she was nervous. (Does *she* refer to Tara or to Emily?)

Clear: When Tara met Emily, Tara was nervous.

Unclear: Stefano and Victor love his DVD collection. (Whose DVD collection—Stefano's, Victor's, or someone else's?)

Clear: Stefano and Victor love Emilio's DVD collection.

(2) Pronoun Placement

Never use a pronoun immediately after the noun it replaces. For example, do not say, "Most of my classmates they are smart"; instead, say, "Most of my classmates are smart." The only exception to this rule occurs with an **intensive pronoun,** which ends in *-self* and emphasizes the preceding noun or pronoun: "Marta *herself* was eager to hear the results."

(3) Indefinite Pronouns

Unlike **personal pronouns** (*I, you, he, she, it, we, they, me, him, her, us,* and *them*), **indefinite pronouns** do not refer to a particular person, place, or thing. Therefore, an indefinite pronoun does not require an antecedent. **Indefinite pronoun subjects** (*anybody, nobody, each, either, someone, something, all, some*), like personal pronouns, must <u>agree</u> in number with the sentence's verb.

See 6b

> *has*
> Nobody ~~have~~ failed the exam. (*Nobody* is a singular subject and requires a singular verb.)

(4) Appositives

Appositives are nouns or noun phrases that identify or rename an adjacent noun or pronoun. An appositive usually follows the noun it explains or modifies but can sometimes precede it.

> My parents, Mary and John, live in Louisiana. (*Mary and John* identifies *parents.*)

See 8a

NOTE: The <u>case</u> of a pronoun in an appositive depends on the case of the word it describes.

If an appositive is *not* necessary to the meaning of the sentence, use commas to set off the appositive from the rest of the sentence. If an appositive *is* necessary to the meaning of the sentence, do not use commas.

> His aunt Trang is in the hospital. (*Trang* is necessary to the meaning of the sentence because it identifies which aunt is in the hospital.)

> Akta's car, a 1994 Jeep Cherokee, broke down last night, so she had to walk home. (*a 1994 Jeep Cherokee* is not necessary to the meaning of the sentence.)

(5) Pronouns and Gender

A pronoun must agree in **gender** with the noun to which it refers.

> My *sister* sold *her* old car.

> Your *uncle* is walking *his* dog.

NOTE: In English, most nonhuman nouns are referred to as *it* because they do not have grammatical gender. However, exceptions are sometimes made for pets, ships, and countries. Pets are often referred to as *he* or *she*, depending on their sex, and ships and countries are sometimes referred to as *she*.

43d Using Adjectives and Adverbs

See
A1.
4–5;
Ch. 9

Adjectives and adverbs are words that **modify** (describe, limit, or qualify) other words.

(1) Position of Adjectives and Adverbs

Adjectives in English usually appear *before* the nouns they modify. A native speaker of English would not say, "*Cars red and black* are involved in more accidents than *cars blue or green*" but would say instead, "*Red and black cars* are involved in more accidents than *blue or green cars.*"

However, adjectives may appear *after* linking verbs ("The name seemed *familiar*"), *after* direct objects ("The coach found them *tired* but *happy*."), and *after* indefinite pronouns ("Anything *sad* makes me cry.")

Adverbs may appear before or after the verbs they describe, but they should be placed as close to the verb as possible: not "I *told* John that I couldn't meet him for lunch *politely*," but "I *politely told* John that I couldn't meet him for lunch" or "I *told* John *politely* that I couldn't meet him for lunch." When an adverb describes an adjective or another adverb, it usually comes *before* that adjective or adverb: "The essay has *basically sound* logic"; "You must express yourself *absolutely clearly*." Never place an adverb between the verb and the direct object.

Incorrect: Rolf drank *quickly* the water.

Correct: Rolf drank the water *quickly* (or, Rolf *quickly* drank the water).

Incorrect: Suong took *quietly* the test.

Correct: Suong *quietly* took the test (or, Suong took the test *quietly*.)

(2) Order of Adjectives

A single noun may be modified by more than one adjective, perhaps even by a whole list of adjectives. Given a list of three or four adjectives, most native speakers would arrange them in a sentence in the same order. If, for example shoes are to be described as *green* and *big*, numbering *two*, and of the type worn for playing *tennis*, a native speaker would say "two big green tennis shoes." Generally, the adjectives that are most important in completing the meaning of the noun are placed closest to the noun.

Close-up: Order of Adjectives

1. Articles (*a*, *the*), demonstratives (*this*, *those*), and possessives (*his*, *our*, *Maria's*, *everybody's*)
2. Amounts (*one*, *five*, *many*, *few*), order (*first*, *next*, *last*)
3. Personal opinions (*nice*, *ugly*, *crowded*, *pitiful*)
4. Sizes and shapes (*small*, *tall*, *straight*, *crooked*)
5. Age (*young*, *old*, *modern*, *ancient*)
6. Colors (*black*, *white*, *red*, *blue*, *dark*, *light*)
7. Nouns functioning as adjectives to form a unit with the noun (*soccer* ball, *cardboard* box, *history* class)

43e Using Prepositions

See A1.6 In English, <u>prepositions</u> (such as *to*, *from*, *at*, *with*, *among*, *between*) give meaning to nouns by linking them with other words and other parts of the sentence. Prepositions convey several different kinds of information:

- Relations to **time** (*at* nine o'clock, *in* five minutes, *for* a month)
- Relations of **place** (*in* the classroom, *at* the library, *beside* the chair) and **direction** (*to* the market, *onto* the stage, *toward* the freeway)
- Relations of **association** (go *with* someone, the tip *of* the iceberg)
- Relations of **purpose** (working *for* money, dieting *to* lose weight)

(1) Commonly Used Prepositional Phrases

In English, the use of prepositions is often idiomatic rather than governed by grammatical rules. In many cases, therefore, learners of English as a second language need to memorize which prepositions are used in which phrases.

In English, some prepositions that relate to time have specific uses with certain nouns, such as days, months, and seasons:

- *On* is used with days and specific dates: *on* Monday, *on* September 13, 1977.
- *In* is used with months, seasons, and years: *in* November, *in* the spring, *in* 1999.
- *In* is also used when referring to some parts of the day: *in* the morning, *in* the afternoon, *in* the evening.
- *At* is used to refer to other parts of the day: *at* noon, *at* night, *at* seven o'clock.

Close-up: Difficult Prepositional Phrases

The following phrases (accompanied by their correct prepositions) sometimes cause difficulties for ESL writers:

according *to*	*at* least	relevant *to*
apologize *to*	*at* most	similar *to*
appeal *to*	refer *to*	subscribe *to*
different *from*		

---

(2) Commonly Confused Prepositions

The prepositions *to*, *in*, *on*, *into*, and *onto* are very similar to one another and are therefore easily confused.

Close-up: Basic Definitions of Common Prepositions

- *To* is the basic preposition of direction. It indicates movement toward a physical place: "She went *to* the restaurant"; "He went *to* the meeting." *To* is also used to form the infinitive of a verb: "He wanted *to deposit* his paycheck before noon"; "Irene offered *to drive* Maria to the baseball game."
- *In* indicates that something is within the boundaries of a particular space or period of time: "My son is *in* the garden"; "I like to ski *in* the winter"; "The map is *in* the car."
- *On* indicates position above or the state of being supported by something: "The toys are *on* the porch"; "The baby sat *on* my lap"; "The book is *on* top of the magazine."
- *Into* indicates movement to the inside or interior of something: "She walked *into* the room"; "I threw the stone *into* the lake"; "He put the photos *into* the box."

(continued)

Basic definitions of common prepositions
(continued)

Although *into* and *in* are sometimes interchangeable, note that usage depends on whether the subject is stationary or moving. *Into* usually indicates movement, as in "I jumped *into* the water." *In* usually indicates a stationary position relative to the object of the preposition, as in "Mary is swimming *in* the water."

- *Onto* indicates movement to a position on top of something: "The cat jumped *onto* the chair"; "Crumbs are falling *onto* the floor." Both *on* and *onto* can be used to indicate a position on top of something (and therefore they can sometimes be used interchangeably), but *onto* specifies that the subject is moving to a place from a different place or from an outside position.

Close-up: Prepositions in Idiomatic Expressions

Common Nonnative Speaker Usage	Native Speaker Usage
according *with*	according *to*
apologize *at*	apologize *to*
appeal *at*	appeal *to*
believe *at*	believe *in*
different *to*	different *from*
for least, *for* most	*at* least, *at* most
refer *at*	refer *to*
relevant *with*	relevant *to*
similar *with*	similar *to*
subscribe *with*	subscribe *to*

43f Understanding Word Order

In English, word order is extremely important, contributing a good deal to the meaning of a sentence.

(1) Standard Word Order

Like Chinese, English is an "SVO" language, or one in which the most typical sentence pattern is "subject-verb-object." (Arabic, by contrast, is an example of a "VSO" language.) Deviation from the SVO pattern tends to confuse English speakers.

(2) Word Order in Questions

Word order in questions can be particularly troublesome for speakers of languages other than English, partly because there are so many different ways to form questions in English.

Close-up: Word Order in Questions

1. To create a **yes/no question** from a statement using the verb *be*, simply invert the order of the subject and the verb:

   <u>Rasheem is</u> researching the depletion of the ozone layer.

   <u>Is Rasheem</u> researching the depletion of the ozone layer?

2. To create a **yes/no question** from a statement using a verb other than *be*, use a form of the auxiliary verb *do* before the sentence without inverting the subject and verb:

   <u>Does</u> Rasheem want to research the depletion of the ozone layer?

   <u>Do</u> Rasheem's friends want to help him with his research?

   <u>Did</u> Rasheem's professors approve his research proposal?

3. You can also form a question by adding a **tag question**—such as *won't he?* or *didn't I?*—to the end of a statement. If the verb of the main statement is *positive*, then the verb of the tag question is *negative*; if the verb of the main statement is *negative*, then the verb of the tag question is *positive:*

   Rasheem <u>is</u> researching the depletion of the ozone layer, <u>isn't he</u>?

   Rasheem <u>doesn't</u> intend to write his dissertation about the depletion of the ozone layer, <u>does</u> he?

4. To create a **question asking for information, use interrogative** words (*who, what, where, when, why, how*), and invert the order of the subject and verb (note that *who* functions as the subject of the question in which it appears):

   <u>Who is</u> researching the depletion of the ozone layer?

   <u>What is Rasheem</u> researching?

   <u>Where is Rasheem</u> researching the depletion of the ozone layer?

A1 Parts of Speech

The **part of speech** to which a word belongs depends on its function in a sentence.

(1) Nouns

Nouns name people, animals, places, things, ideas, actions, or qualities.

A **common noun** names any of a class of people, places, or things: *artist, judge, building, event, city.*

A **proper noun,** always <u>capitalized</u>, refers to a particular person, place, or thing: *Mary Cassatt, World Trade Center, Crimean War.*   <small>See 23a</small>

A **collective noun** designates a group thought of as a unit: *committee, class, family.*

An **abstract noun** refers to an intangible idea or quality: *love, hate, justice, anger, fear, prejudice.*

(2) Pronouns

Pronouns are words used in place of nouns. The noun for which a pronoun stands is its **antecedent.**

Although different types of pronouns may have the same form, they are distinguished from one another by their function in a sentence.

A **personal pronoun** stands for a person or thing: *I, me, we, us, my, mine, our, ours, you, your, yours, he, she, it, its, him, his, her, hers, they, them, their, theirs.*

The firm made Debbie an offer, and <u>she</u> couldn't refuse <u>it</u>.

An <u>indefinite pronoun</u> does not refer to any particular person or thing, so it does not require an antecedent. Indefinite pronouns include *another, any, each, few, many, some, nothing, one, anyone, everyone, everybody, everything, someone, something, either,* and *neither.*   <small>See 6a4, 6b3</small>

<u>Many</u> are called, but <u>few</u> are chosen.

A **reflexive pronoun** ends with -*self* and refers to a recipient of the action that is the same as the actor: *myself, yourself, himself, herself, itself, oneself, themselves, ourselves, yourselves.*

They found <u>themselves</u> in downtown Pittsburgh.

Intensive pronouns have the same form as reflexive pronouns. An intensive pronoun emphasizes a preceding noun or pronoun.

Darrow <u>himself</u> was sure his client was innocent.

A **relative pronoun** introduces an adjective or noun clause in a sentence. Relative pronouns include *which, who, whom, that, what, whose, whatever, whoever, whomever,* and *whichever.*

Gandhi was the man <u>who</u> led India to independence. (introduces adjective clause)

<u>Whatever</u> happens will be a surprise. (introduces noun clause)

An **interrogative pronoun** introduces a question. Interrogative pronouns include *who, which, what, whom, whose, whoever, whatever,* and *whichever.*

<u>Who</u> was that masked man?

A **demonstrative pronoun** points to a particular thing or group of things. *This, that, these,* and *those* are demonstrative pronouns.

<u>This</u> is one of Shakespeare's early plays.

A **reciprocal pronoun** denotes a mutual relationship. The reciprocal pronouns are *each other* and *one another. Each other* indicates a relationship between two individuals; *one another* denotes a relationship among more than two.

Cathy and I respect <u>each other</u> for our differences.

Many of our friends do not respect <u>one another</u>.

(3) Verbs

Verbs can be classified into two groups: *main verbs* and *auxiliary verbs.*

Main Verbs **Main verbs** carry most of the meaning in a sentence or clause. Some main verbs are action verbs.

He <u>ran</u> for the train. (physical action)

He <u>thought</u> about taking the bus. (emotional action)

Other main verbs are linking verbs. A **linking verb** does not show any physical or emotional action. Its function is to link the subject to a **subject complement,** a word or phrase that renames or describes the subject. Linking verbs include *be, become,* and *seem* and verbs that describe sensations—*look, appear, feel, taste, smell,* and so on.

Carbon disulfide <u>smells</u> bad.

Auxiliary Verbs **Auxiliary verbs** (also called **helping verbs**), such as *be* and *have,* combine with main verbs to form **verb phrases.** Auxiliary verbs indicate tense, voice, or mood.

[auxiliary] [main verb] [auxiliary] [main verb]

The train <u>has started</u>. We <u>are leaving</u> soon.

[verb phrase]   [verb phrase]

Certain auxiliary verbs, known as **modal auxiliaries,** indicate necessity, possibility, willingness, obligation, or ability. These include *must, shall, might, will, should, can, would, may, could, need* [to], and *ought* [to].

Verbals **Verbals,** such as *known* or *running* or *to go,* are verb forms that act as adjectives, adverbs, or nouns. A verbal can never serve as a sentence's main verb unless it is used with one or more auxiliary verbs (*He is running*). Verbals include *participles, infinitives,* and *gerunds.*

Participles

Virtually every verb has a **present participle,** which ends in *-ing* (*loving, learning*) and a **past participle,** which usually ends in *-d* or *-ed* (*agreed, learned*). Some verbs have <u>irregular</u> past participles (*gone, begun, written*). Participles may function in a sentence as adjectives or as nouns.

See 7a

Twenty brands of <u>running</u> shoes were on display. (participle serves as adjective)

The <u>wounded</u> were given emergency first aid. (participle serves as noun)

Infinitives

An **infinitive** is made up of *to* and the base form of the verb (*to defeat*). An infinitive may function as an adjective, an adverb, or a noun.

Ann Arbor was clearly the place <u>to be</u>. (infinitive serves as adjective)

Carla went outside <u>to think</u>. (infinitive serves as adverb)

<u>To win</u> was everything. (infinitive serves as subject)

Gerunds

Gerunds, which like present participles end in *-ing*, always function as nouns.

<u>Seeing</u> is <u>believing</u>.

Andrew loves <u>skiing</u>.

(4) Adjectives

Adjectives describe, limit, qualify, or in some other way modify nouns or pronouns.

Descriptive adjectives name a quality of the noun or pronoun they modify.

After the game, they were <u>exhausted</u>.

They ordered a <u>chocolate</u> soda and a <u>butterscotch</u> sundae.

When articles, pronouns, numbers, and the like function as adjectives, limiting or qualifying nouns or pronouns, they are referred to as <u>determiners</u>.

ESL
43b3

(5) Adverbs

Adverbs describe the action of verbs or modify adjectives or other adverbs (or complete phrases, clauses, or sentences). They answer the questions "How?" "Why?" "When?" "Under what conditions?" and "To what extent?"

He walked <u>rather hesitantly</u> toward the front of the room.

Let's meet <u>tomorrow</u> for coffee.

Adverbs that modify other adverbs or adjectives limit or qualify the words they modify.

He pitched an <u>almost perfect</u> game yesterday.

Interrogative Adverbs   The **interrogative adverbs** (*how, when, why,* and *where*) introduce questions.

See
3b

Conjunctive Adverbs   **Conjunctive adverbs** act as <u>transitional words</u>, joining and relating independent clauses.

Frequently Used Conjunctive Adverbs			
accordingly	furthermore	meanwhile	similarly
also	hence	moreover	still
anyway	however	nevertheless	then
besides	incidentally	next	thereafter
certainly	indeed	nonetheless	therefore
consequently	instead	now	thus
finally	likewise	otherwise	undoubtedly

(6) Prepositions

A **preposition** introduces a noun or pronoun (or a phrase or clause functioning in the sentence as a noun), linking it to other words in the sentence. The word or word group that the preposition introduces is its **object**.

$$\text{prep} \quad \text{obj} \qquad\qquad \text{prep} \quad \text{obj}$$

They received a postcard <u>from</u> Bobby telling <u>about</u> his trip.

Frequently Used Prepositions			
about	beneath	inside	since
above	beside	into	through
across	between	like	throughout
after	beyond	near	to
against	by	of	toward
along	concerning	off	under
among	despite	on	underneath
around	down	onto	until
as	during	out	up
at	except	outside	upon
before	for	over	with
behind	from	past	within
below	in	regarding	without

(7) Conjunctions

Conjunctions connect words, phrases, clauses, or sentences.

Coordinating Conjunctions **Coordinating conjunctions** (*and, or, but, nor, for, so, yet*) connect words, phrases, or clauses of equal weight.

Should I order chicken <u>or</u> fish?

Thoreau wrote *Walden* in 1854, <u>and</u> he died in 1862.

Correlative Conjunctions Always used in pairs, **correlative conjunctions** also link items of equal weight.

<u>Both</u> Hancock <u>and</u> Jefferson signed the Declaration of Independence.

<u>Either</u> I will renew my lease, <u>or</u> I will move.

Frequently Used Correlative Conjunctions	
both . . . and	neither . . . nor
either . . . or	not only . . . but also
just as . . . so	whether . . . or

Subordinating Conjunctions Words such as *since, because,* and *although* are **subordinating conjunctions.** They introduce adverb clauses and thus connect the sentence's independent (main) clause to a dependent (subordinate) clause to form a <u>complex sentence</u>.

See 10a2

<u>Although</u> people may feel healthy, they can still have medical problems.

It is best to diagram your garden <u>before</u> you start to plant.

(8) Interjections

Interjections are words used as exclamations to express emotion: *Oh! Ouch! Wow! Alas! Hey!*

A2 Sentences

(1) Basic Sentence Elements

A **sentence** is an independent grammatical unit that contains a <u>subject</u> (a noun or noun phrase) and a <u>predicate</u> (a verb or verb phrase) and expresses a complete thought.

<u>The quick brown fox</u> <u>jumped over the lazy dog</u>.

<u>It</u> <u>came from outer space</u>.

(2) Basic Sentence Patterns

A **simple sentence** consists of at least one subject and one predicate. Simple sentences conform to one of five patterns.

Subject + Intransitive Verb (s + v)

$$\underset{\text{s}}{\underline{\text{Stock prices}}} \; \underset{\text{v}}{\underline{\text{may fall}}}.$$

Stock prices may fall.

Subject + Transitive Verb + Direct Object (s + v + do)

Van Gogh created *The Starry Night*.
s   v   do

Caroline saved Jake.
s   v   do

Subject + Transitive Verb + Direct Object + Object Complement (s + v + do + oc)

I found the exam easy.
s   v   do   oc

The class elected Bridget treasurer.
s   v   do   oc

Subject + Linking Verb + Subject Complement (s + v + sc)

The injection was painless.
s   v   sc

Tony Blair became prime minister.
s   v   sc

Subject + Transitive Verb + Indirect Object + Direct Object (s + v + io + do)

Cyrano wrote Roxanne a poem. (Cyrano wrote a poem *for* Roxanne.)
s   v   io   do

Hester gave Pearl a kiss. (Hester gave a kiss *to* Pearl.)
s   v   io   do

(3) Phrases and Clauses

Phrases A **phrase** is a group of related words that lacks a subject or predicate or both and functions as a single part of speech. It cannot stand alone as a sentence.

A **verb phrase** consists of a **main verb** and all its auxiliary verbs. (Time *is flying*.) A **noun phrase** includes a noun or pronoun plus all related modifiers. (I'll climb *the highest mountain*.)

A **prepositional phrase** consists of a <u>preposition</u>, its object, and any modifiers of that object (They considered the ethical implications *of the animal studies*). See A1.6

See
A1.3
A **verbal phrase** consists of a <u>verbal</u> and its related objects, modifiers, or complements. A verbal phrase may be a **participial phrase** (*encouraged by the voter turnout*), a **gerund phrase** (*taking it easy*), or an **infinitive phrase** (*to evaluate the evidence*).

An **absolute phrase** usually consists of a noun and a participle, accompanied by modifiers. It modifies an entire independent clause rather than a particular word or phrase.

<u>Their toes tapping</u>, they watched the auditions.

Clauses A **clause** is a group of related words that includes a subject and a predicate. An **independent** (main) **clause** may stand alone as a sentence, but a **dependent** (subordinate) **clause** cannot. It must always be combined See
10a2 with an independent clause to form a <u>complex sentence</u>.

[Lucretia Mott was an abolitionist.] [She was also a pioneer for women's rights.] (two independent clauses)

[Lucretia Mott was an abolitionist] [who was also a pioneer for women's rights.] (independent clause, dependent clause)

Dependent clauses may be *adjective*, *adverb*, or *noun* clauses.

Adjective clauses, sometimes called **relative clauses,** modify nouns or pronouns and always follow the nouns or pronouns they modify. They are introduced by relative pronouns—*that, what, which, who,* and so forth—or by the adverbs *where* and *when*.

Celeste's grandparents, <u>who were born in Romania</u>, speak little English.

Adverb clauses modify verbs, adjectives, adverbs, entire phrases, or independent clauses. They are always introduced by subordinating conjunctions.

Mark will go <u>wherever there's a party</u>.

Noun clauses function as subjects, objects, or complements. A noun clause may be introduced by a relative pronoun or by *whether; when, where, why,* or *how*.

<u>What you see</u> is <u>what you get</u>.

(4) Types of Sentences

A **simple sentence** is a single independent clause. A simple sentence can consist of just a subject and a predicate.

Jessica <u>fell</u>.

Or, a simple sentence can be expanded with modifying words and phrases.

Jessica fell in love with the mysterious Henry Goodyear on Halloween.

A <u>compound sentence</u> consists of two or more simple sentences linked by a coordinating conjunction (preceded by a comma), by a semicolon (alone or followed by a transitional word or phrase), by correlative conjunctions, or by a colon. See 10a1

[The moon rose in the sky], <u>and</u> [the stars shone brightly].

[José wanted to spend a quiet afternoon]; <u>however</u>, [his aunt surprised him with a new set of plans.]

A <u>complex sentence</u> consists of an independent clause along with one or more dependent clauses. See 10a2

independent clause   dependent clause
[It was hard for us to believe] [that anyone could be so cruel].

A **compound-complex sentence** is a compound sentence—made up of at least two independent clauses—that also includes at least one dependent clause.

[My mother always worried] [when my father had to work late], and [she could rarely sleep more than a few minutes at a time].

Sentences can also be classified according to their function. **Declarative sentences** make statements; they are the most common. **Interrogative sentences** pose questions, usually by inverting standard subject-verb order (often with an interrogative word) or by adding a form of *do* (*Is Maggie at home? Where is Maggie? Does Maggie live here?*). **Imperative sentences** express commands or requests, using the second-person singular of the verb and generally omitting the pronoun subject *you* (*Go to your room. Please believe me.*). **Exclamatory sentences** express strong emotion and end with an exclamation point (*The killing must stop now!*).

Usage Review

This usage review lists words and phrases that are often troublesome for writers.

a, an   Use *a* before words that begin with consonants and words that have initial vowels that sound like consonants: *a* person, *a* one-horse carriage, *a* uniform. Use *an* before words that begin with vowels and words that begin with a silent *h*: *an* artist, *an* honest person.

accept, except   *Accept* is a verb that means "to receive"; *except* can be a preposition, a conjunction, or a verb. As a preposition or conjunction, *except* means "other than," and as a verb, it means "to leave out": The auditors will *accept* all your claims *except* the last two. Some businesses are *excepted* from the regulation.

advice, advise   *Advice* is a noun meaning "opinion or information offered"; *advise* is a verb that means "to offer advice to": The broker *advised* her client to take his attorney's *advice*.

affect, effect   *Affect* is a verb meaning "to influence"; *effect* can be a verb or a noun. As a verb it means "to bring about," and as a noun it means "result": We know how the drug *affects* patients immediately, but little is known of its long-term *effects*. The arbitrator tried to *effect* a settlement between the parties.

all ready, already   *All ready* means "completely prepared"; *Already* means "by or before this or that time": I was *all ready* to help, but it was *already* too late.

all right, alright   Although the use of *alright* is increasing, current usage calls for *all right*.

allusion, illusion   An *allusion* is a reference or hint; an *illusion* is something that is not what it seems: The poem makes an *allusion* to the Pandora myth. The shadows created an optical *illusion*.

a lot   *A lot* is always two words.

among, between   *Among* refers to groups of more than two things; *between* refers to just two things: The three parties agreed *among* themselves to settle the case. There will be a brief intermission *between* the two acts.

amount, number *Amount* refers to a quantity that cannot be counted; *number* refers to things that can be counted: Even a small *amount* of caffeine can be harmful. Seeing their commander fall, a large *number* of troops ran to his aid.

an, a See **a, an**.

and/or In business or technical writing, use *and/or* when either or both of the items it connects can apply. In college writing, however, the use of *and/or* should generally be avoided.

as . . . as . . . In such constructions, *as* signals a comparison; therefore, you must always use the second *as*: *East of Eden* is *as* long *as The Grapes of Wrath*.

as, like *As* can be used as a conjunction (to introduce a complete clause) or as a preposition; *like* should be used as a preposition only: In *The Scarlet Letter*, Hawthorne uses imagery *as* (not *like*) he does in his other works. After classes, Amy works *as* a manager of a fast-food restaurant. Writers *like* Carl Sandburg appear once in a generation.

at, to Many people use the prepositions *at* and *to* after *where* in conversation: *Where* are you working *at? Where* are you going *to?* This usage is redundant and should not appear in college writing.

bad, badly *Bad* is an adjective, and *badly* is an adverb: The school board decided that *Huckleberry Finn* was a *bad* book. American automobile makers did not do *badly* this year. After verbs that refer to any of the senses or after any other linking verb, use the adjective form: He looked *bad*. He felt *bad*. It seemed *bad*.

being as, being that These awkward phrases add unnecessary words and weaken your writing. Use *because* instead.

beside, besides *Beside* is a preposition meaning "next to"; *besides* can be either a preposition meaning "except" or "other than," or an adverb meaning "as well": *Beside* the tower was a wall that ran the length of the city. *Besides* its industrial uses, laser technology has many other applications. Edison invented not only the lightbulb but the phonograph *besides*.

between, among See **among, between**.

bring, take *Bring* means to transport from a farther place to a nearer place; *take* means to carry or convey from a nearer place to a farther one: *Bring* me a souvenir from your trip. *Take* this message to the general, and wait for a reply.

can, may *Can* denotes ability, and *may* indicates permission: If you *can* play, you *may* use my piano.

capital, capitol *Capital* refers to a city that is an official seat of government; *capitol* refers to a building in which a legislature meets: Washington, DC, is the *capital* of the United States. When we were there, we visited the *Capitol* building.

center around This imprecise phrase is acceptable in speech and informal writing but not in college writing. Use *center on* instead.

cite, site *Cite* is a verb meaning "to quote as an authority or example"; *site* is a noun meaning "a place or setting": Jeff *cited* five sources in his research paper. The builder cleared the *site* for the new bank.

climactic, climatic *Climactic* means "of or related to a climax"; *climatic* means "of or related to climate": The *climactic* moment of the movie occurs unexpectedly. If scientists are correct, the *climatic* conditions of Earth are changing.

coarse, course *Coarse* is an adjective meaning "inferior" or "having a rough, uneven texture"; *course* is a noun meaning "a route or path," "an area on which a sport is played," or "a unit of study": *Coarse* sandpaper is used to smooth the surface. The *course* of true love never runs smoothly. Last semester I had to drop a *course*.

complement, compliment *Complement* means "to complete or add to"; *compliment* means "to give praise": A double-blind study would *complement* their preliminary research. My instructor *complimented* me on my improvement.

conscious, conscience *Conscious* is an adjective meaning "having one's mental faculties awake"; *conscience* is a noun that means the moral sense of right and wrong: The patient will remain *conscious* during the procedure. His *conscience* wouldn't allow him to lie.

continual, continuous *Continual* means "recurring at intervals"; *continuous* refers to an action that occurs without interruption: A pulsar is a star that emits a *continual* stream of electromagnetic radiation. (It emits radiation at regular intervals.) A small battery allows the watch to run *continuously* for five years. (It runs without stopping.)

could of, should of, would of The contractions *could've*, *should've*, and *would've* are often misspelled as the nonstandard constructions *could of, should of,* and *would of.* Use *could have, should have,* and *would have* in college writing.

council, counsel A *council* is "a body of people who serve in a legislative or advisory capacity"; *counsel* means "to offer advice or guidance": The city *council* argued about the proposed ban on smoking. The judge *counseled* the couple to settle their differences.

couple of *Couple* means "a pair," but *couple of* is used colloquially to mean "several" or "a few." In your college writing, specify "four points" or "two examples" rather than using "a couple of."

criterion, criteria *Criteria*, from the Greek, is the plural of *criterion*, meaning "standard for judgment": Of all the *criteria* for hiring graduating seniors, class rank is the most important *criterion*.

data *Data* is the plural of the Latin *datum*, meaning "fact." In everyday speech and writing, *data* is used for both singular and plural. In college writing, you should use *data* only for the plural: The *data* discussed in this section *are* summarized in Appendix A.

different from, different than *Different than* is widely used in American speech. In college writing, use *different from*.

disinterested, uninterested *Disinterested* means "objective" or "capable of making an impartial judgment"; *uninterested* means "indifferent or unconcerned": The American judicial system depends on *disinterested* jurors. Finding no treasure, Hernando de Soto was *uninterested* in going farther.

don't, doesn't *Don't* is the contraction of *do not; doesn't* is the contraction of *does not*. Do not confuse the two: My dog *doesn't* (not *don't*) like to walk in the rain.

effect, affect See **affect, effect.**

e.g. *E.g.* is an abbreviation for the Latin *exempli gratia*, meaning "for example" or "for instance." In college writing, do not use *e.g.* Instead, use its English equivalent.

emigrate from, immigrate to To *emigrate* is "to leave one's country and settle in another"; to *immigrate* is "to come to another country and reside there." The noun forms of these words are *emigrant* and *immigrant*: My great-grandfather *emigrated from* Warsaw along with many other *emigrants* from Poland. Many people *immigrate* to the United States for economic reasons, but such *immigrants* still face great challenges.

enthused *Enthused*, a colloquial form of *enthusiastic*, should not be used in college writing.

etc. *Etc.*, the abbreviation of *et cetera*, means "and the rest." Do not use it in your college writing. Instead, say "and so on" or, better, specify exactly what *etc.* stands for.

everyday, every day *Everyday* is an adjective that means "ordinary" or "commonplace"; *every day* means "occurring daily": In the Gettysburg Address, Lincoln used *everyday* language. She exercises almost *every day*.

everyone, every one *Everyone* is an indefinite pronoun meaning "every person"; *every one* means "every individual or thing in a particular group": *Everyone* seems happier in the spring. *Every one* of the packages had been opened.

except, accept See **accept, except.**

explicit, implicit *Explicit* means "expressed or stated directly"; *implicit* means "implied" or "expressed or stated indirectly": The director *explicitly* warned the actors to be on time for rehearsals. Her *implicit* message was that lateness would not be tolerated.

farther, further *Farther* designates distance; *further* designates degree: I have traveled *farther* from home than any of my relatives. Critics charge that welfare subsidies encourage *further* dependence.

fewer, less Use *fewer* with nouns that can be counted: *fewer* books, *fewer* people, *fewer* dollars. Use *less* with quantities that cannot be counted: *less* pain, *less* power, *less* enthusiasm.

firstly (secondly, thirdly, . . .) Archaic forms meaning "in the first . . . second . . . third place." Use *first, second, third.*

further, farther See **farther, further.**

good, well *Good* is an adjective, never an adverb: She is a *good* swimmer. *Well* can function as an adverb or as an adjective. As an adverb it means "in a good manner": She swam *well* (not *good*) in the meet. *Well* is used as an adjective with verbs that denote a state of being or feeling. Here *well* can mean "in good health": I feel *well*.

got to *Got to* is not acceptable in college writing. To indicate obligation, use *have to, has to,* or *must.*

hanged, hung Both *hanged* and *hung* are past participles of *hang. Hanged* is used to refer to executions; *hung* is used to mean "suspended": Billy Budd was *hanged* for killing the master-at-arms. The stockings were *hung* by the chimney with care.

he, she Traditionally *he* has been used in the generic sense to refer to both males and females. To acknowledge the equality of the sexes, however, avoid the generic *he.* Use plural pronouns whenever possible. **See 15c2.**

hopefully The adverb *hopefully*, meaning "in a hopeful manner," should modify a verb, an adjective, or another adverb. Do not use *hopefully* as a sentence modifier meaning "it is hoped." Rather than "*Hopefully*, scientists will soon discover a cure for AIDS," write "Scientists *hope* they will soon discover a cure for AIDS."

i.e. The abbreviation *i.e.* stands for the Latin *id est*, meaning "that is." In college writing, do not use *i.e.* Instead, use its English equivalent.

if, whether When asking indirect questions or expressing doubt, use *whether*: He asked *whether* (not *if*) the flight would be delayed. The flight attendant was not sure *whether* (not *if*) it would be delayed.

illusion, allusion See **allusion, illusion.**

immigrate to, emigrate from See **emigrate from, immigrate to.**

implicit, explicit See **explicit, implicit.**

imply, infer *Imply* means "to hint" or "to suggest"; *infer* means "to conclude from": Mark Antony *implied* that the conspirators had murdered Caesar. The crowd *inferred* his meaning and called for justice.

infer, imply See **imply, infer.**

inside of, outside of *Of* is unnecessary when *inside* and *outside* are used as prepositions. *Inside of* is colloquial in references to time: He waited *inside* (not *inside of*) the coffee shop. He could run a mile in *under* (not *inside of*) eight minutes.

irregardless, regardless *Irregardless* is a nonstandard version of *regardless*. Use *regardless* instead.

is when, is where These constructions are faulty when they appear in definitions: A playoff *is* an additional game played to establish the winner of a tie. (not "A playoff *is when* an additional game is played. . . . ")

its, it's *Its* is a possessive pronoun; *it's* is a contraction of *it is*: It's no secret that the bank is out to protect *its* assets.

kind of, sort of *Kind of* and *sort of* to mean "rather" or "somewhat" are colloquial and should not appear in college writing: It is well known that Napoleon was *rather* (not *kind of*) short.

lay, lie See **lie, lay.**

leave, let *Leave* means "to go away from" or "to let remain"; *let* means "to allow" or "to permit": *Let* (not *leave*) me give you a hand.

less, fewer   See **fewer, less.**

let, leave   See **leave, let.**

lie, lay   *Lie* is an intransitive verb (one that does not take an object) that means "to recline." Its principal forms are *lie, lay, lain, lying:* Each afternoon she would *lie* in the sun and listen to the surf. *As I Lay Dying* is a novel by William Faulkner. By 1871, Troy had *lain* undisturbed for two thousand years. The painting shows a nude *lying* on a couch.

    Lay is a transitive verb (one that takes an object) meaning "to put" or "to place." Its principal forms are *lay, laid, laid, laying:* The Federalist Papers *lay* the foundation for American conservatism. In October of 1781, the British *laid* down their arms and surrendered. He had *laid* his money on the counter before leaving. We watched the stonemasons *laying* a wall.

like, as   See **as, like.**

loose, lose   *Loose* is an adjective meaning "not rigidly fastened or securely attached"; *lose* is a verb meaning "to misplace": The marble facing of the building became *loose* and fell to the sidewalk. After only two drinks, most people *lose* their ability to judge distance.

lots, lots of, a lot of   These words are colloquial substitutes for *many, much,* or *a great deal of.* Avoid their use in college writing: This point of view has many (not *lots of* or *a lot of*) advantages.

man   Like the generic pronoun *he, man* has been used in English to denote members of both sexes. This usage is being replaced by *human beings, people,* or similar terms that do not specify gender. **See 15c2.**

may, can   See **can, may.**

may be, maybe   *May be* is a verb phrase; *maybe* is an adverb meaning "perhaps": She *may be* the smartest student in the class. *Maybe* her experience has given her an advantage.

media, medium   *Medium,* meaning a "means of conveying or broadcasting something," is singular; *media* is the plural form and requires a plural verb: The *media* have distorted the issue.

might have, might of   *Might of* is a nonstandard spelling of the contraction of *might have* (*might've*).

number, amount   See **amount, number.**

OK, O.K., okay   All three spellings are acceptable, but this term should be avoided in college writing. Replace it with a more specific word or words: The lecture was *adequate* (not *okay*), if uninspiring.

outside of, inside of See **inside of, outside of.**

passed, past *Passed* is the past tense of the verb *pass; past* means "belonging to a former time" or "no longer current": The car must have been going eighty miles per hour when it *passed* us. In the envelope was a bill marked *past* due.

percent, percentage *Percent* indicates a part of a hundred when a specific number is referred to: "*10%* of his salary." *Percentage* is used when no specific number is referred to: "a *percentage* of next year's receipts." In technical and business writing, it is permissible to use the % sign after percentages you are comparing. In other college writing, % is acceptable only when used with a numeral (6%).

precede, proceed *Precede* means "to go or come before"; *proceed* means "to go forward in an orderly way": Robert Frost's *North of Boston* was *preceded* by an earlier volume. In 1532, Francisco Pizarro landed at Tumbes and *proceeded* south.

principal, principle As a noun, *principal* means "a sum of money (minus interest) invested or lent" or "a person in the leading position"; as an adjective it means "most important." A *principle* is a rule of conduct or a basic truth: He wanted to reduce the *principal* of the loan. The *principal* of the high school is a talented administrator. Women are the *principal* wage earners in many American households. The Constitution embodies certain fundamental *principles*.

quote, quotation *Quote* is a verb. *Quotation* is a noun. In college writing, do not use *quote* as a shortened form of *quotation*: Scholars attribute those *quotations* (not *quotes*) to Shakespeare.

raise, rise *Raise* is a transitive verb, and *rise* is an intransitive verb—that is, *raise* takes an object, and *rise* does not: My grandparents *raised* a large family. The sun will *rise* at 6:12 this morning.

real, really *Real* means "genuine" or "authentic"; *really* means "actually." In your college writing, do not use *real* as an adjective meaning "very."

reason is that, reason is because *Reason* should be used with *that* and not with *because*, which is redundant: The *reason* he left *is that* (not *is because*) you insulted him.

regardless, irregardless See **irregardless, regardless.**

respectably, respectfully, respectively *Respectably* means "worthy of respect"; *respectfully* means "giving honor or deference"; *respectively* means "in the order given": He skated quite *respectably* at his first Olympics. The seminar taught us to treat others *respectfully*. The first- and second-place winners were Tai and Kim, *respectively.*

rise, raise See **raise, rise.**

set, sit *Set* means "to put down" or "to lay." Its principal forms are *set* and *setting:* After rocking the baby to sleep, he *set* her down carefully in her crib. *Sit* means "to assume a sitting position." Its principal forms are *sit, sat, sat,* and *sitting:* Many children *sit* in front of the television five to six hours a day.

shall, will *Will* has all but replaced *shall* to express all future action.

should of See **could of, should of, would of.**

since Do not use *since* for *because* if there is any chance of confusion. In the sentence "*Since* President Nixon traveled to China, trade between China and the United States has increased," *since* could mean either "from the time that" or "because."

sit, set See **set, sit.**

so Avoid using *so* alone as a vague intensifier meaning "very" or "extremely." Follow *so* with *that* and a clause that describes the result: She was *so* pleased with their work *that* she took them out to lunch.

sometime, sometimes, some time *Sometime* means "at some time in the future"; *sometimes* means "now and then"; *some time* means "a period of time": The president will address Congress *sometime* next week. All automobiles, no matter how reliable, *sometimes* need repairs. It has been *some time* since I read that book.

sort of, kind of See **kind of, sort of.**

take, bring See **bring, take.**

than, then *Than* is a conjunction used to indicate a comparison; *then* is an adverb indicating time: The new shopping center is bigger *than* the old one. He did his research; *then*, he wrote a report.

that, which, who Use *that* or *which* when referring to a thing; use *who* when referring to a person: It was a speech *that* inspired many. The movie, *which* was a huge success, failed to impress her. Anyone *who* (not *that*) takes the course will benefit.

their, there, they're *Their* is a possessive pronoun; *there* indicates place and is also used in the expressions *there is* and *there are*; *they're* is a contraction of *they are:* Watson and Crick did *their* DNA work at Cambridge University. I love Los Angeles, but I wouldn't want to live *there*. *There* is nothing we can do to resurrect an extinct species. When *they're* well treated, rabbits make excellent pets.

themselves; theirselves, theirself *Theirselves* and *theirself* are nonstandard variants of *themselves.*

then, than See **than, then.**

till, until, 'til *Till* and *until* have the same meaning, and both are acceptable. *Until* is preferred in college writing. *'Til*, a contraction of *until*, should be avoided.

to, at See **at, to.**

to, too, two *To* is a preposition that indicates direction; *too* is an adverb that means "also" or "more than is needed"; *two* expresses the number 2: Last year we flew from New York *to* California. "Tippecanoe and Tyler, *too*" was Harrison's campaign slogan. The plot was *too* complicated for the average reader. Just north of *Two* Rivers, Wisconsin, is a petrified forest.

try to, try and *Try and* is the colloquial equivalent of *try to:* He decided to *try to* (not *try and*) do better.

-type Deleting this empty suffix eliminates clutter and clarifies meaning: Found in the wreckage was an *incendiary* (not *incendiary-type*) device.

uninterested, disinterested See **disinterested, uninterested.**

unique Because *unique* means "the only one," not "remarkable" or "unusual," you should never use constructions like "the most unique" or "very unique."

until See **till, until, 'til.**

utilize In most cases, it is best to replace *utilize* with *use* (*utilize* often sounds pretentious).

wait for, wait on To *wait for* means "to defer action until something occurs." To *wait on* means "to act as a waiter": I am *waiting for* (not *on*) dinner.

weather, whether *Weather* is a noun meaning "the state of the atmosphere"; *whether* is a conjunction used to introduce an alternative: The *weather* outside is frightful, but the fire inside is delightful. It is doubtful *whether* we will be able to ski tomorrow.

well, good   See **good, well.**

were, we're   *Were* is a verb; *we're* is the contraction of *we are:* The Trojans *were* asleep when the Greeks attacked. We must act now if *we're* going to succeed.

whether, if   See **if, whether.**

which, who, that   See **that, which, who.**

who, whom   When a pronoun serves as the subject of its clause, use *who* or *whoever*; when it functions in a clause as an object, use *whom* or *whomever:* Sarah, *who* is studying ancient civilizations, would like to visit Greece. Sarah, *whom* I met in France, wants me to travel to Greece with her.

who's, whose   *Who's* means "who is"; *whose* indicates possession: *Who's* going to take calculus? The writer *whose* book was in the window was autographing copies.

will, shall   See **shall, will.**

would of   See **could of, should of, would of.**

your, you're   *Your* indicates possession, and *you're* is the contraction of *you are:* You can improve *your* stamina by jogging two miles a day. *You're* certain to be the winner.

Credits

This page constitutes an extension of the copyright page. We have made every effort to trace the ownership of all copyrighted material and to secure permission from copyright holders. In the event of any question arising as to the use of any material, we will be pleased to make the necessary corrections in future printings. Thanks are due to the following authors, publishers, and agents for permission to use the material indicated.

Text and Illustrations

p. 136: Excerpt from "Freedom of Hate Speech?" by Phil Sudo from *Scholastic Update*, 124.14 (1992), pp. 17–20. Copyright © 1992 by Scholastic Inc. Reprinted by permission of Scholastic Inc.

p. 154: Figure 29.1. Screen shot used by permission of the University of Texas Libraries, The University of Texas at Austin.

p. 162: Figure 30.1. Screen shot from <http://home.netscape.com>. An AOL company.

p. 163: Figure 30.2. Screen shot reproduced with permission of Yahoo! Inc. YAHOO! and the YAHOO! logo are trademarks of Yahoo! Inc.

p. 310: Figure 38.4. Screen shot reprinted by permission of the Lyric Opera of Waco.

p. 314: Figure 39.1. Screen shot courtesy of Chris Rusu. Accessed 8/4/2004.

Photos

Part Openers
p. 1: © Photodisc Green/Getty Images; **p. 123:** © Photodisc Red/Getty Images; **p. 179:** © John Coletti; **p. 297:** © Taxi/Getty Images; **p. 331:** © NASA Goddard Space Flight Center. Image by Reto Stockli. Enhancement by Robert Simmon

Icons
Computer tips, p. iii: © Keith Brofsky/PhotoDisc/Getty Images
Grammar checker, p. iii: © Siede Preis/Photodisc/Getty Images
Checklists, p. iv: © John Coletti
Close-up, p. iv: © Photodisc/Getty Images
Print sources, p. iv: © Simon Battensby/Stone/Getty Images
ESL tips, p. v: © NASA Goddard Space Flight Center. Image by Reto Stockli. Enhancement by Robert Simmon

Photos
Chapter 38, p. 311: Figure 38.5. Courtesy of Deb Martin
Chapter 40, p. 316: Figure 40.1. © Ken Reid/The Image Bank/Getty Images; **p. 321:** Figure 40.2. © David Chasey/PhotoDisc Green/Getty Images

Index

Note: Page numbers in blue refer to definitions.

A, an, use as articles, 360
A lot, 360
A lot of, lots, lots of, 366
Abbreviation(s), 78–79, 117–20
  acronyms, 78, 118
  addresses, 78, 79, 119
  editing misused, 119–20
  measurements before, 121
  in MLA-style paper, 79, 118–19
  organization names, 78, 118
  with periods, 78
  without periods, 78–79, 118
  titles of people, 74, 78, 86, 109–10, 117–18
-able, -ible endings, 108
Absolute phrase(s), 85, 358
Abstract(s), 150
  APA reference list, 243
  APA-style paper, 248
  CSE documentation style, 289
  in online databases, 150
Abstract noun(s), 351
Abstract word(s), 72
Academic course(s)
  abbreviating, 119
  capitalizing, 111
  requirements of, 4, 300
Academic degree(s)
  abbreviating, 78, 86, 110, 117–18
  capitalizing, 110
  commas with, 86
Academic success, 298–305
  active learning, 300–02
  college services, 302
  contacts, 304
  library resources, 303
  lifelong learning, 304–05
  school and course requirements, 300
  study as priority, 299
  technological competence, 303–04
  time management, 298–99
Accept, except, 360
Accuracy, 166
Acronym(s), 78, 118
Action verb(s), 51
Active learning, 300–02
Active voice, 44–45, 64–65, 71, 339
AD, 118
Address(es). *See also* Electronic address
  abbreviations in, 78, 79, 119
  commas in, 86
  numbers in, 121
Adjective(s), 50–53, 345, 354
  comparative degree, 51–53
  compound, 116
  coordinate, 81
  descriptive, 354

order of, 345–46
position of, 345–46
proper, 111
superlative degree, 51–53
using, 50–51
Adjective (relative) clause(s), 358
  commas with, 62, 83
  eliminating, 62
  in formation of complex sentences, 27–28
  misplaced, revising, 70
Adverb(s), 50–53, 345, 354
  comparative degree, 51–53
  conjunctive, 354–55
  interrogative, 354
  position of, 345
  superlative degree, 51–53
  using, 51
Adverb clause(s), 70, 358
Adverbial conjunction(s). *See* Conjunctive
    adverb(s)
Advertisement(s), MLA works-cited list, 202
Advice, advise, 360
Affect, effect, 360
Afterword
  APA reference list, 237
  MLA works-cited list, 193
Agreement, 32–38
  in number, 32–38
  in person, 32–38, 336
  pronoun-antecedent, 35, 36–38, 48–50,
    65
  subject-verb, 32–36, 336
Aircraft, italicizing names of, 113
All ready, already, 360
All right, alright, 360
Allusion, illusion, 360
Almanacs, 152–53
a.m., 118
Ambiguous antecedent(s), 48–49
American Psychological Association (APA).
    See APA documentation style
Among, between, 360
Amount, number, 361
Amount, numbers to indicate, 343
Ampersand, in APA in-text citations, 233
An, a, use as articles, 360
And
  compound subjects joined by, 33
  in series, comma with, 88
AND, as Boolean operator, 149, 151, 162
And/or, 361
Annotated bibliography, 127–28
Anonymous/unsigned work(s)
  APA in-text citations, 234
  APA reference list, 237, 242
  Chicago-style endnotes and bibliography,
    268
  CSE reference list, 287

MLA parenthetical references, 186
MLA works-cited list, 195–96, 198–99
Antecedent(s), 35, 48, 351
    agreement with pronouns, 35, 36–38,
        48–50, 65
    ambiguous, 48–49
    collective noun, 37
    compound, 36
    indefinite pronoun, 37
    nonexistent, 49–50
    pronoun, 343
    relative pronoun, 35–36
    remote, 49
Anthology(ies)
    APA reference list, 237–38
    Chicago-style endnotes and bibliographies,
        266
    MLA works-cited list, 194–95
APA documentation style, 230–59
    content footnotes, 243
    defined, 232
    in-text citations, 232–35
    manuscript guidelines, 244–46
    numbers versus numerals in, 120
    parenthetical references, 232–35
    reference list, 236–43, 246, 258–59
    sample research paper, 246–59
Apostrophe(s), 90–92
    editing misused, 92
    in forming plurals, 92
    to indicate omissions, 91–92
    in possessive case, 90–91
Appositive(s), 344
    commas with, 83
    creating, for concise sentences, 62
    explanatory material, 99
    fragments, revising, 30
    pronoun case in, 47–48
Art
    italicizing titles of, 113
    MLA works-cited list, 202, 206–07
Article(s) (grammatical), 360
    with nouns, 341–42
    in titles of works, 111–12, 199, 269
Article(s) (publications). *See* Journal article(s);
    Magazine article(s); Newsletter
    article(s); Newspaper article(s)
As
    comparisons with, 47
    paired elements linked by, 67
As, like, 361
As . . . as . . . , in comparisons, 361
At, as preposition, 347
At, to, 361
Atlas(es), 153
    CSE reference list, 288
    MLA works-cited list, 207
Audience, 3
    academic, 4–6
    for essay, 3–6
    identifying, 3–6
    for oral presentation, 324

Audiocassette recording(s)
    APA reference list, 240
    CSE reference list, 288
Author name(s)
    APA in-text citations, 232–35
    APA reference list, 236–43
    Chicago-style endnotes and bibliographies,
        263–74
    CSE reference list, 285
    MLA parenthetical references, 185–86,
        188
    MLA works-cited list, 191–92
AutoCorrect tool, 109, 213
Auxiliary (helping) verb(s), 337, 353
    in forming verb phrases, 337
    modal, 337, 353
Awkward sentence(s), 64–66

Bad, badly, 361
Base form, 38–41
BC, 118
BCE, 118
Be
    as auxiliary (helping) verb, 336
    faulty predication, 66
Being as, being that, 361
Beside, besides, 361
Between, among, 360
Biased language, 74–75
Bible
    abbreviating books of, 188
    capitalizing name of, 111
    Chicago-style endnotes and bibliographies,
        266
    MLA parenthetical references, 188
    MLA works-cited list, 194
    periods to mark divisions in, 79
Bibliography(ies) (documentation styles)
    APA reference list, 236–43, 246, 258–59
    Chicago-style, 263–74, 276, 281
    CSE reference list, 284–89, 293
    MLA works-cited list, 190–210, 212–13,
        227–29
Bibliography(ies) (reference tools)
    general, 151–52
    specialized, 151
Bibliography(ies) (student)
    formatting, 126–28
    working, 126–28
Bilingual writer(s). *See* ESL (English as a
    Second Language) tip(s); ESL (English
    as a Second Language) writer(s)
Biographical references, 152
Body paragraph(s), 19–24
    essay, 8, 19–24
    oral presentation, 325
    research paper, 142
    unified, 20
    well-developed, 22
    when to begin new paragraph, 19–20
Book(s)
    APA reference list, 236–38

Book(s) *(continued)*
   Chicago-style endnotes and bibliographies,
     263–66
   CSE reference list, 284–86, 288–89
   italicizing titles of, 112
   in library research, 153, 154
   MLA parenthetical references, 185–89
   MLA works-cited list, 190–97, 205
   in online catalogs, 153, 154
   in working bibliography, 126
Book review(s), MLA works-cited list, 199,
   205–06
Bookmark, 164
Boolean operators, 149, 151, 162
Boolean search, 149, 151, 162
Borrowed word(s), 97, 174–77
Bracket(s)
   with additional ellipses in quotation, 171
   to indicate additions to quotations, 102
   to indicate omissions in quoted passage,
     104
   to indicate substitutions within quotations,
     102
   to replace parentheses within parentheses,
     102
   to set off comments within quotations, 102
Brainstorming, 7
Brand names, capitalizing, 111
Bring, take, 361
Business letter(s). *See also* Workplace
    communication
   follow-up, 318
   format of, 100, 317
   job application, 316–18
Button(s), in Web site design, 314
Byline(s), APA-style paper, 244, 247

Call number(s), 153
Can, may, 362
Capital, capitol, 362
Capitalization, 109–12. *See also* Proper
    adjective(s); Proper noun(s); *specific*
    documentation styles
   of abbreviations, 109–10
   with colons, 99
   of course names, 111
   editing misused capitals, 112
   of important words in titles, 111–12, 190
   of material within parentheses, 101
Caption(s), in APA-style paper, 245
Cardinal number(s), as determiners, 343
Cartoon(s), MLA works-cited list, 202, 207
Case, 45–48, 344. *See also specific types of case*
CBE documentation style. *See* CSE
    documentation style
CD(s), APA reference list, 240
CD-ROMs
   MLA works-cited list, 210
   reference works on, 151
CE, 118
Center around, 362
Chapter(s)
   APA in-text citations, 234

Chicago-style endnotes and bibliographies,
   266
   CSE reference list, 285–86, 286
   quotation marks for titles, 97
Chemistry, style manual, 294
Chicago documentation style, 260–81
   bibliography, 263–74, 276, 281
   defined, 261
   endnotes and footnotes, 261, 262, 263–74,
     276, 280
   manuscript guidelines, 274–76
   sample research paper, 276–81
Chicago Manual of Style. See Chicago
    documentation style
Circumlocution, eliminating, 60–61
Citation-sequence format, in CSE
    documentation style, 283, 284–89,
    290–93
Cite, site, 362
Cited in, APA-style paper, 251
Civic groups, capitalizing names of, 111
Classical literature, CSE reference list, 286
Clause(s), 358. *See also specific types of clause*
   nonrestrictive/restrictive, 50, 83
   in series, 67
   types of, 358
Clichés, 73
Climactic, climatic, 362
Clipped form(s), 79
Coarse, course, 362
Coherent paragraphs, 20–22
   key words and phrases in, 21–22
   parallel structure in, 21–22
   transitional words and phrases in, 20–22
Coinage, 97
Collaborative work. *See also* Peer review
   study groups, 299, 304
Collection of work(s), MLA works-cited list,
   194–95, 200–01
Collective noun(s), 34–35, 351
   as antecedents, 37
   fixed amounts as, 35
   subject-verb agreement with, 34–35
College services, 302
Colon(s), 99–100
   in business letters, 100
   capitalization with, 99
   in compound sentences, 56
   editing misused, 100
   for emphasis, 100
   with identifying tags for quoted passages,
    94
   to introduce lists, 30, 89, 99
   to introduce quotations, 99
   to introduce series, 99
   to set off explanations, 99
Color
   defined, 306
   in document design, 306
Comic strip(s), MLA works-cited list, 202,
   207
Comma(s), 80–87
   in addresses, 86

with adjective clauses, 62, 83
between coordinating elements, 81
in dates, 86
between dependent and independent clauses, 57
before dependent clauses at end of sentence, 87
editing misused, 87
with identifying tags for quoted passages, 93–95, 170
with personal titles, 86
to prevent misreading, 86–87
with quotation marks, 86, 89, 93–96, 97
to set off independent clauses, 27, 56, 80–81, 87
to set off introductory elements, 82
to set off items in series, 81–82
to set off nonessential material, 82–85
with *that*, 50, 84, 170
with transitional elements, 27, 31, 50, 82, 85
Comma splice(s), 26–28, 88
Command(s), exclamation points for, 80
Comment(s)
of instructor, 10, 143–44
in peer review, 5–6, 10, 144–46
within quotations, 102
Comment feature, 143
Common knowledge, 174
Common noun(s), 351
Comparative degree, 51–53
Comparison(s)
as . . . as . . . , 361
with *than* or *as,* 47
with *who* and *whom,* 47
Complement(s). *See* Subject complement(s)
Complement, compliment, 362
Complex sentence(s), 57, 359
as concise sentences, 62
constructing, 27–28, 57
relative clauses in formation of, 27–28, 57
subordinating conjunctions in formation of, 27–28, 57
using, 57
Compound adjective(s), 116
Compound antecedents, 36
Compound-complex sentence(s), 359
Compound construction(s). *See also specific types*
objective case in, 46
Compound noun(s), 90–91, 108
Compound sentence(s), 56, 359
constructing, 62, 80–81
excessive coordination, eliminating, 62
using, 56
Compound subject(s), 33
Compound word(s), 115–17
adjectives, 116
dividing, 115–17
fractions, 117
nouns, 90–91
numerals, 117
Computer(s). *See also* Computer software; Computer tip(s)
managing printouts, 134–35

note-taking and, 132, 133, 134–35
technological competence and, 303–04
Computer software. *See also* Grammar checker(s); Spell checker(s); *specific software names*
APA reference list, 241
italicizing titles of, 113
personal organizer, 298
presentation, 327
visuals and, 308–12, 327
Computer tip(s)
capitalization errors, 109
editing, 12
electronic addresses, dividing, 115
formatting features, 306
outline file, 141
plagiarism avoidance, 176
proofreading, 12
revising, 147
Concise sentence(s), 59–63
Concluding paragraph(s)
of essay, 8, 23–24
of oral presentation, 325
of research paper, 142
Concrete word(s), 72
Conditional statements, 44
Conference(s), with instructor, 333
Confusing sentence(s), 64–66
Conjunction(s), 355–56. *See also specific types of conjunction*
Conjunctive adverb(s), 354–55
Connotation, 71–72
Conscious, conscience, 362
Consistency, of headings, 307
Contacts, 304
Content note(s)
APA documentation style, 243
MLA documentation style, 187, 210–11, 226
Continual, continuous, 362
Contraction(s), 91–92
Contradiction, commas with contradictory phrases, 85
Coordinate adjective(s), 81
Coordinate elements, 67, 81–82. *See also* Coordination; *specific types*
Coordinating conjunction(s), 56, 355
commas before, 81
in compound sentences, 56, 80
list of, 27, 355
in revising comma splices, 27
in revising fused sentences, 27
in revising run-on sentences, 27
in titles of works, 111–12
Coordination, 58
to combine sentences, 58
excessive, eliminating, 62
Copyright, Web sites and, 312–13
Corporate author(s)
APA in-text citations, 234
APA reference list, 237
Chicago-style endnotes and bibliographies, 264–65

Corporate author(s) *(continued)*
MLA parenthetical references, 188–89
MLA works-cited list, 192
Correlative conjunction(s), 356
in compound sentences, 33, 56, 80
paired items linked by, 67
Could of, should of, would of, 362
Council, counsel, 363
Council of Biology Editors (CBE). *See* CSE
documentation style
Council of Science Editors (CSE). *See* CSE
documentation style
Couple, couple of, 363
Course, coarse, 362
Course names. *See* Academic course(s)
Coverage, 168
Credibility, 166–67
Criterion, criteria, 363
Critical thinking, in research papers, 124
Cross-references, parentheses with, 101
CSE documentation style, 283–93
citation-sequence format, 283, 284–89,
290–93
defined, 283
in-text, 283–84
manuscript guidelines, 289–90
name-year format, 283–84
reference list, 284–89, 293
sample research paper, 290–93
Currency, 156, 168

Dangling modifier(s), 70–71
Dash(es), 100
for emphasis, 100
to indicate interruptions, 101
with quotation marks, 97–98
to set off nonessential material, 100
to set off summaries, 101
Data, 363
Database(s). *See* Online database(s)
Date(s). *See also* Publication date(s)
abbreviating, 118
commas in, 86
numbers in, 121
parentheses with, 102
questionable, marking, 79
Days of the week
abbreviating, 119
capitalizing names of, 110
Deadwood, eliminating, 59–60
Decimal(s), numbers in, 121
Declarative sentence(s), 359
Def. (definition), MLA works-cited list,
195–96
Definite article(s), 341–42
Definition(s)
italics or underlining in, 114
quoting dictionary, 114, 195–96
Delivery, of oral presentation, 329–30
Demonstrative pronoun(s), 352
as determiners, 343
list of, 352
Denotation, 71–72

Dependent (subordinate) clause(s), 28–29,
358
avoiding commas before, 82
commas before ending, 87
commas with introductory, 82
in complex sentences, 57
as introductory elements, 82
as modifiers, 70
as sentence fragments, 28–29, 30
Descriptive adjective(s), 354
Design. *See* Document design; Web site
design
Determiner(s), 342–43
Diagram(s), in document design, 309–10
Dialogue, 93–96
interruptions in, 101
quotation marks with, 93–96
Diction, 71–75
biased language, 74
inappropriate language, 73
informal, 98
word choice, 71–75
Dictionary(ies)
connotations, 72
definitions in MLA works-cited list, 195–96
quoting definitions from, 114, 195–96
specialized, 151, 152
unabridged, 152
Different from, different than, 363
Direct address, commas with names in, 85
Direct object(s), 46, 357
Direct question(s), question marks with, 79
Direct quotation(s)
colons to introduce, 99
commas with, 86, 89
identifying tags with, 86
quotation marks with, 93–96
when to use, 93–96, 171–72
Direction, in thesis statement, 9
Discussion list(s), 164–65, 204
Disinterested, uninterested, 363
Diskette(s), MLA works-cited list, 201, 210
Dissertation(s), MLA works-cited list, 196
Document design, 305–12. *See also* Web site
design
APA manuscript guidelines, 244–46
Chicago manuscript guidelines, 274–76
CSE manuscript guidelines, 289–90
effective format in, 305–06
headings in, 306–08
lists in, 307–08
MLA manuscript guidelines, 211–13
visuals in, 308–12
in Web site design, 312–15
Document name(s), capitalizing, 110
Documentation, 4, 183
to avoid plagiarism, 175–76
in idea generation stage, 176–77
Documentation style(s). *See* APA
documentation style; Chicago
documentation style; CSE
documentation style; MLA
documentation style

Don't, doesn't, 363
Double negative(s), 337
Drafting, 9
  essay, 9
  final draft, 147
  instructor comments in, 10
  peer review in, 5
  research paper, 141–43, 147
  rough draft, 9, 141–43, 147
  in writing process, 332
Dramatic work(s). *See also* Literature
  italicizing titles of, 113
  MLA parenthetical references, 187–88
  MLA works-cited list, 194–95
  periods to mark divisions in, 79
DVD(s) (digital videodiscs)
  Chicago-style endnotes and bibliography, 270
  CSE reference list, 288
  MLA works-cited list, 201, 210
  reference works on, 151

-e endings, 107
Each, with compound antecedents, 36
Ed./Eds. (edited by), MLA works-cited list, 192
Edited work(s)
  APA reference list, 237
  Chicago-style endnotes and bibliographies, 265
  CSE reference list, 285
  MLA works-cited list, 192
Editing, 11. *See also* Revision
  ESL writers and, 334–35
  essay, 11–12
  research paper, 147
  Web site, 314
Editorial(s), MLA works-cited list, 199
Effect, affect, 360
e.g. (for example), 363
ei, ie combinations, 107
Either . . . or, 33, 56
Electronic address. *See also* URL (uniform resource locator)
  divisions of, 79, 115, 203, 241
  entering, 161
Electronic résumés, 318, 320
Electronic source(s), 150–51. *See also* Internet research; Online catalog(s); Online database(s); Source(s)
  APA in-text citations, 235
  APA reference list, 241–43
  Chicago-style endnotes and bibliographies, 271–74
  CSE reference list, 288–89
  evaluating, 166–68
  in library research, 148–49, 150, 151, 154–55
  MLA parenthetical references, 189–90
  MLA works-cited list, 202–10
  online catalogs, 148–49, 153, 154
  online databases, 150–51, 154–55, 207–09, 243

Electronic version, APA documentation style, 241–42
Ellipses, 103–04, 171–72
Email
  APA in-text citations, 234
  APA reference list, 242
  Chicago-style endnotes and bibliography, 273
  MLA works-cited list, 204
  as research tool, 164
  in the workplace, 323
  writing, 323
Embedding, 58
Emigrate from, immigrate to, 363
Emphasis
  colons for, 100
  dashes for, 100
  exclamation points for, 80
  italics for, 114
  in thesis statement, 9
Encyclopedia(s)
  general, 151
  MLA works-cited list, 206
  specialized, 151
End punctuation. *See* Exclamation point(s); Period(s); Question mark(s)
Endnote(s), 261
  Chicago documentation style, 261, 262, 263–74, 276, 280
  MLA documentation style, 187, 210–11, 226
English as a Second Language (ESL). *See* ESL (English as a Second Language) tip(s); ESL (English as a Second Language) writer(s)
Enthused, 363
Entire works, MLA parenthetical references, 188
-er, in comparative degree, 51–53
ESL (English as a Second Language) tip(s). *See also* ESL (English as a Second Language) writer(s)
  adjective placement, 345
  adverb placement, 345
  connotations, 72
  idea generation, 7
  instructor expectations, 300, 301
  oral presentations, 330
  plagiarism avoidance, 134, 138, 174
  varying sentences, 58
  writing labs, 302
ESL (English as a Second Language) writer(s), 331–49. *See also* ESL (English as a Second Language) tip(s)
  adjusting to the US classroom, 332–35
  capitalization issues, 112
  editing and, 334–35
  English languages basics and, 334
  nouns, 341–43
  prepositions, 346–48
  pronouns, 343–45
  spelling issues, 334
  understanding writing process, 332–33

ESL writer(s) *(continued)*
using native language, 333
verbs, 336–41
word order, 334, 345–46, 348–49
Essay(s), 6–19
audience for, 3–6
Chicago-style endnotes and bibliographies,
266
drafting, 9
editing, 11–12
idea generation for, 7
MLA works-cited list, 194–95
outlines of, 9
paragraphs, 8, 10, 19–24
planning, 6–7, 9
proofreading, 11–12
purpose of, 2–3
quotation marks for titles, 96
revising, 9–11
sample essay, 13–19
shaping, 7–9
thesis and support in, 7–9
title selection for, 11
topic selection for, 6–7
-est, in superlative degree, 51–53
Et al.
APA documentation style, 233, 237
MLA documentation style, 186, 191
Etc. (and so forth), 363
Ethnic group(s)
capitalizing names of, 110
offensive labels, 74
Euphemism(s), 72
Evaluation, 127
of Internet sites, 166–68
Evaluation *(continued)*
of sources, 156–58, 166–68
Evaluative writing, 2
Event names, capitalizing, 110
Every, with compound antecedents, 36
Everyday, every day, 364
Everyone, 37, 75
Everyone, every one, 364
Exact time(s), numbers in, 121
Except, accept, 360
Exclamation(s), avoiding question marks
after, 80
Exclamation point(s)
with quotation marks, 94, 97–98
using, 80
Exclamatory sentence(s), 359
Explanation(s), colons to set off, 99
Explicit, implicit, 364
Exploratory research, 125–26
in library, 151–52
working bibliography in, 126–28

-f, -fe endings, plurals with, 108
Fair use doctrine, 313
Farther, further, 364
Faulty modification, 68–71
Faulty parallelism, 67–68
Faulty predication, 66

Fewer, less, 364
Fiction. *See* Literature; Prose
Fig. (Figure), with MLA-style visuals, 212
Figure(s)
in APA-style paper, 245, 257
in Chicago-style paper, 275
in CSE documentation style, 290, 292
in MLA-style paper, 212, 219
Film(s)
APA reference list, 240
CSE reference list, 288
italicizing titles of, 113
MLA works-cited list, 201
Final draft, research paper, 147
Find command, 12
Firstly (secondly, thirdly,...), 364
Fixed amounts, as collective nouns, 35
Focused research, 129–31. *See also* Research
in library, 152–53
note-taking in, 131–38
primary sources in, 130–31
reading sources in, 129–30
secondary sources in, 130–31
Follow-up letter(s), 318
Footnote(s)
APA documentation style, 243
Chicago documentation style, 261, 262,
263–74, 276, 280
MLA documentation style, 187, 210–11,
226
Foreign words and phrase(s). *See also* Latin
expression(s)
foreign plurals, 108
italics to set off, 113–14
Foreword
APA reference list, 237
MLA works-cited list, 193
Formal outline(s), 139–41
Format
of APA-style research paper, 236, 244–59
of business letters, 100, 317
of Chicago-style research paper, 274–81
of CSE-style research paper, 289–93
of essay, 13–19
of follow-up letters, 318
of job application letters, 317
of long quotations within paper, 95, 99,
171, 185, 211, 222–23, 232, 244
of memos, 321–22
of MLA-style research paper, 211–29
of résumés, 318–20
of student bibliographies, 126–28
Fraction(s), hyphenating compound, 117
Fragment(s), 28–32. *See also* Phrase
fragment(s)
Freewriting, 7
FTP (file transfer protocol), 165, 315
Further, farther, 364
Fused sentence(s), 26–28, 88
Future perfect progressive tense, 43
Future perfect tense, 43
Future progressive tense, 43
Future tense, 42

Gender
  pronoun, 344–45
  sexist language, 37, 74–75
General reference works, 151–52
General word(s), 72
Generic *he, him*, 74, 75
Geographical regions, capitalizing names of, 110
Geology, style manual, 294
Gerund(s)
  defined, 354
  possessive case before, 46–47
Gerund phrase(s), 358
Good, well, 364
Got to, 364
Government agencies, capitalizing names of, 111
Government document(s)
  APA reference list, 238
  Chicago-style endnotes and bibliographies, 270
  finding, 156
  MLA parenthetical references, 188–89
  MLA works-cited list, 196–97, 206
  style manuals, 294
Grammar. *See* Parts of speech; *specific concepts*
Grammar checker(s)
  checking quotation marks, 94
  comma splices, 26
  contractions, revising, 92
  faulty parallelism, 68
  hyphenating compound words, 116
  passive construction, eliminating, 63
  pronoun-antecedent agreement, 38
  redundancy, deleting, 61
  semicolons, misused, 89
  sentence fragments, 29
  spelled-out numbers, 121
  subject-verb agreement, 34
  that and *which*, 84
Graph(s)
  in document design, 309
  sample, 310

Hanged, hung, 364
He, him, generic, 74, 75
He, she, 364
He or she, 74
Heading(s)
  APA-style paper, 244
  consistency of, 307
  in document design, 306–08
  indentation of, 307
  number of, 307
  phrasing of, 307
  research paper, 142, 244
  subject, 151
  typographical emphasis in, 307
  uses of, 306–07
Headword, 68
Helping verbs. *See* Auxiliary (helping) verb(s)
Him, he, generic, 74

His or her, 75
Historical periods, capitalizing names of, 110
Hits, 162
Holiday(s)
  abbreviating, 119
  capitalizing names of, 110
Home page(s), 159. *See also* Web site(s); Web site design
  Chicago-style endnotes and bibliography, 272
  for course, 203–04
  italicizing, 113
  MLA works-cited list, 203–04
  personal, 204, 312
Homophone(s), 72–73
Hopefully, 365
HTML (hypertext markup language), 314
Humanities. *See* Chicago documentation style; Literature; MLA documentation style
Hung, hanged, 364
Hyperlinks, hypertext link(s), 159, 314
Hypertext markup language (HTML), 314
Hyphen(s), 115–17
  to break word at end of line, 115
  in compound adjectives, 116
  to divide compound words, 115–17
  MLA works-cited list, 191–92, 197
  suspended, 116

I, me, in compound constructions, 46
-ible, -able endings, 108
Ibid. (in the same place), 262
Idea(s)
  generating, 7
  plagiarism avoidance, 176–77
Identification number(s), 121
Identifying tag(s), 86, 93, 169
  with direct quotations, 86
  at end of quoted passage, 94–95, 170
  to introduce source material, 94, 169, 185
  location of, 169–70
  in middle of quoted passage, 93–95, 170
  for paraphrases, 172
  punctuating, 170
  for quotations, 93–95, 169–70
  for summaries, 172
Idiomatic expressions, prepositions in, 348
i.e. (that is), 365
ie, ei combinations, 107
If, in conditional statements, 44
If, whether, 365
Illusion, allusion, 360
Illustration(s). *See* Figure(s)
Immigrate to, emigrate from, 363
Imperative mood, 44, 80
Imperative sentence(s), 359
Implicit, explicit, 364
Imply, infer, 365
In, as preposition, 347
In-text citation(s)
  APA documentation style, 232–35
  Chicago documentation style, 261, 262, 263–74, 276, 280

In-text citation(s) *(continued)*
   CSE documentation style, 283–84
   MLA documentation style, 184–90
Inappropriate language, 73
Indefinite article(s), 341
Indefinite pronoun(s), 32, 344, 351
   as antecedents, 37
   forming possessive case of, 90
   list of, 34, 351
   subject-verb agreement with, 32, 34
Indentation
   in APA-style paper, 244
   in Chicago-style paper, 274, 278
   in CSE-style paper, 291
   of headings, 307
   of long prose passages, 95, 211, 244
   in MLA-style paper, 211
Independent (main) clause(s), 358
   attaching sentence fragments to, 29–30
   commas to set off, 27, 56, 80–81, 87
   in complex sentences, 57
   in compound sentences, 56
   semicolons to set off, 88, 89
   transitional words and phrases to connect,
      27, 56
Index(es), periodical, 154
Index card(s)
   in note-taking, 132, 133
   oral presentation notes on, 326
Indicative mood, 44
Indirect object(s), 46, 357
Indirect question(s)
   commas in, 87
   periods in, 78, 80
Indirect quotation(s)
   avoiding quotation marks with, 98
   commas in, 87
Indirect source(s)
   APA in-text citations, 234
   MLA parenthetical references, 186–87
Infer, imply, 365
Infinitive(s), 353
   recognizing, 353–54
   in titles of works, 111–12
Infinitive phrase(s), 358
Informal diction, 98
Informative writing, 2
Inseparable elements, commas between, 87
Inseparable phrasal verb(s), 339
Inside of, outside of, 365
Instant messaging, as research tool, 165
Instructor(s)
   as audience for essay, 4
   comments of, 10, 143–44
   conferences with, 333
   course requirements, 300
   expectations of, 300, 301
   as mentor, 304
Integrating source material, 142–43, 169–72
   identifying tags, 94, 169–70, 185
   paraphrases, 172
   quotations, 169–70
   summaries, 172

Intensive pronoun(s), 343, 352
Intentional plagiarism, 173
Interjection(s), 356
   commas with, 85
   exclamation points for, 80
   list of, 356
Interlibrary loans, 156
Internet, 158. *See also* Electronic source(s);
     Internet research
Internet research, 158–68. *See also* Electronic
     source(s)
   email, 164
   evaluating sources, 166–68
   FTP (file transfer protocol), 165, 315
   instant messaging, 165
   IRCS, 165
   listservs, 164–65, 204, 273
   MOOS, 165, 204
   MUDS, 165, 204
   newsgroups, 165, 204, 242–43
   plagiarism avoidance, 176
   resources for, 159–61
   search engines in, 159–64, 167
   telnet, 165
   tips for effective, 163–64
   World Wide Web, 159–64
Internet server, 315
Internships, 302
Interrogative adverb(s), 354
Interrogative pronoun(s), 352
Interrogative sentence(s), 359
Interruption(s), dashes to indicate, 101
Interview(s)
   APA in-text citations, 234
   Chicago-style endnotes and bibliography,
     269–70
   MLA works-cited list, 200
Into, as preposition, 347–48
Intransitive verb(s), 340–41, 357
Introductory element(s), 59, 82
Introductory paragraph(s)
   of essay, 8, 22–23
   of oral presentation, 325
   of research paper, 142
Intrusive modifier(s), 70
Invented word(s), 97
Inversion, of word order, 35, 59, 349
IRCS, as research tool, 165
Irregardless, regardless, 365
Irregular verb(s), 38–41
Is when, is where, faulty predication, 66, 365
Italic(s), 112–14. *See also* Underlining
   in APA reference list, 236–43
   for emphasis, 114
   to set off foreign words and phrases, 113–14
   to set off letters as letters, 114
   to set off numerals as numerals, 114
   to set off titles and names, 97, 112–13
   to set off words as words, 97, 114
   for terms being defined, 114
   underlining versus, in MLA works-cited
     list, 97, 113, 190–210
Its, it's, 365

Jargon, 73
Job application letter(s), 316–18
Journal(s)
    italicizing titles of, 113
    personal, in idea generation, 7
Journal article(s)
    APA reference list, 239, 241–42
    Chicago-style endnotes and bibliographies, 267, 271, 273–74
    continuous pagination, 198, 209, 239, 267, 287
    CSE reference list, 286–87, 289
    electronic version based on print source, 241–42
    in library research, 154–55
    MLA parenthetical references, 185–87
    MLA works-cited list, 198, 205, 208–09
    in periodical indexes, 154–55
    quotation marks for titles, 96
    separate pagination, 198, 208, 239, 267, 286
    in subscription databases, 150, 154–55
    in working bibliography, 126
Journalism, style manual, 294
Journalistic questions, 7
Justification, 305

Key words and phrase(s)
    repeating, 21–22, 68
    in searching online subscription services, 151, 207
Keyword search, 149, 151
    Boolean operators in, 149, 151
    Boolean search in, 149, 151
    of online catalogs, 149
    of online databases, 151, 207–09
    search engine, 162, 167
    subject search versus, 151
Kind of, sort of, 365

Label(s)
    in APA-style paper, 245
    in Chicago-style paper, 275
    in MLA-style paper, 212
Language(s). See also Foreign words and phrase(s); Latin expression(s); Offensive language
    capitalizing names of, 110
    documentation style. See MLA documentation style
    hypertext markup language (HTML), 314
    inappropriate, 73
Laser disc(s), MLA works-cited list, 201
Latin expression(s)
    editing misused, 119
    et al. (and others), 186, 191, 233, 237
    ibid. (in the same place), 262
    i.e. (that is), 365
    [sic] (thus), 102
Law
    legal case names, abbreviating, 189, 197
    legal case names, capitalizing, 110
    style manual, 294

Lay, lie, 40, 366
Leave, let, 365
Lecture(s), MLA works-cited list, 200
Legal source(s)
    case name abbreviation, 189, 197
    MLA parenthetical references, 189
    MLA works-cited list, 197
    style manual, 294
Length
    paragraph, 22
    sentence, 57–58
Less, fewer, 364
Let, leave, 365
Letter(s) (of alphabet)
    apostrophes for omitted, 91–92
    apostrophes in plurals of, 92
    as letters, setting off, 114
    silent, 106, 107
Letter(s) (correspondence)
    APA in-text citations, 234
    APA reference list, 240
    business, writing, 100, 316–18
    Chicago-style endnotes and bibliography, 270
    job application, 316–18
    MLA works-cited list, 200–01
    punctuation of, 100
Letter(s) of application, 316–18
Letter(s) to the editor
    APA reference list, 239
    MLA works-cited list, 199, 206
Library of Congress Classification System, 149
Library research, 148–58
    books, 153, 154
    electronic sources, 148–51, 153
    evaluating sources, 156–58
    exploratory, 151–52
    focused, 152–53
    library classification systems, 149
    library resources, 303
    online catalogs, 148–49, 153, 154
    periodicals, 153–55
    popular publications, 157–58
    primary sources, 130–31
    print sources, 151–55
    reference collection, 151–53
    scholarly publications, 157–58
    secondary sources, 130–31
    special library services, 155–56
Library subscription services, 207–09
Lie, lay, 40, 366
Lifelong learning, 304–05
Like, as, 361
Limiting modifier(s), 69
Line/lines, MLA parenthetical references, 187
Line spacing, in document design, 305
Link(s), in Web site design, 314
Linking verb(s), 50–51, 353
    in simple sentences, 50–51, 357
    subject-verb agreement with, 35
List(s)
    appositive fragments as, 30
    colons to introduce, 30, 89, 99

List(s) *(continued)*
  in document design, 307–08
  parentheses for points on, 102
  punctuating, 30, 89, 99, 102
Listserv(s), 164–65, 204
  Chicago-style endnotes and bibliography, 273
Literature. *See also* Poetry; Prose
  CSE reference list, 286
  long quotations of, 95, 99, 171, 185, 211
  MLA parenthetical references, 171, 185, 187–88
  MLA works-cited list, 194–95
  periods to mark divisions in, 79
Long quotation(s)
  colons to introduce, 99
  of poetry, 96, 171, 185, 211, 232
  of prose, 95, 99, 171, 185, 211, 222–23, 232, 244
Loose, lose, 366
Lots, lots of, a lot of, 366
-ly, in comparative degree, 51–53

Magazine(s), italicizing titles of, 113
Magazine article(s)
  APA reference list, 239
  Chicago-style endnotes and bibliographies, 268, 272
  CSE reference list, 287
  in library research, 154–55
  MLA parenthetical references, 185–87
  MLA works-cited list, 198–99, 205, 209
  in periodical indexes, 154–55
  quotation marks for titles, 96
  in subscription databases, 150, 154–55
  in working bibliography, 126
Main clause(s). *See* Independent (main) clause(s)
Main idea. *See* Thesis; Thesis statement; Topic sentence(s)
Main verb(s), 352, 357
Man, 366
Manuscript guidelines
  APA documentation style, 244–46
  Chicago documentation style, 274–76
  CSE documentation style, 289–90
  MLA documentation style, 211–13
Map(s)
  CSE reference list, 288
  MLA works-cited list, 207
Margin(s), 305
Mathematics, style manual, 294
May, can, 362
May be, maybe, 366
Me, I, in compound constructions, 46
Media, medium, 366
Medicine, style manual, 294
Medium, media, 366
Memo(s), 321–322
  APA in-text citations, 234
Mentor(s), 304
Metacrawler engine(s), 161
Microfiche, in library research, 155

Microfilm
  in library research, 155
  MLA works-cited list, 196
Microsoft Internet Explorer, 159
Microsoft PowerPoint, 327
Microsoft Word. See also Grammar checker(s); Spell checker(s)
  AutoCorrect tool, 109, 213
  Comment feature, 143
  Find command, 12
  Search command, 12
  Track Changes feature, 144–46
Might have, might of, 366
Misplaced modifier(s), 69–70
Miss, Ms. Mrs., 74
Mixed construction, 65–66
MLA documentation style, 180–229
  abbreviations in, 79, 118–19
  content notes, 187, 210–11, 226
  defined, 184
  manuscript guidelines, 211–13
  numbers in, 120–21
  parenthetical references, 79, 184–90
  quoting long prose passages, 95
  quoting poetry, 96
  sample research paper, 213–29
  underlining versus italics in, 97, 113, 190–210
  works-cited list, 190–210, 212–13, 227–29
Modal auxiliary(ies), 337, 353
Modern Language Association (MLA). *See* MLA documentation style
Modifier(s), 68–71
  dangling, 70–71
  intrusive, 70
  limiting, 69
  misplaced, 69–70
  negative, 337
  nonrestrictive, 83–84
  phrases, 69–70
  restrictive, 83–84, 87
  squinting, 69
Money amounts, numbers in, 121
Month(s)
  abbreviating, 119
  capitalizing names of, 110
Monthly calendar, 298
Monument names, capitalizing, 110
MOO(s)
  MLA works-cited list, 204
  as research tool, 165
Mood, 43–44. *See also specific types of mood*
  shift in, 65
  types of, 44
More, in comparative degree, 52
Most, in superlative degree, 52
Movie(s). *See* Film(s)
Mrs., Miss, Ms., 74
MUD(s)
  MLA works-cited list, 204
  as research tool, 165
Multiple author(s)
  APA in-text citations, 233

APA reference list, 237, 258
Chicago-style endnotes and bibliographies, 263–64
CSE reference list, 285
MLA parenthetical references, 185–86
MLA works-cited list, 191–92
Multivolume work(s)
  APA reference list, 237
  Chicago-style endnotes and bibliographies, 265–66
  MLA parenthetical references, 186
  MLA works-cited list, 193
Music
  APA reference list, 240
  Chicago-style endnotes and bibliography, 270–71
  italicizing titles of, 113
  MLA works-cited list, 201–02
  quotation marks for titles, 96
  style manual, 295
Musical(s). *See* Dramatic work(s)

Name(s). *See* Author name(s); Place name(s); Proper noun(s); Publisher's name
Name-year format, in CSE documentation style, 283–84
Narrowing of focus, for essay topic, 6–7
Nationalities
  capitalizing names of, 110
  offensive labels, 74
n.d. (no date), APA documentation style, 242
Negative modifiers, 337
Negative verb(s), 337
Neither . . . nor, 33, 36
Netscape Navigator, 159
News service(s), MLA works-cited list, 209
Newsgroup(s), 165
  APA reference list, 242–43
  MLA works-cited list, 204
Newsletter article(s), MLA works-cited list, 205
Newspaper(s), italicizing titles of, 112
Newspaper article(s)
  APA reference list, 239, 243
  Chicago-style endnotes and bibliographies, 269, 272
  CSE reference list, 287
  in library research, 154–55
  MLA parenthetical references, 185–87
  MLA works-cited list, 199–200, 205, 209
  in periodical indexes, 154–55
  quotation marks for titles, 96
  in subscription databases, 150, 154–55
  in working bibliography, 126
Noncount noun(s), 341, 342
Nonessential material
  commas to set off, 82–85
  dashes to set off, 100
  eliminating, 59–61
  nonrestrictive modifiers, 83–84
  parentheses to set off, 101
Nonexistent antecedent(s), 49–50

Nonrestrictive clause(s), 50
Nonrestrictive modifier(s), 83–84
Nor, singular antecedents joined by, 36
NOT, as Boolean operator, 149, 151, 162
Not only . . . but also, 33
Note(s). *See* Content note(s); Endnote(s); Footnote(s); Note-taking
Note-taking, 131–38
  to avoid plagiarism, 175–77
  computer printouts in, 132, 133, 134–35
  index cards in, 132, 133
  notes for oral presentations, 325–26
  photocopies in, 134–35
  recording source information, 131–34
Noun(s), 341, 351. *See also specific types of noun*
  articles with, 341–42
  ESL writers and, 341–43
  forming possessive case of, 46–47, 90–91
  noncount, 341, 342
  plural, 90, 108, 342
  possessive, 342
  singular, 32–36, 89
  types of, 351
  we, us before, 48
Noun clause(s), 358
Noun phrase(s), 63, 357
Number, 65
  agreement in, 32–38
  plural, 32–38
  shift in, 65
  singular, 32–38
Number(s), 120–21
  abbreviating, 118
  apostrophes for omitted, 92
  cardinal, 343
  compound, hyphenating, 117
  conventional uses of, 121
  italics to set off, 114
  ordinal, 343
  questionable, marking, 79
  spelled-out, versus numerals, 120–21
Number, amount, 361
Numeral(s). *See* Number(s)

-o endings, plurals with, 108
Object(s)
  direct, 46, 357
  indirect, 46, 357
  of prepositions, 46, 355
Object of preposition, 46, 355
Objective case, 46
Objectivity, 167–68
Observing, in idea generation, 7
O'clock, 121
Offensive labels, 74
Offensive language
  labels, 74
  sexist language, 37, 74–75
OK, O.K., okay, 366–67
Omission(s)
  apostrophes to indicate, 91–92
  commas to indicate, 87
  ellipsis to indicate, 103–04, 171–72

On, as preposition, 347
One-page article(s), MLA parenthetical references, 186
Online catalog(s), 148–49, 153, 154
Online database(s), 150–51
  APA reference list, 243
  italicizing names of, 113
  searching, 151, 207–09
  subscription, 150, 154–55
  types of, 150
Online forum(s)
  MLA works-cited list, 204
  types of, 165–66
Onto, as preposition, 348
Or
  compound subjects joined by, 33
  singular antecedents joined by, 36
OR, as Boolean operator, 149, 151, 162
Oral presentation(s), 324–30
  delivering, 329–30
  getting started, 324
  notes for, 325–26
  planning, 325, 326
  rehearsing, 329
  visual aids for, 326–29
Order
  of adjectives, 345–46
  of adverbs, 345
  numbers to indicate, 343
Ordinal number(s), as determiners, 343
Organization, of research paper, 139–42, 244
Organization name(s)
  abbreviating, 78, 118
  capitalizing, 111
Outline(s)
  essay, 9
  formal, 139–41
  oral presentation, 325, 326
  research paper, 139–41
Outside of, inside of, 365

P., pp.
  APA in-text citations, 232, 234
  APA reference list, 237–38
  MLA works-cited list, 197
Page header(s), APA-style paper, 244, 247
Page number(s)
  APA in-text citations, 232
  APA reference list, 236–40
  Chicago-style endnotes and bibliography, 267, 269
  Chicago-style paper, 274
  continuous pagination, 198, 209, 239, 267, 287
  CSE reference list, 286–87
  CSE-style paper, 290, 291
  MLA parenthetical references, 185–89
  MLA-style paper, 212
  MLA works-cited list, 195–96, 200
  separate pagination, 198, 208, 239, 267, 286
Painting(s)
  italicizing names of, 113
  MLA works-cited list, 202, 206

Pamphlet(s)
  italicizing titles of, 113
  MLA works-cited list, 196
Paper(s). *See* Essay(s); Research paper(s)
par./pars., MLA parenthetical references, 189
Paragraph(s), 19–24
  APA in-text citations, 234, 235
  body. *See* Body paragraph(s)
  concluding. *See* Concluding paragraph(s)
  introductory. *See* Introductory paragraph(s)
  key words and phrases in, 21–22
  length of, 22
  MLA parenthetical references, 189–90
  parallel structure in, 21–22
  revising, 10, 23, 24
  topic sentences in, 20
  transitional words and phrases in, 20–22
  unified, 20
  well-developed, 22
  when to begin new paragraph, 19–20
Parallelism, 21–22, 66–68
  faulty, 67–68
  in series, 67
Paraphrase(s)
  to avoid plagiarism, 175
  identifying tags to introduce, 172
  integrating, 172
  MLA parenthetical references for, 184
  of source information, 137–38
Parentheses, 101–02
  for cross-references, 101
  for dates, 102
  with other punctuation, 101
  within parentheses, brackets for, 102
  with points on list, 102
  question marks in, 79
  to set off nonessential material, 101
Parenthetical reference(s), 184
  APA documentation style, 232–35
  MLA documentation style, 79, 184–90
  placement of, 184
  quotation with ellipses before, 104
Part of source
  APA in-text citations, 234
  Chicago-style endnotes and bibliographies, 266
  CSE reference list, 285–86
  MLA works-cited list, 194–96
Participial phrase(s), 358
Participle(s), 353. *See also specific types of participle*
Parts of speech, 351–56. *See also specific parts of speech*
Passed, past, 367
Passive voice, 45, 339–40
  with dangling modifiers, 71
  eliminating, 63
  intentional use of, 45
  in rambling sentences, 63
  shift from or to active voice, 64–65, 71
Past, passed, 367
Past participle(s), 38–40, 353

Past perfect progressive tense, 43
Past perfect tense, 42
Past progressive tense, 43
Past tense, 38–40, 42
Peer review, 5
    audience in, 5–6
    comments in, 5–6, 10, 144–46
    drafts in, 5
    in revision process, 5–6, 10, 144–46, 333
Percentage
    numbers in, 121
    percent, percentage, defined, 367
Perfect tense(s), 41, 42–43
Period(s), 78–80
    with ellipses, 103
    at end of sentence, 78
    with identifying tags for quoted passages,
        94–95
    in indirect questions, 78, 80
    to mark abbreviations, 78
    to mark divisions in electronic addresses,
        79, 115
    to mark divisions in literary works, 79
    with other punctuation, 78, 94–96, 97
    with quotation marks, 94–96, 97
    in revising comma splices, 26–28
    in revising fused sentences, 26–28
    in revising run-on sentences, 26–28
Periodical(s), 153–55. *See also* Journal
        article(s); Magazine article(s);
        Newspaper article(s)
Periodical index(es), 154
Person, 65, 336
    agreement in, 32–38, 336
    shift in, 65
Personal communication. *See also* Business
        letter(s); Email
    APA in-text citations, 234
    APA reference list, 240
    audience in, 3
    Chicago-style endnotes and bibliography,
        270, 273
    MLA works-cited list, 200–01, 204
Personal home page(s)
    defined, 312
    MLA works-cited list, 204
Personal organizer, 298
Personal pronoun(s), 344, 351
Personal subscription services, 207
Personal title(s). *See* Titles of people
Persuasive writing, 2
Photocopies, managing, 134–35
Photograph(s)
    in document design, 311
    MLA works-cited list, 202, 206
Phrasal verb(s), 338–39
Phrase(s), 357. *See also* Transitional words and
        phrase(s); *specific types of phrase*
    commas with, 83
    key, 21–22, 68
    misplaced, relocating, 69–70
    phrase fragments, 29–30
    plagiarism avoidance, 175

    in series, 67
    between subject and verb, 33
    types of, 357–58
    wordy, eliminating, 61
Phrase fragment(s), 29–30
    appositive, 30
    prepositional phrase, 29
    revising, 29–30
    verbal phrase, 29
Physics, style manual, 295
Place name(s)
    abbreviating, 78, 79, 119
    capitalizing, 110
    numbers in, 121
Plagiarism, 173–77
    avoiding, 130, 133–34, 138, 173–77
    intentional, 173
    revising to eliminate, 174–77
    unintentional, 173–74
Planning
    of essay, 6–7, 9
    idea generation in, 7
    of oral presentations, 325
    topic selection in, 6–7
    in Web site design, 313
    in writing process, 332
Play(s). *See* Dramatic work(s)
Plural(s)
    apostrophes in, 92
    foreign, 108
    forming, 92, 108
    subject-verb agreement, 32–36
Plural noun(s)
    articles with, 342
    forming, 108
    forming possessive case of, 90
Plural pronoun(s), 36
p.m., 118
Poetry. *See also* Literature
    italicizing titles of long poems, 113
    long quotations of, 96, 171, 185, 211,
        232
    MLA parenthetical references, 171, 185,
        187
    MLA works-cited list, 194–95
    periods to mark divisions in, 79
    quotation marks for titles, 96
    slashes to separate lines of, 96, 103
Point(s), 306
Political groups, capitalizing names of, 111
Popular publication(s), 157–58. *See also*
        Magazine article(s); Newspaper
        article(s)
Positive degree, 51
Possessive case, 46–47, 90–91
Possessive noun(s), 342
Possessive pronoun(s), 342
Postal abbreviation(s), 79
PowerPoint, 327
Precede, proceed, 367
Predicate(s), 356. *See also* Verb(s)
    commas between subject of sentence and,
        87

Predicate(s) *(continued)*
  faulty predication, 66, 365
  as function of word, 334
  in simple sentences, 356–57, 358–59
Preface
  APA reference list, 237
  MLA works-cited list, 193
Prefix(es), hyphenating with, 116–17
Preposition(s), 355
  ESL writers and, 346–48
  list of, 347–48, 355
  object of, 46, 355
  in titles of works, 111–12
Prepositional phrase(s), 357
  commas with, 82, 83
  fragments, revising, 29
  misplaced, 70
  as modifiers, 70
  pronouns in, 346–47
  in rambling sentences, 63
  wordy, eliminating, 63
Present participle(s), 353
Present perfect progressive tense, 43
Present perfect tense, 42
Present progressive tense, 43
Present subjunctive mood, 44
Present tense, 41
  special uses of, 42
  subject-verb agreement with, 32
  in verb forms, 38–40
Presentation(s). *See* Oral presentation(s)
Presentation software, 327
Pretentious diction, 73
Prewriting stage, 6–7
Primary source(s), 130–31
Principal, principle, 367
Principal part(s), 38–41
  irregular verbs, 38–41
  regular verbs, 38
Principle, principal, 367
Print résumés, 318
Print source(s). *See also* Source(s); *specific print sources*
  APA in-text citations, 233–35
  Chicago-style endnotes and bibliographies, 263–70
  CSE reference list, 284–88
  in library research, 151–55
  MLA parenthetical references, 185–89
  MLA works-cited list, 190–202
Proceed, precede, 367
Professor. *See* Instructor(s)
Progressive tense(s), 41, 43
Pronoun(s), 343, 351–52. *See also* Antecedent(s); *specific types of pronoun*
  case, 45–48, 344
  ESL writers and, 343–45
  forming possessive case of, 90
  gender, 344–45
  placement in sentence, 343
  possessive, 342
  in prepositional phrases, 346–47
  reference, 48–50, 343

revising reference errors, 48–50
  sexist use of, 74–75
  singular/plural, 86
  subject-verb agreement with, 34, 35–36
  types of, 351–52
Pronoun reference, 48–50, 343
Pronunciation, spelling and, 106
Proofreading, 11
  essay, 11–12
  research paper, 147
Proper adjective(s), 111
Proper noun(s), 109, 351
  categories of, 109–11
  commas with names in direct address, 85
Prose
  indicating omissions in, 103–04, 171–72
  long quotations of, 95, 99, 171, 185, 211, 222–23, 232, 244
  MLA parenthetical references, 171, 185, 187, 188
  MLA works-cited list, 194–95
Publication date(s)
  APA in-text citations, 233–35
  APA reference list, 236–43, 246
  MLA parenthetical references, 185–89
  MLA works-cited list, 191–210
Publication Manual of the American Psychological Association. See APA documentation style
Publisher's name
  APA reference list, 236–43
  Chicago-style bibliography, 263–74, 276, 281
  colons to separate publication place from, 100
  CSE reference list, 284–89, 293
  MLA works-cited list, 118, 190
Punctuation, 78–104. *See also specific documentation styles; specific punctuation marks*
  for identifying tags, 170
  to indicate changes to quotations, 170
  of lists, 30, 89, 99, 102
Purpose, 2
  of essay, 2–3
  of memos, 321
  of oral presentation, 324
  of Web site, 313

Qtd. in (quoted in), MLA parenthetical references, 186–87
Question(s)
  in idea generation, 7
  indirect, 78, 80, 87
  for information, 349
  journalistic, 7
  research, 125–26
  tag, 85, 349
  word order in, 349
Question mark(s), 79–80
  and abbreviations with periods, 78
  with other punctuation, 78, 79, 80, 94, 97–98
  with quotation marks, 94, 97–98

Quotation(s), 138, 169–72. *See also* Direct
   quotation(s)
   additions within, 171
   APA in-text citations, 232
   APA-style paper, 244
   brackets in, 102, 104, 171
   colons to introduce, 99
   comments within, 102
   identifying tags for, 93–95, 169–70
   indirect, 87
   integrating, 169–72
   long, 95, 96, 99, 171, 185, 211, 222–23,
      232, 244
   MLA parenthetical references, 185
   MLA-style paper, 185, 211
   omissions within, 103–04, 171–72
   of poetry, 96, 171, 185, 211, 232
   of prose, 95, 99, 171, 185, 211, 222–23,
      232, 244
   quotation marks with, 93–96
   within quotations, 98
   run in with text, 185
   set off from text, 185
   of source information, 138
   substitutions within, 171
   when to quote, 93–96, 138
Quotation, quote, 367
Quotation book, 153
Quotation mark(s), 93–98
   for borrowed words, 97, 174–75
   commas with, 86, 89, 93–96, 97
   editing misused, 98
   with other punctuation marks, 93–96,
      97–98
   for titles of unpublished dissertations,
      196
   for titles of works, 96–97, 196
   for titles within titles, 194, 200
   when to use, 93–98, 171–72
Quote, quotation, 367

Race(s)
   capitalizing names of, 110
   offensive labels, 74
Radio program(s)
   italicizing titles of, 113
   MLA works-cited list, 201, 204
   quotation marks for episodes, 97
Raise, rise, 367
Rambling sentence(s), 62–63
Ratio(s), numbers in, 121
Reading, in idea generation, 7
Real, really, 367
Reason is that, reason is because, 367
Reasonableness. *See* Objectivity
Reciprocal pronoun(s), 352
Recording(s)
   APA reference list, 240
   Chicago-style endnotes and bibliography,
      270–71
   MLA works-cited list, 201–02
Redundancy, deleting, 61
Reference, pronoun, 48–50, 343

Reference list(s), 236. *See also*
   Bibliography(ies) (reference tools)
   APA-style, 236–43, 246, 258–59
   CSE-style, 284–89, 293
Reference work(s), 151–53
   APA reference list, 238
   general, 151–52
   MLA works-cited list, 195–96
   specialized, 151, 152–53
Reflective writing, 2
Reflexive pronoun(s), 352
Regardless, irregardless, 365
Regular verb(s), 38
Rehearsal, of oral presentation, 329
Relative clause(s). *See* Adjective (relative)
   clause(s)
Relative pronoun(s), 352
   in complex sentences, 27–28, 57
   in dependent clause fragments, 28–29
   list of, 57
   in revising comma splices, 27–28
   in revising fused sentences, 27–28
   in revising run-on sentences, 27–28
   in revising sentence fragments, 30–31
   subject-verb agreement with, 35–36
Religion(s), capitalizing names of, 111
Religious work(s)
   capitalizing names of, 111
   Chicago-style endnotes and bibliographies,
      266
   CSE reference list, 286
   MLA parenthetical references, 188
   MLA works-cited list, 194
Remote antecedent(s), 49
Repetition
   commas to indicate omissions, 87
   of key words and phrases, 21–22, 68
   parallelism and, 68
Republished work(s), MLA works-cited list,
   193
Requirements, school and course, 4
Research, 124, 148–68. *See also* Exploratory
   research; Focused research; Internet
   research; Library research
   Internet research, 158–68
   library research, 148–58
Research paper(s), 124–47
   APA-style, 246–59
   Chicago-style, 276–81
   CSE-style, 290–93
   editing, 147
   exploratory research, 125–26
   final draft, 147
   focused research, 129–31
   MLA-style, 213–29
   note-taking, 131–38
   organizing, 139–42, 244
   outlines, 139–41
   plagiarism avoidance, 173–77
   research question, 125–26
   rough draft, 141–43
   search strategy, 151–52
   sources for, 126–28, 129–31, 142–43

Research paper(s) *(continued)*
  thesis statement, 128–29
  topic selection for, 124–25
  working bibliography, 126–28
Research question, 125–26
Respectably, respectfully, respectively, 368
Restrictive clauses, 50
Restrictive modifier(s), 83–84, 87
Résumé(s), 318–20
  print, 318
  sample, 319
  scannable, 318, 320
  templates, 319, 320
Review(s), MLA works-cited list, 199, 205–06
Revision, 9. *See also* Editing
  of agreement errors, 32–38
  of comma splices, 26–28
  computer software in, 144–46
  of dangling modifiers, 70–71
  to eliminate plagiarism, 174–77
  of essays, 9–11
  of faulty parallelism, 67–68
  of fused sentences, 26–28
  instructor's comments in, 10, 143–44
  of misplaced modifiers, 69–70
  of misused abbreviations, 119–20
  of misused colons, 100
  of misused commas, 87
  of misused question marks, 80
  of misused quotation marks, 98
  of mixed constructions, 65–66
  of paragraphs, 10, 23, 24
  peer review in, 5–6, 10, 144–46, 333
  of pronoun reference errors, 48–50
  of run-on sentences, 26–28
  of sentence fragments, 29–31
  of sentences, 10–11, 26–28, 29, 56–71
  with Track Changes, 144–46
  of unwarranted shifts, 64–65
  of words, 11, 71–75
Rise, raise, 367
Rough draft. *See also* Revision
  essay, 9
  research paper, 141–43, 147
Run-on sentence(s), 26–28
  comma splice, 26–28, 88
  fused sentences, 26–28, 88
  revising, 26–28
Running head(s), APA-style paper, 244, 247

-*s*
  in forming plurals, 108
  possessive form of nouns ending in, 90
-'*s*
  in forming plurals, 92
  in forming possessive case, 90–91
Sacred books, 111, 113
Salutation(s), punctuation of, 100
Sarcasm, 80
Scannable résumés, 318, 320
Scholarly publication(s), 157–58. *See also*
  Journal article(s)

Scientific writing
  documentation style. *See* CSE
    documentation style
  style manuals, 294–95
  symbols in, 120
  units of measurement, abbreviating, 119
Scope, 168
  in thesis statement, 9
  of Web site content, 168
Score(s), numbers in, 121
Sculpture, italicizing names of, 113
Search command, 12
Search engine(s), 159–64
  keyword searches, 162, 167
  lists of, 160–61
  metasearch/metacrawler, 161
  subject guides, 162–63
Search operators, 149
Search strategy
  exploratory research, 125–26, 151–52
  focused research, 129–31
Secondary source(s), 130–31
Section(s)
  APA in-text citations, 234
  book, quotation marks for titles, 97
-*seed* endings, 108
Semicolon(s), 88–89
  APA in-text citations, 235
  in compound sentences, 56
  with quotation marks, 97
  in revising comma splices, 27
  in revising fused sentences, 27
  in revising run-on sentences, 27
  to separate independent clauses, 88, 89
  to separate multiple works in MLA
    parenthetical citation, 187
  in series, 88–89
  with transitional elements, 27, 88
Sentence(s), 356–59. *See also* Complex
    sentence(s); Compound-complex
    sentence(s); Compound sentence(s);
    Punctuation; Simple sentence(s);
    Subject of sentence; Topic sentence(s)
  agreement errors, 32–38, 336
  awkward, 64–66
  basic elements, 356
  basic patterns, 356–57
  comma splice, 26–28, 88
  concise, 59–63
  confusing, 64–66
  fused, 26–28, 88
  length of, 57–58
  mixed construction, 65–66
  periods to end, 78–80
  phrases and clauses in, 357–58
  rambling, tightening, 62–63
  revising, 10–11, 26–28, 29, 56–71
  run-on, 26–28
  tenses in, 41–43
  types of, 358–59
  varied, 56–59
  wordiness, eliminating, 59–63
Sentence fragment(s), 28–32

Separable phrasal verb(s), 338
Series
  colons to introduce, 99
  commas in, 81–82
  MLA works-cited list, 193
  parallelism in, 67
  semicolons in, 88–89
Set, sit, 40–41, 368
Sexist language, 37, 74–75
Shall, will, 368
Shaping
  essay, 7–9
  research paper, 141–42
  in writing process, 332
She, he, 364
Shift(s)
  in mood, 65
  in number, 65
  in person, 65
  in tense, 64
  unwarranted, revising, 64–65
  in voice, 64–65
Ship(s), italicizing names of, 113
Short story(ies)
  MLA works-cited list, 194–95
  quotation marks for titles, 96
Should of, could of, would of, 362
[*Sic*] (thus), 102
Silent letter(s), 106, 107
Simple sentence(s), 50–51, 56, 356–57, 358–59
Simple tenses, 41–42, 336–37
Since, 368
Singular noun(s)
  forming possessive case of, 89
  subject-verb agreement, 32–36
Singular pronoun(s), 36
Sit, set, 40–41
Site, cite, 362
Slang, 98
Slash(es), 102–03
  dividing electronic addresses with, 79, 115, 203, 241
  in quotations of poetry, 96, 103
  to separate options, 102–03
So, 368
Social groups, capitalizing names of, 110
Social science(s), documentation styles. *See* APA documentation style
Software. *See* Computer software
Sometime, sometimes, some time, 368
Sort of, kind of, 365
Source(s). *See also* Documentation; Electronic source(s); Print source(s)
  evaluating, 156–58, 166–68
  integrating into paper, 142–43, 169–72
  note-taking from, 131–38
  paraphrasing, 137–38
  plagiarism avoidance, 130, 133–34, 134, 138, 173–77
  primary, 130–31
  quoting, 138
  reading, 129–30
  recording source information, 131–34
  secondary, 130–31
  summarizing, 135–37
  working bibliography for, 126–28
Source, with MLA-style visuals, 212
Spacecraft, italicizing names of, 113
Special collections, 156
Special event names, capitalizing, 110
Specialized reference works, 151, 152–53
Specific word(s), 72
Speech(es). *See* Oral presentation(s)
Spell checker(s), 12, 109
Spelling, 106–09. *See also* Spell checker(s)
  ESL writers and, 334
  homophones, 72–73
  pronunciation and, 106
  rules of, 106–08
Squinting modifier(s), 69
Stability, 168
Statistic(s)
  documenting, 175
  numbers in, 121
Street name(s), abbreviating, 119
Structure names, capitalizing, 110
Study groups, 299, 304
Style manuals, by specific subject, 294–95
Subject complement(s), 50–51, 353
  linking verbs and, 353
  in simple sentences, 50–51, 357
  in subjective case, 46
Subject guide(s), search engine, 162–63
Subject heading(s), 151
Subject of sentence, 356
  agreement with verb, 32–36, 336
  collective nouns as, 34–35
  commas between predicate and, 87
  compound, 33
  creating new, to correct dangling modifier, 71
  indefinite pronouns as, 34
  lack of, in sentence fragments, 28
  singular subjects with plural forms, 35
  supplying missing, 31
Subject of verb, subjective case with, 46
Subject search, 149, 151
  keyword search versus, 151
  of online catalogs, 149
  of online databases, 151
  search engine, 162–63
  subject headings in, 151
Subject-verb agreement, 32–36, 336
Subjective case, 46
Subjunctive mood, 44
Subordinate clause(s). *See* Dependent (subordinate) clause(s)
Subordinating conjunction(s), 356
  in complex sentences, 27–28, 57
  in dependent clause fragments, 28–29
  list of, 57
  in revising comma splices, 27–28
  in revising fused sentences, 27–28
  in revising run-on sentences, 27–28
  in revising sentence fragments, 30–31
Subordination, 58

Subscription database(s), 150, 154–55. *See also* Online database(s)

Subscription service(s)
  Chicago-style endnotes and bibliography, 273–74
  library, 207–09
  MLA works-cited list, 207–09
  personal, 207

Subsequent edition(s)
  Chicago-style endnotes and bibliographies, 265
  MLA works-cited list, 192

Subtitles, colons to separate titles from, 100

Success. *See* Academic success

Suffix(es)
  -able, -ible, 108
  doubling final consonants before, 107
  hyphenating with, 116–17
  -seed, 108
  silent *-e* before, 107
  spelling rules, 107–08
  -y before, 107

Summary(ies). *See also* Abstract(s)
  dashes to introduce, 101
  identifying tags to introduce, 172
  integrating, 172
  MLA parenthetical references for, 184
  of source information, 135–37

Superlative degree, 51–53

Superscript(s), 262
  Chicago documentation style, 262, 274–75, 278
  CSE documentation style, 283, 291
  MLA documentation style, 210, 226

Suspended hyphen(s), 116

Symbol(s)
  as abbreviations, 120
  measurements before, 121

Synchronous communication, 165
  MLA works-cited list, 204
  types of, 165–66

Syntax, plagiarism avoidance, 175

Table(s)
  in APA-style paper, 235, 245, 255
  in Chicago-style paper, 275
  in CSE documentation style, 290
  in document design, 309
  in MLA-style paper, 212
  sample, 309

Tag question(s), 85, 349

Take, bring, 361

Talk(s). *See* Oral presentation(s)

Technical terms
  abbreviating, 118
  quotation marks with, 98

Technical writing
  documentation style. *See* CSE documentation style
  style manual, 295
  symbols in, 120
  units of measurement, abbreviating, 119

Technology. *See entries beginning with* "Computer"

Television program(s)
  APA reference list, 240
  italicizing titles of, 113
  MLA works-cited list, 201
  quotation marks for episodes, 97

Telnet, 165

Temperature(s), abbreviating, 118

Tense, 41–43, 336
  perfect tenses, 41, 42–43
  progressive tenses, 41, 43
  shift in, 64
  simple tenses, 41–42, 336–37

Tentative thesis, 128–29

Than
  comparisons with, 47
  paired elements linked by, 67

Than, then, 368

That, commas with, 50, 84, 170

That, which, who, 49–50, 368–69

That clauses, in subjunctive mood, 44

The, within titles of works, 111–12, 199, 269

The reason . . . is because, faulty predication, 66

Their
  in eliminating sexist language, 74
  pronoun-antecedent agreement with, 36

Their, there, they're, 369

Theirselves, theirself, themselves, 369

Themselves, theirselves, theirself, 369

Then, than, 368

There, their, they're, 369

There is, there are, 35

Thesis
  of essay, 8
  fine-tuning, 139
  of research paper, 128–29
  tentative, 128–29

Thesis and support
  essay, 7–9
  oral presentation, 325

Thesis statement
  essay, 8–9
  fine-tuning, 139
  oral presentation, 325
  research paper, 128–29
  writing effective, 8–9

They
  in eliminating sexist language, 74
  pronoun-antecedent agreement with, 36

They're, their, there, 369

Thinking critically. *See* Critical thinking

Till, until, 'til, 369

Time management, 298–99

Time measure(s)
  abbreviating, 78, 118, 119
  colons in, 100
  numbers in, 121

Title page(s)
  APA-style paper, 247
  Chicago-style paper, 274, 277
  CSE-style paper, 291

essay, 13
 MLA-style paper, 211, 214
Titles of people
 abbreviating, 74, 78, 86, 109–10, 117–19
 capitalizing, 109–10
 commas with, 86
 Miss, Ms., Mrs., 74
 sexist use of, 74
Titles of work(s). *See also specific documentation*
  styles
 articles in, 111–12, 119, 269
 capitalizing important words in, 111–12,
  190
 choosing essay, 11
 colons to separate subtitles from, 100
 italicizing, 97, 112–13
 long, italics or underlining for, 97
 quotation marks with, 96–97, 196
 short, quotation marks for, 96
 student papers, 98, 147
 the within, 111–12, 199, 269
 within titles, in MLA works-cited list, 194,
  200
 underlined, in MLA works-cited list, 97,
  113, 190–210
To, as preposition, 347
To, at, 361
To, too, two, 369
Too, two, to, 369
Topic labels, in keyword searches, 207
Topic selection
 essay, 6–7
 idea generation and, 7
 narrowing, 6–7
 oral presentation, 324
 research paper, 124–25
Topic sentence(s), 20
 placement of, 20
 in unified paragraphs, 20
Track Changes feature, 144–46
Train(s), italicizing names of, 113
Transitional words and phrase(s), 20–22
 in coherent paragraphs, 20–22
 commas with, 27, 31, 50, 82, 85
 in compound sentences, 56
 to connect independent clauses, 27, 56
 list of, 21
 semicolons to introduce, 27, 88
Transitive verb(s), 340–41, 357
Translation(s), MLA works-cited list, 194
Try to, try and, 369
Two, to, too, 369
-type, 369
Type size, in document design, 306
Typeface, in document design, 306, 307

Unabridged dictionaries, 152
Underlining. *See also* Italic(s)
 in MLA-style papers, 97, 113, 190–210
 for terms being defined, 114
Unified paragraphs, 20
Unintentional plagiarism, 173–74
Uninterested, disinterested, 363

Unique, 369
Units of measurement, abbreviating, 119
University Microfilms International (UMI),
  196
Unsigned work(s). *See* Anonymous/unsigned
  work(s)
Until, 'til, till, 369
URL (uniform resource locator)
 APA reference list, 241–43
 division of, 79, 115, 203, 241
 entering electronic address, 161
 MLA works-cited list, 115, 202–09, 203
 understanding, 167
Us, we, before a noun, 48
Usenet newsgroup(s), 165, 204
Utility word(s), eliminating, 60, 72
Utilize, 369

Varied sentence(s), 56–59
Verb(s), 38–45, 352–54. *See also* Tense;
  Verbal(s); Voice; *specific types of verb*
 agreement with subject, 32–36, 336
 base form, 38–41
 commas between indirect question and, 87
 commas between indirect quotation and,
  87
 ESL writers and, 336–41
 intransitive, 340–41, 357
 to introduce source material, 170
 irregular, 38–41
 lack of, in sentence fragments, 28
 mood, 43–44
 negative, 337
 phrasal, 338–39
 principal parts, 38–41
 regular, 38
 subject of, 46
 supplying missing, 31
 transitive, 340–41, 357
 types of, 352–54
Verb phrase(s), 337, 353, 357
Verbal(s), 353. *See also specific types of verbal*
Verbal phrase(s), 358
 commas with, 83
 commas with introductory, 82
 fragments, revising, 29
 misplaced, 69
Vertical file, 156
Videotape(s)
 Chicago-style endnotes and bibliography,
  270
 CSE reference list, 288
 MLA works-cited list, 201
Visual(s), 308. *See also* Document design;
  Web site design
 in APA-style paper, 235, 245, 255, 257
 in Chicago-style paper, 275
 in CSE documentation style, 290, 292
 in document design, 308–12
 in MLA-style paper, 212, 219
 in oral presentations, 326–29
 types of, 309–11
Visual text(s). *See* Visual(s)

Voice, 44–45, 339–40. *See also* Active voice;
    Passive voice
    shift in, 64–65

Wait for, wait on, 369
We, us, before a noun, 48
Weather, whether, 369–70
Web. *See* World Wide Web
Web browser(s), 159–61
    bookmarks, 164
Web page. *See* Home page(s); Web site(s);
    Web site design
Web site(s), 312
    APA reference list, 242
    audience for, 313
    Chicago-style endnotes and bibliography,
       272
    design of. *See* Web site design
    italicizing, 113
    MLA works-cited list, 203–04
Web site design, 312–15
    components of, 313
    editing in, 314
    linking content, 314
    planning in, 313
    posting site in, 315
Well, good, 364
Well-developed paragraphs, 22
Were, we're, 370
Whether, if, 365
Whether, weather, 369–70
Which, commas with, 84
Which, who, that, 49–50, 368–69
White space, 306
Who, that, which, 49–50, 368–69
Who, whom, 47, 370
Who? What? Where? When? and *How?*
    questions, 7
Whoever, whomever, 47
Who's, whose, 370
Will, shall, 368
Word. See Microsoft Word
Word(s). *See also* Parts of speech; Transitional
    words and phrase(s); Word order
    abstract, 72
    borrowed, 174–77
    breaking at end of line, 115
    clichés, 73
    compound, 115–17
    concrete, 72
    deadwood, eliminating, 60
    dividing, 115–17
    euphemisms, 72
    general, 72
    inappropriate, 73

    invented, 97
    jargon, 73
    key, 21–22, 68, 149, 151, 207
    misplaced, revising, 69–70
    offensive, 74
    plagiarism avoidance, 130, 133–34, 138,
       173–77
    revising, 11, 71–75
    in series, 67
    sexist language, 37, 74–75
    specific, 72
    utility, eliminating, 60, 72
    as words, apostrophes in plurals of, 92
    as words, setting off, 97, 114
Word order
    ESL writers and, 334, 345–46, 348–49
    inverting, 35, 59, 349
    position of adjectives, 345–46
    position of adverbs, 345
    standard, 348
Word processor(s). *See* Computer tip(s);
    Grammar checker(s); *Microsoft Word;*
    Spell checker(s)
Wordiness, eliminating, 59–63
Working bibliography, 126–28
Workplace communication, 315–23. *See also*
    Business letter(s); Oral presentation(s)
    audience in, 3
    emails, 323
    follow-up letters, 318
    letters of application, 316–18
    memos, 234, 321–22
    résumés, 318–20
Works-cited list(s), 190. *See also*
    Bibliography(ies) (documentation
    styles)
    MLA style, 190–210, 212–13, 227–29
World Wide Web, 159–64. *See also* URL
    (uniform resource locator)
    plagiarism avoidance, 176
    search engines, 159–64
    Web browsers, 159–61, 164
Would of, should of, could of, 362
Writing center(s), 333
Writing process. *See also* ESL (English as a
    Second Language) writer(s); Essay(s);
    Research paper(s)
    stages of, 6–12

-y endings, 108
    plurals with, 108
    suffixes with, 107, 108
Yearbooks, 152
Yes/no question(s), 349
Your, you're, 370